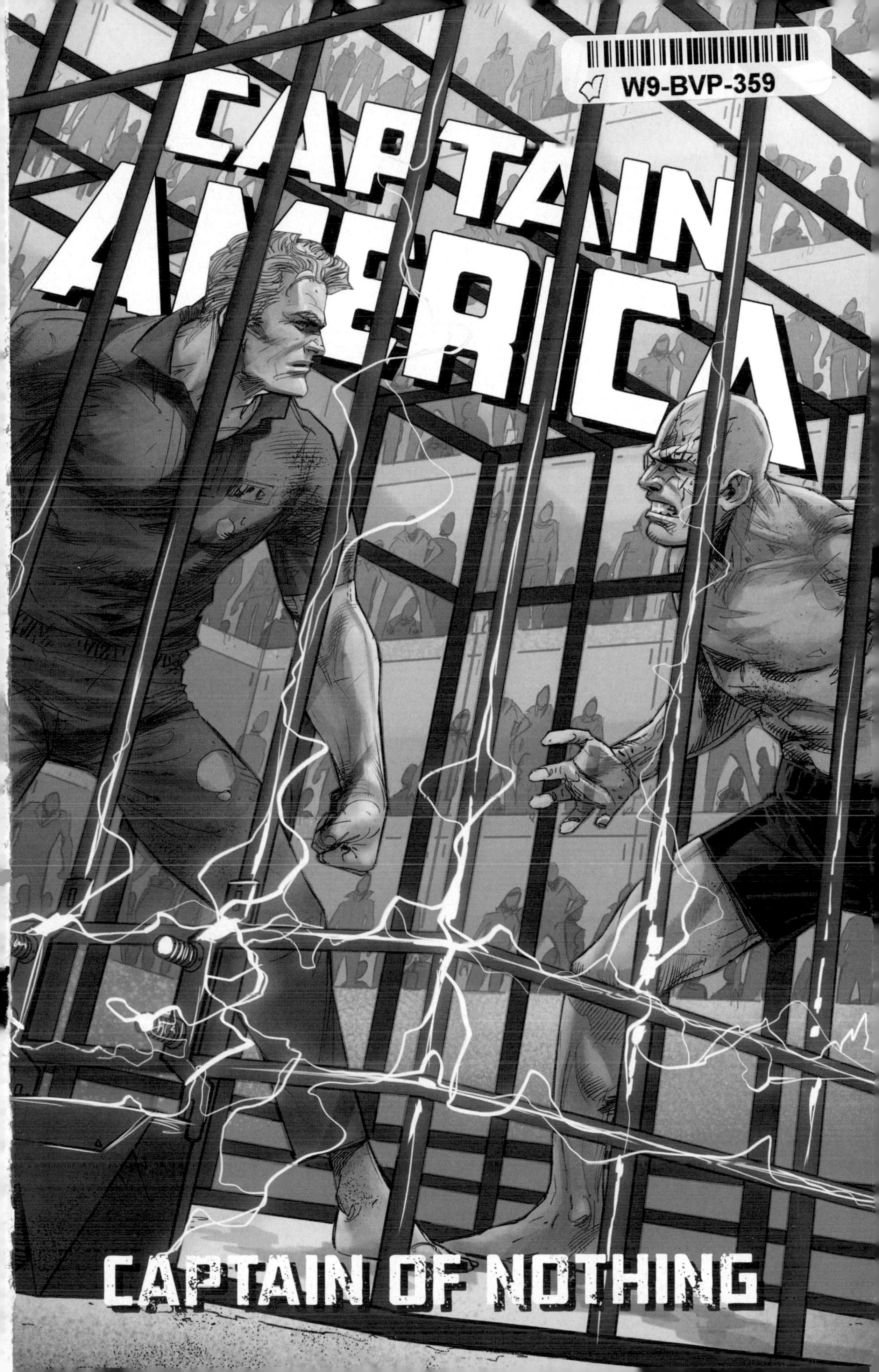
CAPTAIN AMERICA
CAPTAIN OF NOTHING

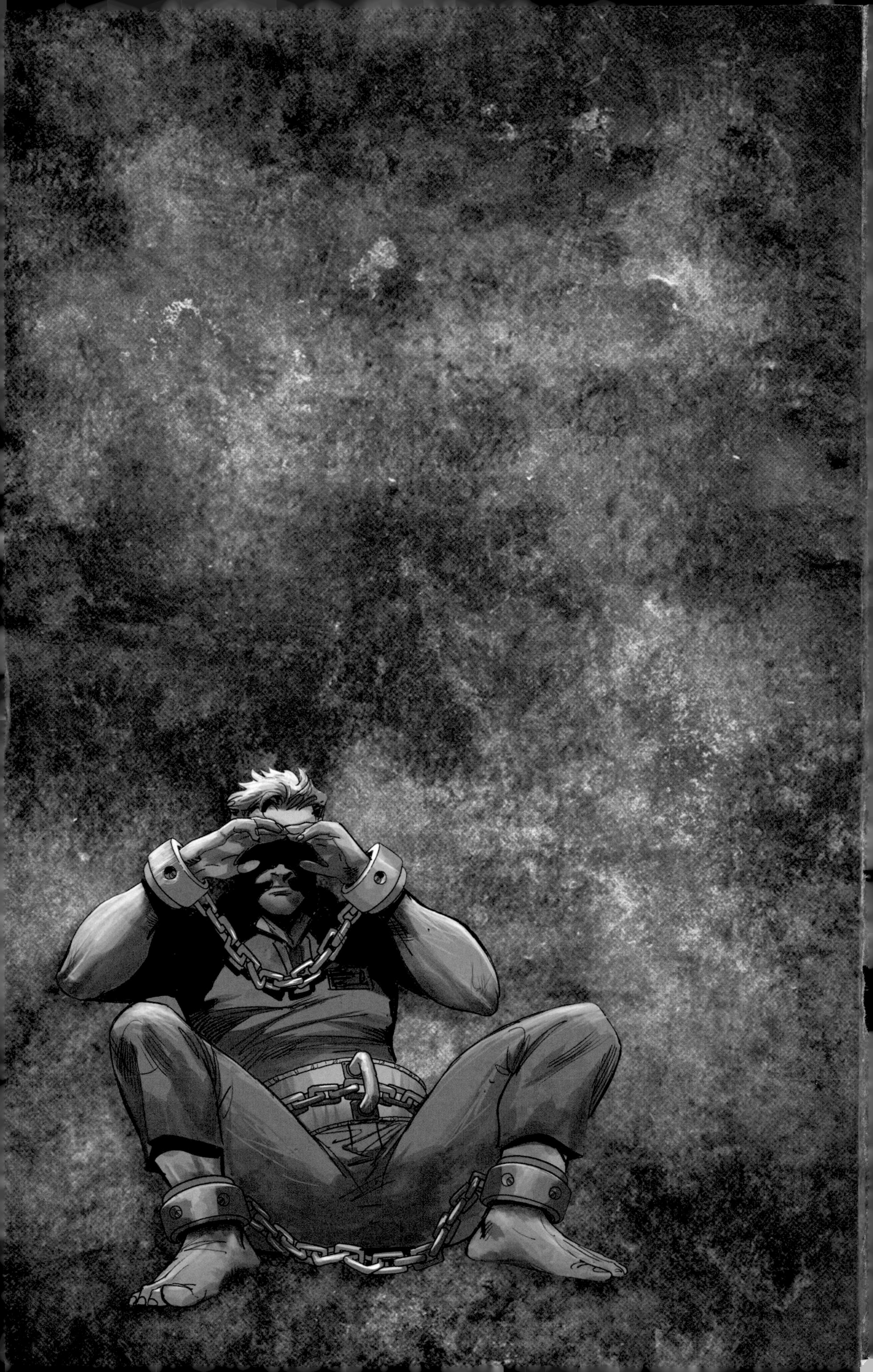

HYDRA CONQUERED THE UNITED STATES, FOLLOWING A LEADER WITH STEVE ROGERS' FACE.

CAPTAIN AMERICA RETURNED AND HYDRA FELL, BUT A NEW THREAT KNOWN AS THE POWER ELITE, SPEARHEADED BY ALEXA LUKIN AND HER NEWLY RESURRECTED HUSBAND ALEKSANDER, HAS EMERGED TO FILL THE VACUUM.

ALEXA'S PEOPLE SEEM TO BE SPREADING THEIR INFLUENCE EVERYWHERE, INCLUDING THE U.S. GOVERNMENT...AND STEVE SUSPECTS THAT SHARON CARTER'S BOSS, THUNDERBOLT ROSS, SENT SHARON INTO AN AMBUSH ON THEIR ORDERS.

BUT HE WASN'T ABLE TO PROVE IT BEFORE ROSS UNEXPECTEDLY TURNED UP DEAD. BECAUSE OF THE RECENT TENSIONS BETWEEN THEM, ALL THE SUSPICION HAS FALLEN ON STEVE...

CAPTAIN AMERICA

CAPTAIN OF NOTHING

Ta-Nehisi Coates
WRITER

Adam Kubert
ARTIST

Frank Martin [#7-10] & **Matt Milla** [#11-12]
COLORISTS

VC's Joe Caramagna
LETTERER

Alex Ross
COVER ART

Shannon Andrews Ballesteros
ASSISTANT EDITOR

Alanna Smith
ASSOCIATE EDITOR

Tom Brevoort
EDITOR

CAPTAIN AMERICA CREATED BY JOE SIMON & JACK KIRBY

COLLECTION EDITOR KATERI WOODY
ASSISTANT EDITOR CAITLIN O'CONNELL
EDITOR, SPECIAL PROJECTS MARK D. BEAZLEY
SENIOR EDITOR, SPECIAL PROJECTS JENNIFER GRÜNWALD
VP PRODUCTION & SPECIAL PROJECTS JEFF YOUNGQUIST
BOOK DESIGNER ADAM DEL RE

SVP PRINT, SALES & MARKETING DAVID GABRIEL
DIRECTOR, LICENSED PUBLISHING SVEN LARSEN
EDITOR IN CHIEF C.B. CEBULSKI
CHIEF CREATIVE OFFICER JOE QUESADA
PRESIDENT DAN BUCKLEY
EXECUTIVE PRODUCER ALAN FINE

CAPTAIN AMERICA VOL. 2: CAPTAIN OF NOTHING. Contains material originally published in magazine form as CAPTAIN AMERICA #7-12. First printing 2019. ISBN 978-1-302-91195-9. Published by MARVEL WORLDWIDE, INC., a subsidiary of MARVEL ENTERTAINMENT, LLC. OFFICE OF PUBLICATION: 135 West 50th Street, New York, NY 10020. **Printed in Canada.** DAN BUCKLEY, President, Marvel Entertainment; JOHN NEE, Publisher; JOE QUESADA, Chief Creative Officer; TOM BREVOORT, SVP of Publishing; DAVID BOGART, Associate Publisher & SVP of Talent Affairs; DAVID GABRIEL, SVP of Sales & Marketing, Publishing; JEFF YOUNGQUIST, VP of Production & Special Projects; DAN CARR, Executive Director of Publishing Technology; ALEX MORALES, Director of Publishing Operations; DAN EDINGTON, Managing Editor; SUSAN CRESPI, Production Manager; STAN LEE, Chairman Emeritus. For information regarding advertising in Marvel Comics or on Marvel.com, please contact Vit DeBellis, Custom Solutions & Integrated Advertising Manager, at vdebellis@marvel.com. For Marvel subscription inquiries, please call 888-511-5480. **Manufactured between 8/2/2019 and 9/3/2019 by SOLISCO PRINTERS, SCOTT, QC, CANADA.**

10 9 8 7 6 5 4 3 2 1

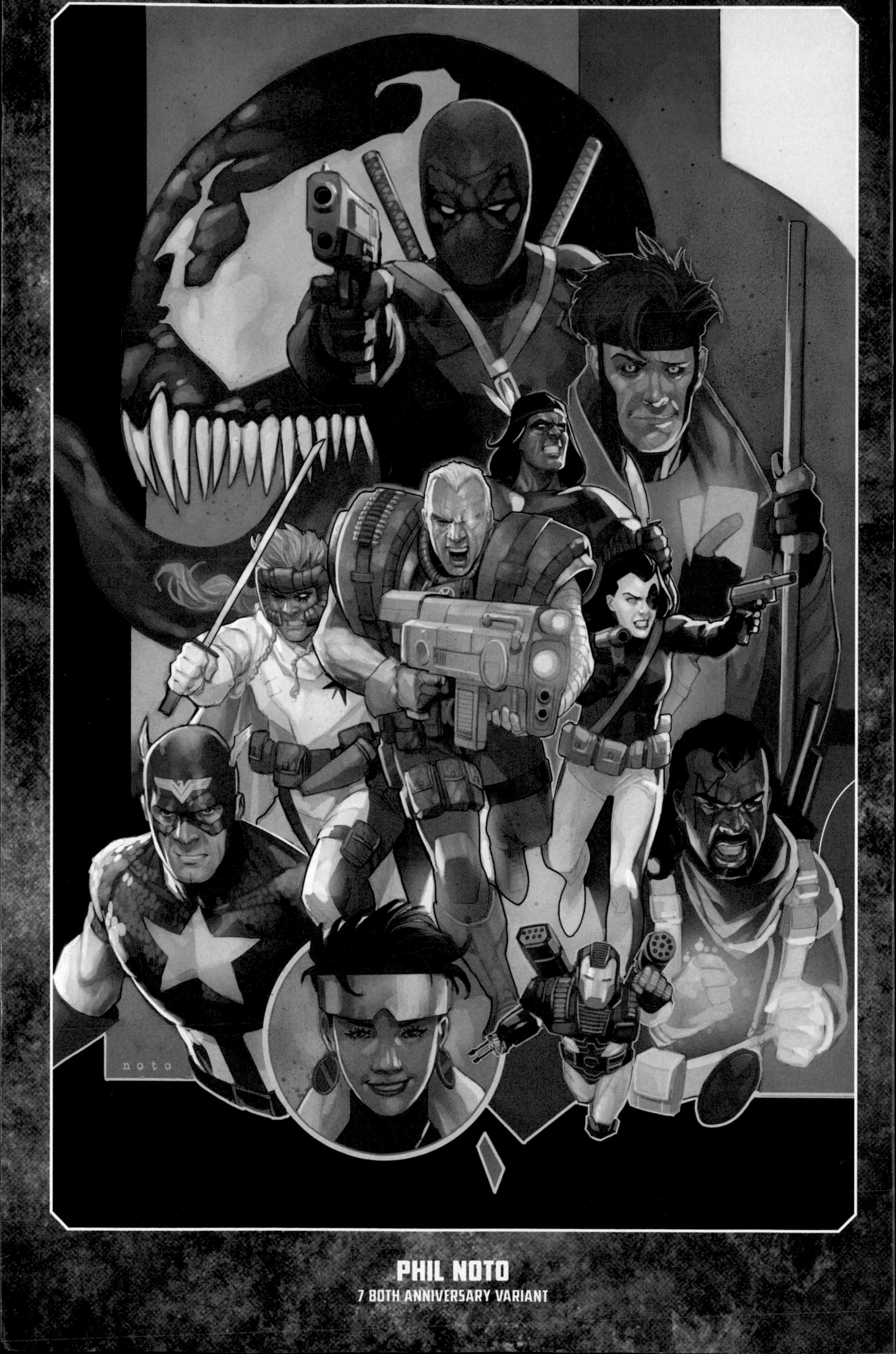
noto

PHIL NOTO

7 80TH ANNIVERSARY VARIANT

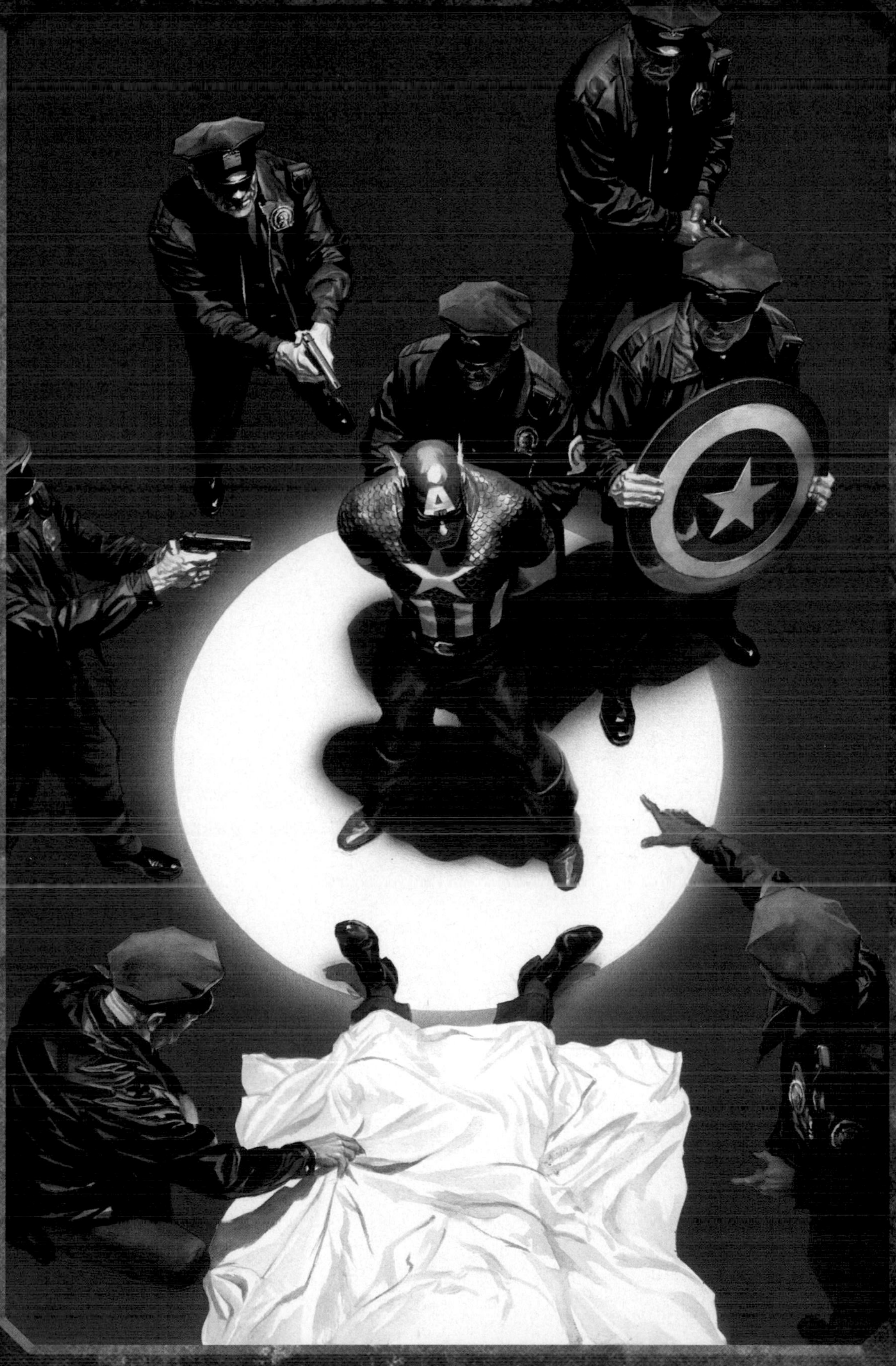

7

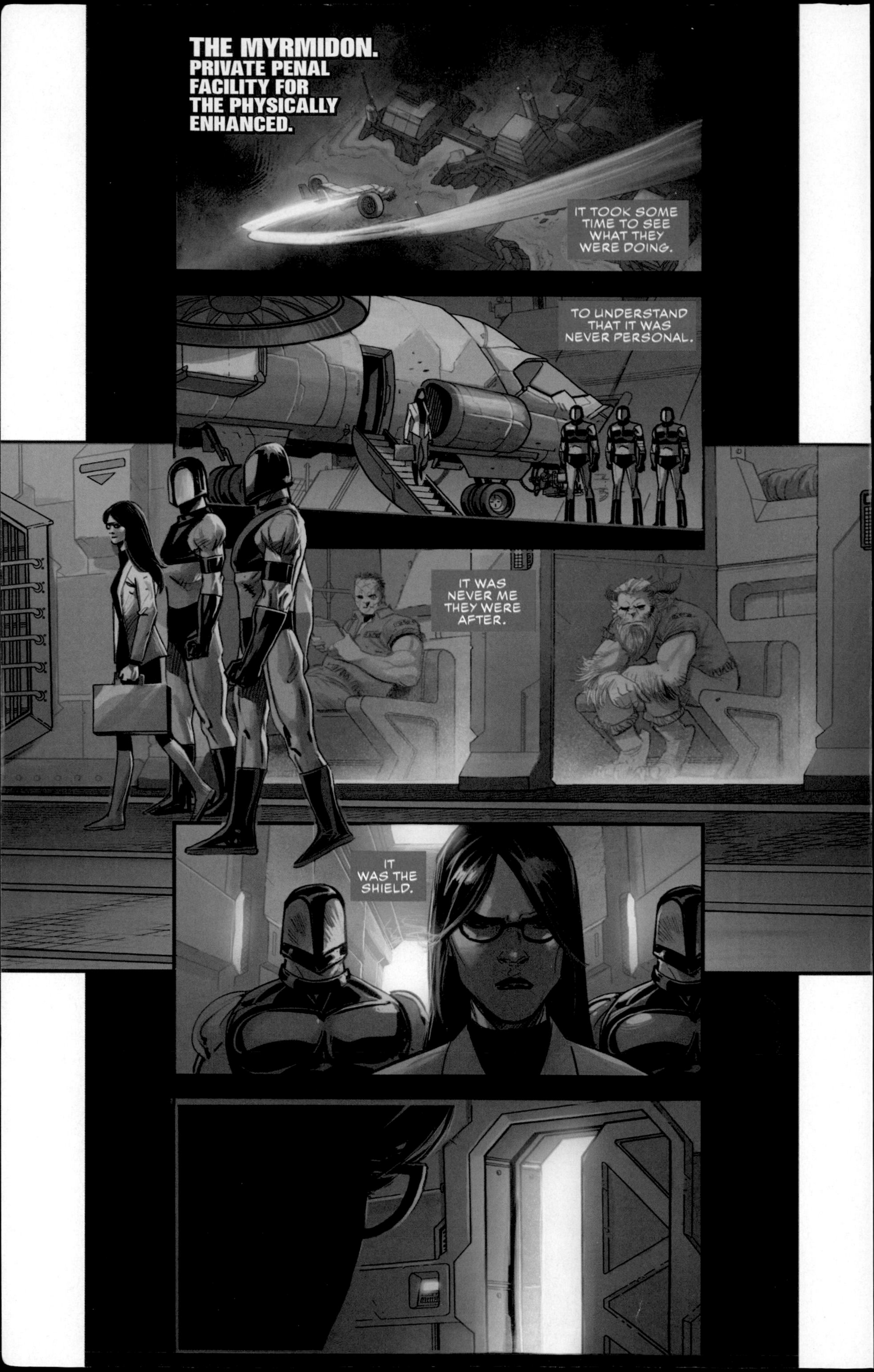
THE MYRMIDON. PRIVATE PENAL FACILITY FOR THE PHYSICALLY ENHANCED.
IT TOOK SOME TIME TO SEE WHAT THEY WERE DOING.
TO UNDERSTAND THAT IT WAS NEVER PERSONAL.
IT WAS NEVER ME THEY WERE AFTER.
IT WAS THE SHIELD.

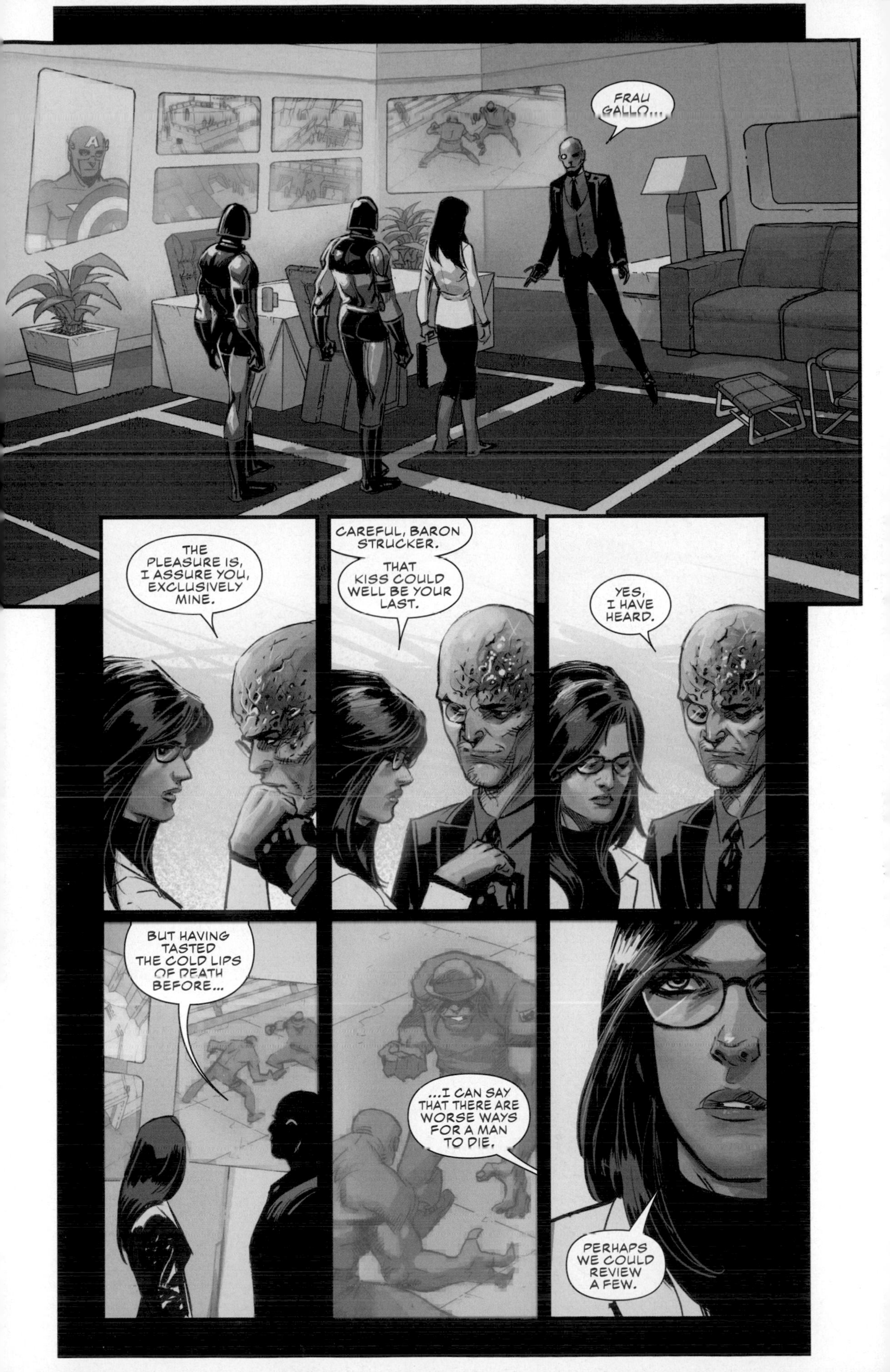
FRAU GALLO...
THE PLEASURE IS, I ASSURE YOU, EXCLUSIVELY MINE.
CAREFUL, BARON STRUCKER.
THAT KISS COULD WELL BE YOUR LAST.
YES, I HAVE HEARD.
BUT HAVING TASTED THE COLD LIPS OF DEATH BEFORE...
...I CAN SAY THAT THERE ARE WORSE WAYS FOR A MAN TO DIE.
PERHAPS WE COULD REVIEW A FEW.

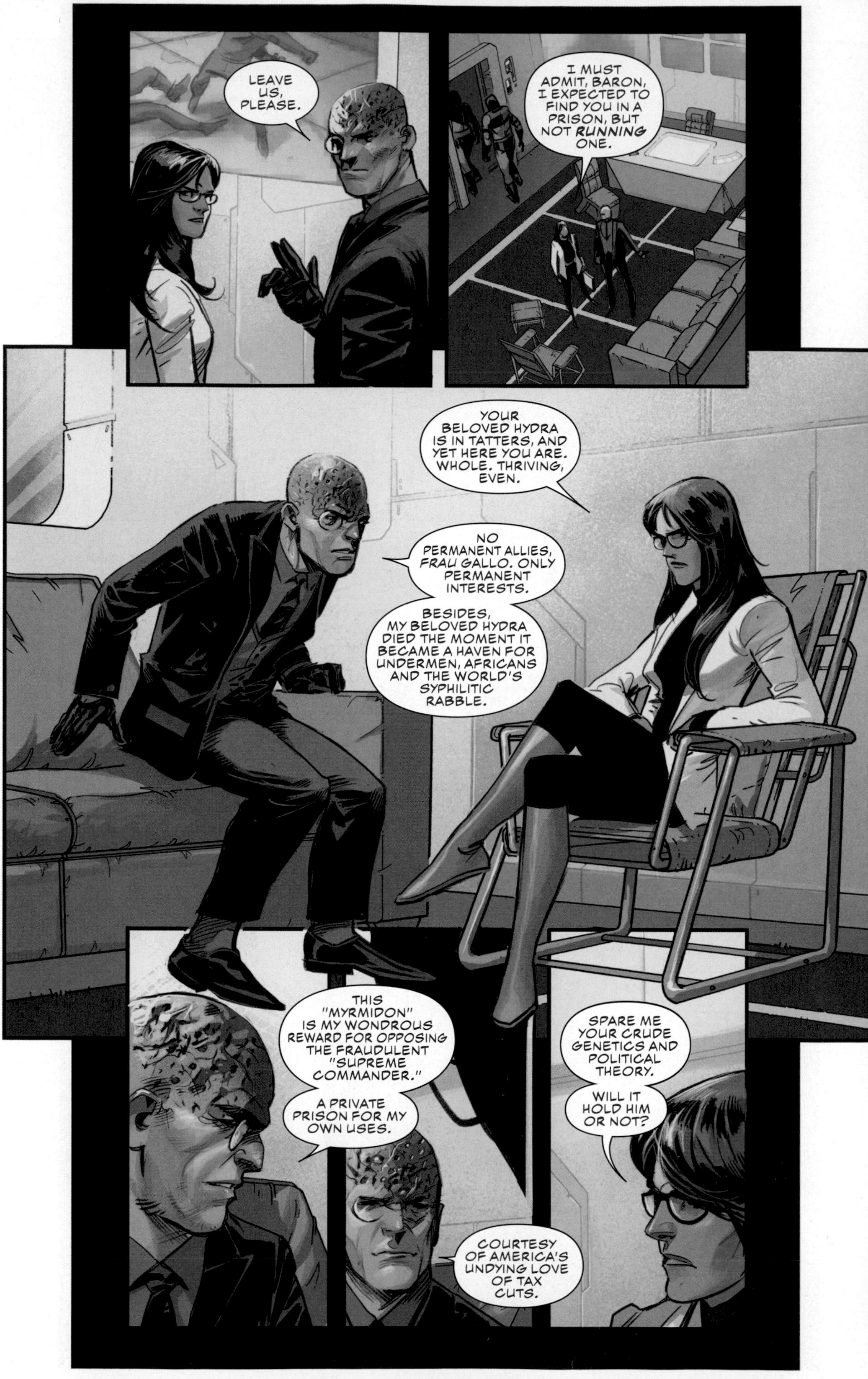
LEAVE US, PLEASE.
I MUST ADMIT, BARON, I EXPECTED TO FIND YOU IN A PRISON, BUT NOT *RUNNING* ONE.
YOUR BELOVED HYDRA IS IN TATTERS, AND YET HERE YOU ARE. WHOLE. THRIVING, EVEN.
NO PERMANENT ALLIES, *FRAU GALLO.* ONLY PERMANENT INTERESTS.
BESIDES, MY BELOVED HYDRA DIED THE MOMENT IT BECAME A HAVEN FOR UNDERMEN, AFRICANS AND THE WORLD'S SYPHILITIC RABBLE.
THIS "MYRMIDON" IS MY WONDROUS REWARD FOR OPPOSING THE FRAUDULENT "SUPREME COMMANDER."
A PRIVATE PRISON FOR MY OWN USES.
COURTESY OF AMERICA'S UNDYING LOVE OF TAX CUTS.
SPARE ME YOUR CRUDE GENETICS AND POLITICAL THEORY.
WILL IT HOLD HIM OR NOT?

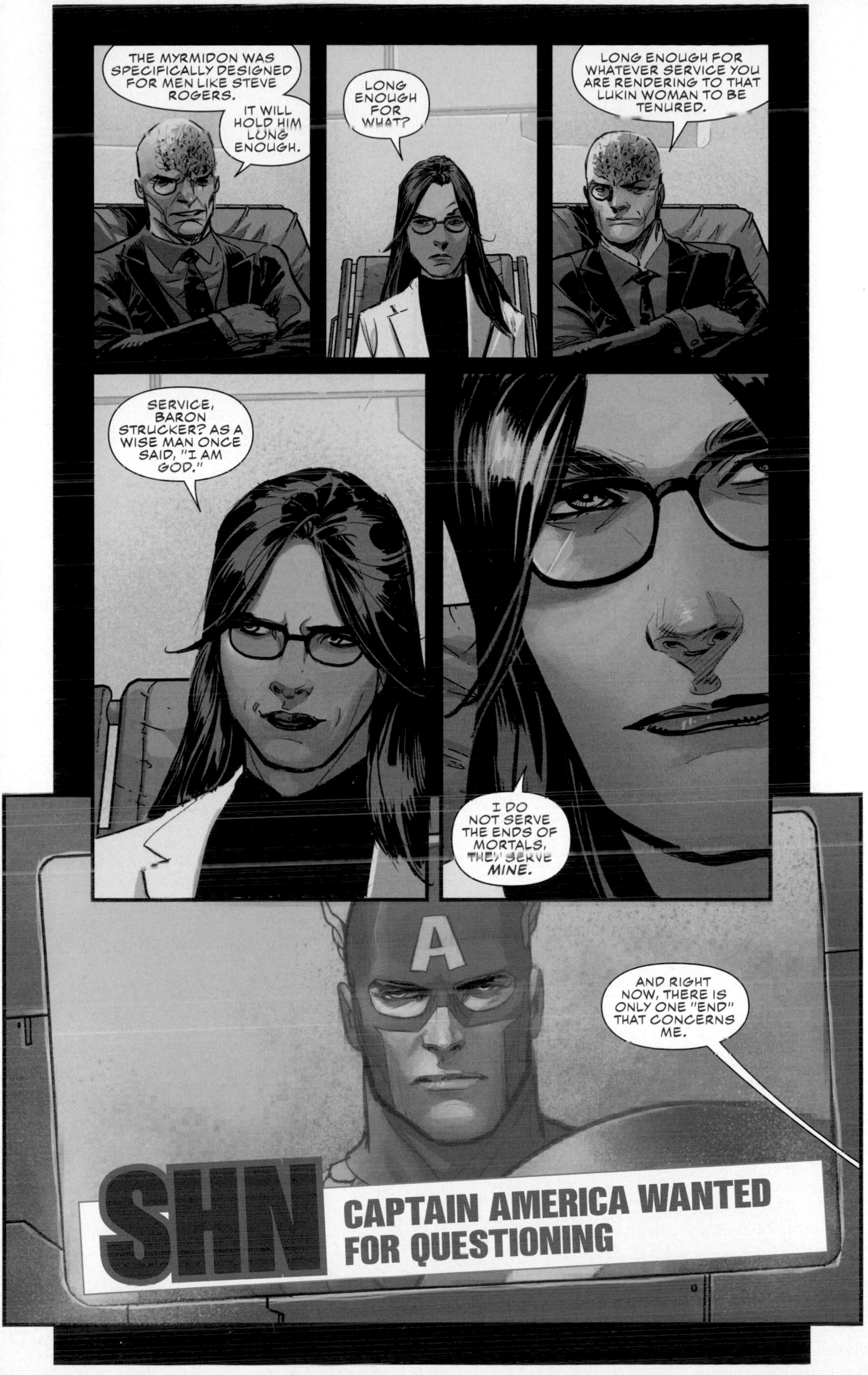
THE MYRMIDON WAS SPECIFICALLY DESIGNED FOR MEN LIKE STEVE ROGERS.
IT WILL HOLD HIM LONG ENOUGH.
LONG ENOUGH FOR WHAT?
LONG ENOUGH FOR WHATEVER SERVICE YOU ARE RENDERING TO THAT LUKIN WOMAN TO BE TENURED.
SERVICE, BARON STRUCKER? AS A WISE MAN ONCE SAID, "I AM GOD."
I DO NOT SERVE THE ENDS OF MORTALS, THEY SERVE MINE.
AND RIGHT NOW, THERE IS ONLY ONE "END" THAT CONCERNS ME.
SHN
CAPTAIN AMERICA WANTED FOR QUESTIONING

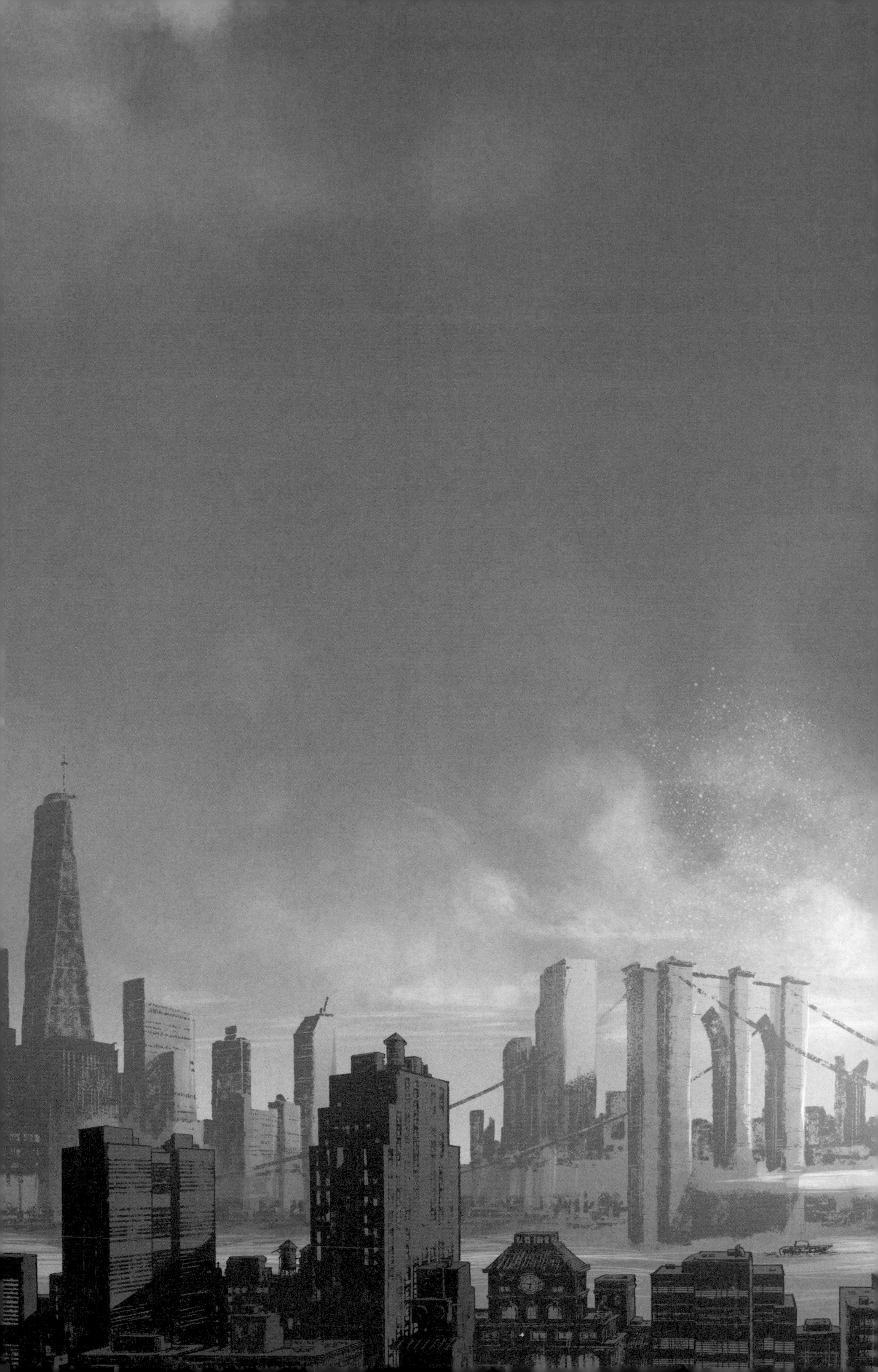

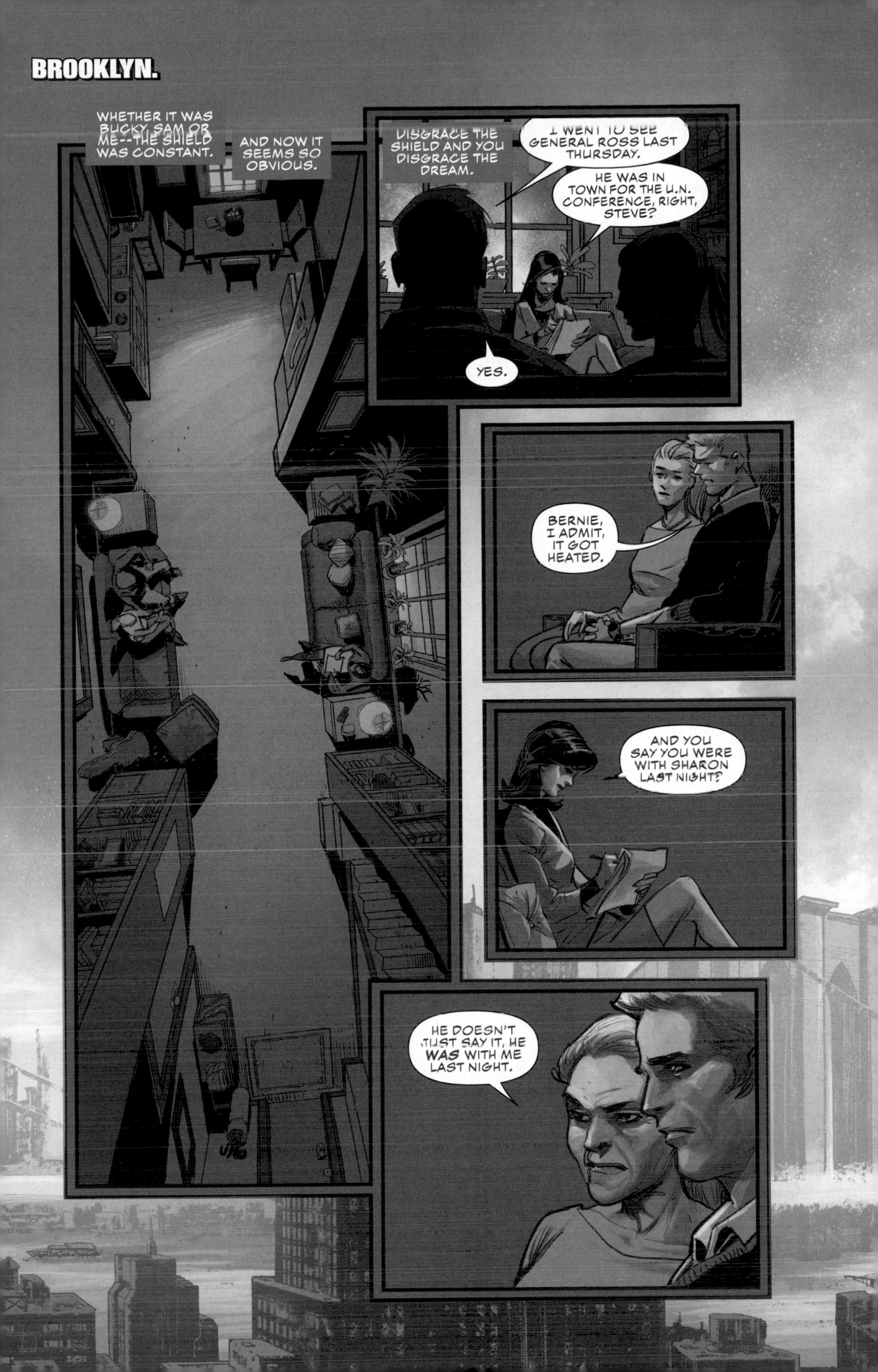
BROOKLYN.
WHETHER IT WAS BUCKY, SAM OR ME--THE SHIELD WAS CONSTANT.
AND NOW IT SEEMS SO OBVIOUS.
DISGRACE THE SHIELD AND YOU DISGRACE THE DREAM.
I WENT TO SEE GENERAL ROSS LAST THURSDAY.
HE WAS IN TOWN FOR THE U.N. CONFERENCE, RIGHT, STEVE?
YES.
BERNIE, I ADMIT, IT GOT HEATED.
AND YOU SAY YOU WERE WITH SHARON LAST NIGHT?
HE DOESN'T JUST SAY IT, HE WAS WITH ME LAST NIGHT.

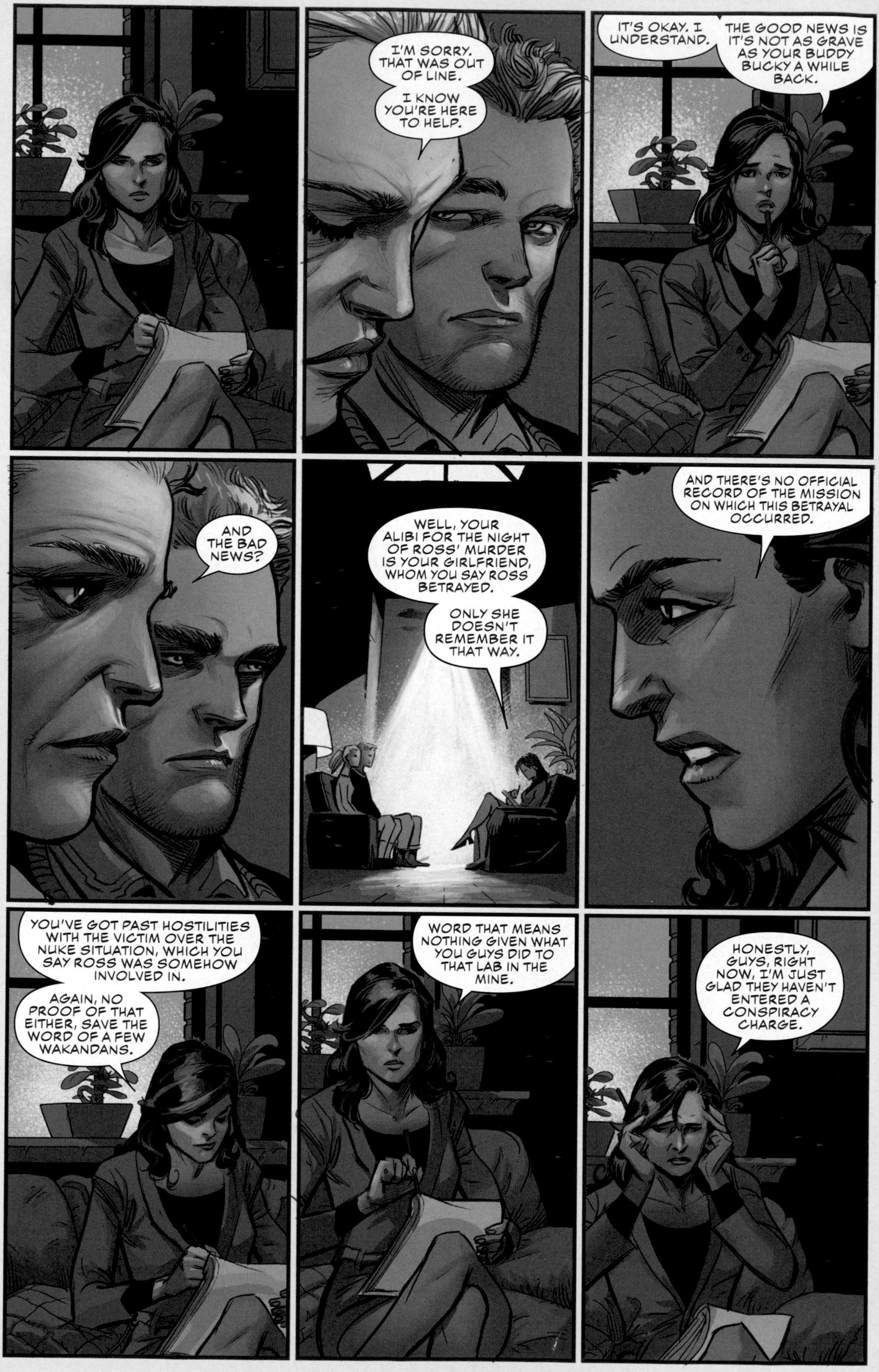
I'M SORRY. THAT WAS OUT OF LINE.
I KNOW YOU'RE HERE TO HELP.
IT'S OKAY. I UNDERSTAND.
THE GOOD NEWS IS IT'S NOT AS GRAVE AS YOUR BUDDY BUCKY A WHILE BACK.
AND THE BAD NEWS?
WELL, YOUR ALIBI FOR THE NIGHT OF ROSS' MURDER IS YOUR GIRLFRIEND, WHOM YOU SAY ROSS BETRAYED.
ONLY SHE DOESN'T REMEMBER IT THAT WAY.
AND THERE'S NO OFFICIAL RECORD OF THE MISSION ON WHICH THIS BETRAYAL OCCURRED.
YOU'VE GOT PAST HOSTILITIES WITH THE VICTIM OVER THE NUKE SITUATION, WHICH YOU SAY ROSS WAS SOMEHOW INVOLVED IN.
AGAIN, NO PROOF OF THAT EITHER, SAVE THE WORD OF A FEW WAKANDANS.
WORD THAT MEANS NOTHING GIVEN WHAT YOU GUYS DID TO THAT LAB IN THE MINE.
HONESTLY, GUYS, RIGHT NOW, I'M JUST GLAD THEY HAVEN'T ENTERED A CONSPIRACY CHARGE.

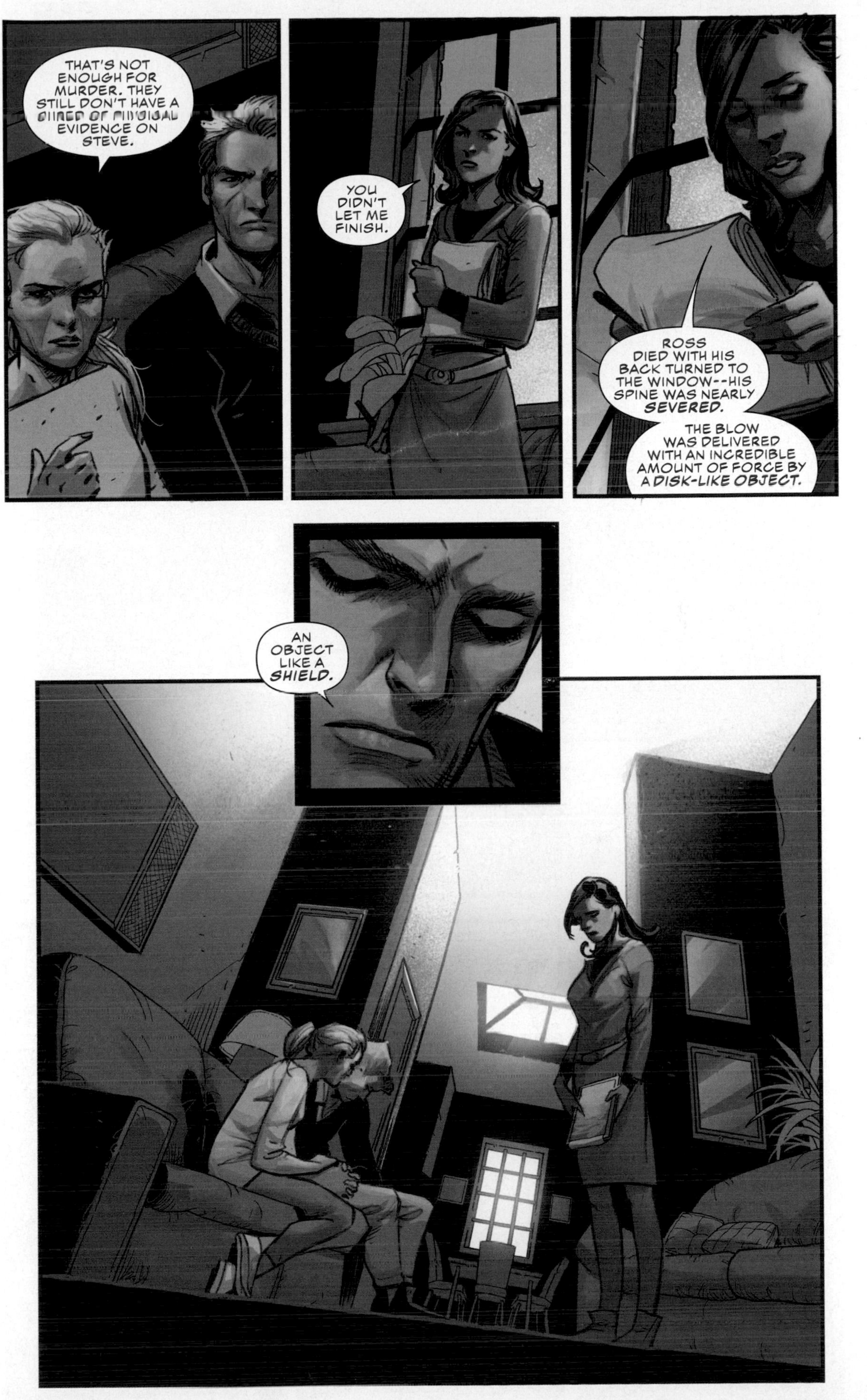
THAT'S NOT ENOUGH FOR MURDER. THEY STILL DON'T HAVE A
EVIDENCE ON STEVE.
YOU DIDN'T LET ME FINISH.
ROSS DIED WITH HIS BACK TURNED TO THE WINDOW--HIS SPINE WAS NEARLY SEVERED.
THE BLOW WAS DELIVERED WITH AN INCREDIBLE AMOUNT OF FORCE BY A DISK-LIKE OBJECT.
AN OBJECT LIKE A SHIELD.

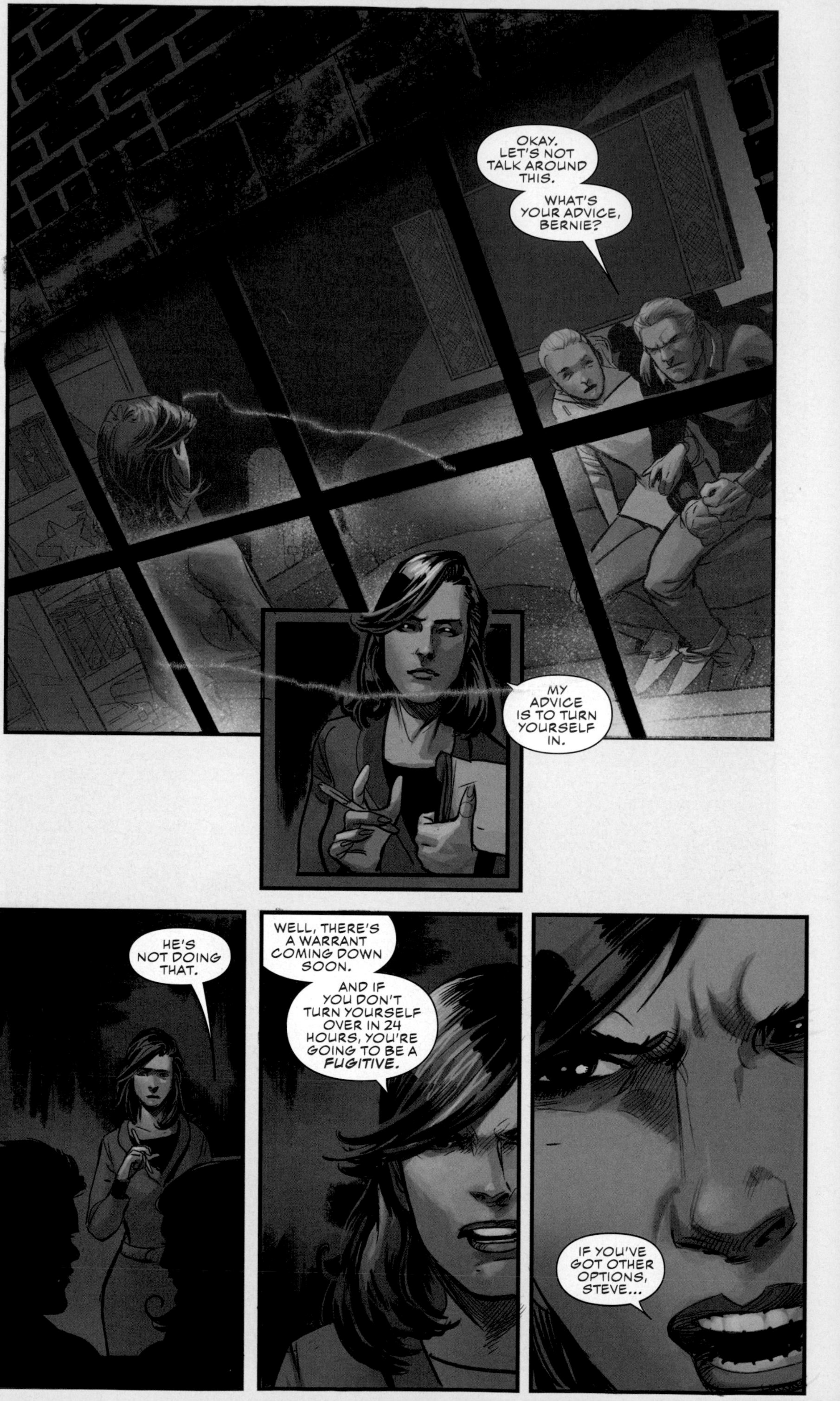
OKAY. LET'S NOT TALK AROUND THIS.
WHAT'S YOUR ADVICE, BERNIE?
MY ADVICE IS TO TURN YOURSELF IN.
HE'S NOT DOING THAT.
WELL, THERE'S A WARRANT COMING DOWN SOON.
AND IF YOU DON'T TURN YOURSELF OVER IN 24 HOURS, YOU'RE GOING TO BE A FUGITIVE.
IF YOU'VE GOT OTHER OPTIONS, STEVE...

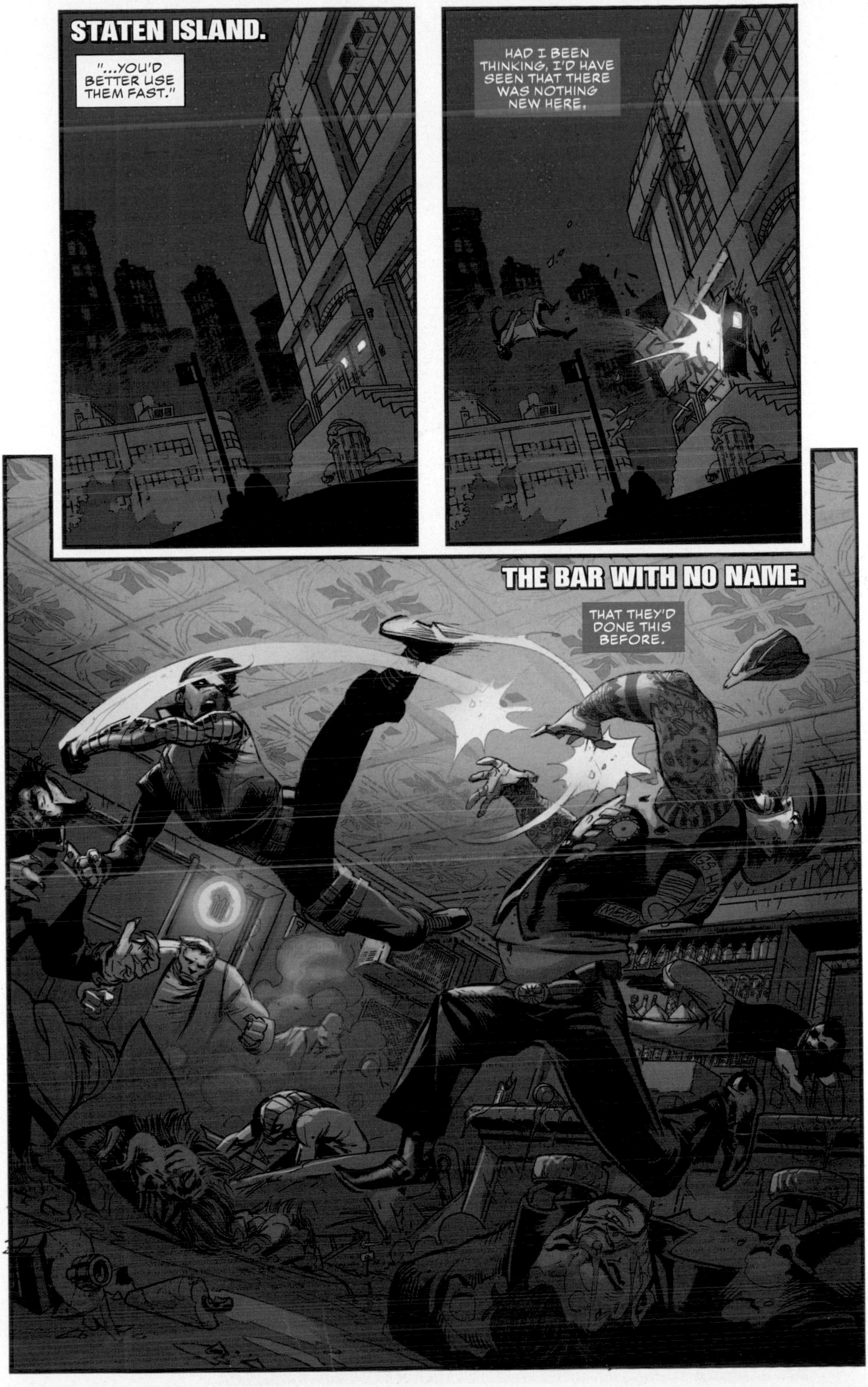
STATEN ISLAND.
"...YOU'D BETTER USE THEM FAST."
HAD I BEEN THINKING, I'D HAVE SEEN THAT THERE WAS NOTHING NEW HERE.
THE BAR WITH NO NAME.
THAT THEY'D DONE THIS BEFORE.

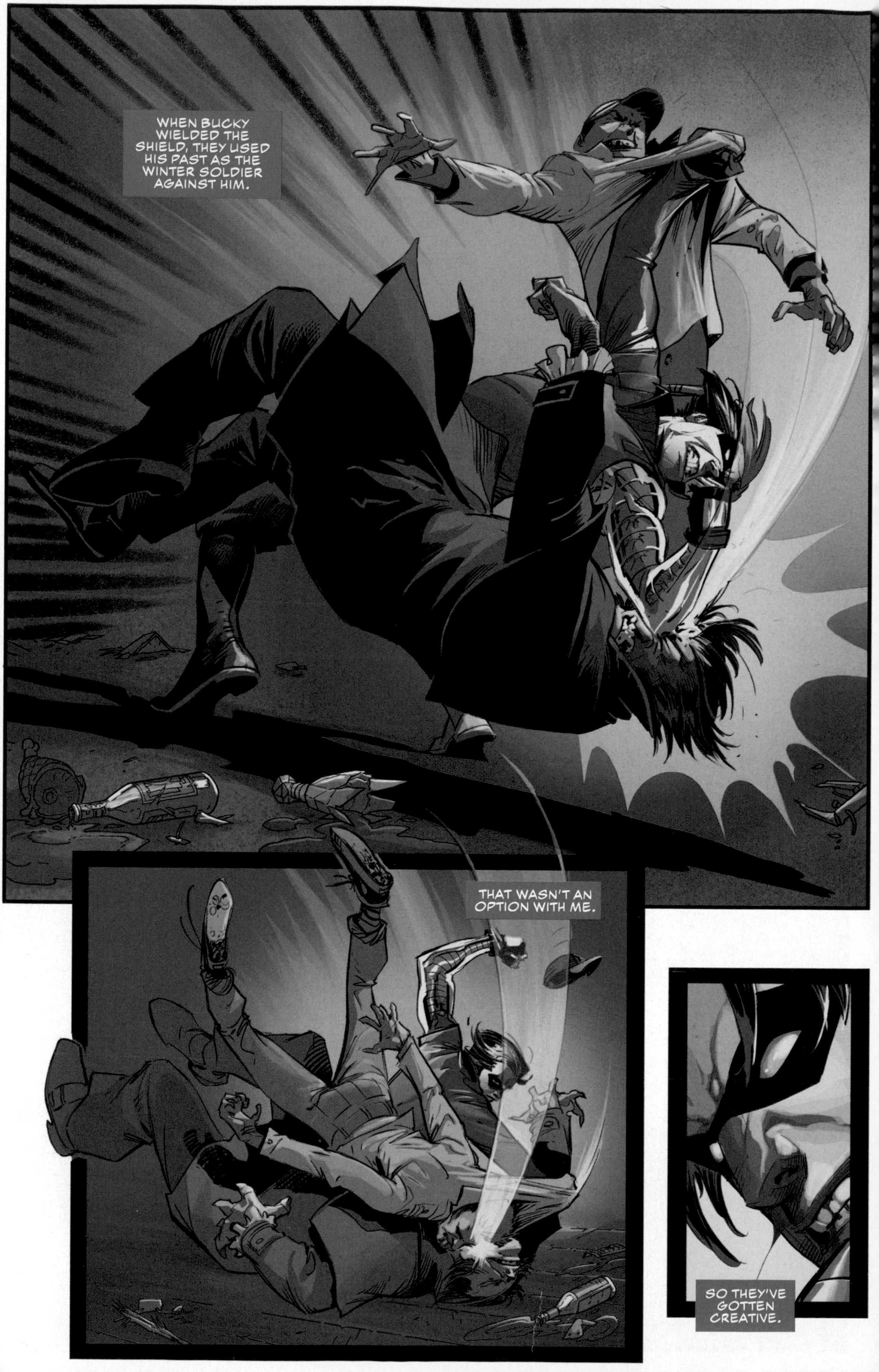
WHEN BUCKY WIELDED THE SHIELD, THEY USED HIS PAST AS THE WINTER SOLDIER AGAINST HIM.
THAT WASN'T AN OPTION WITH ME.
SO THEY'VE GOTTEN CREATIVE.

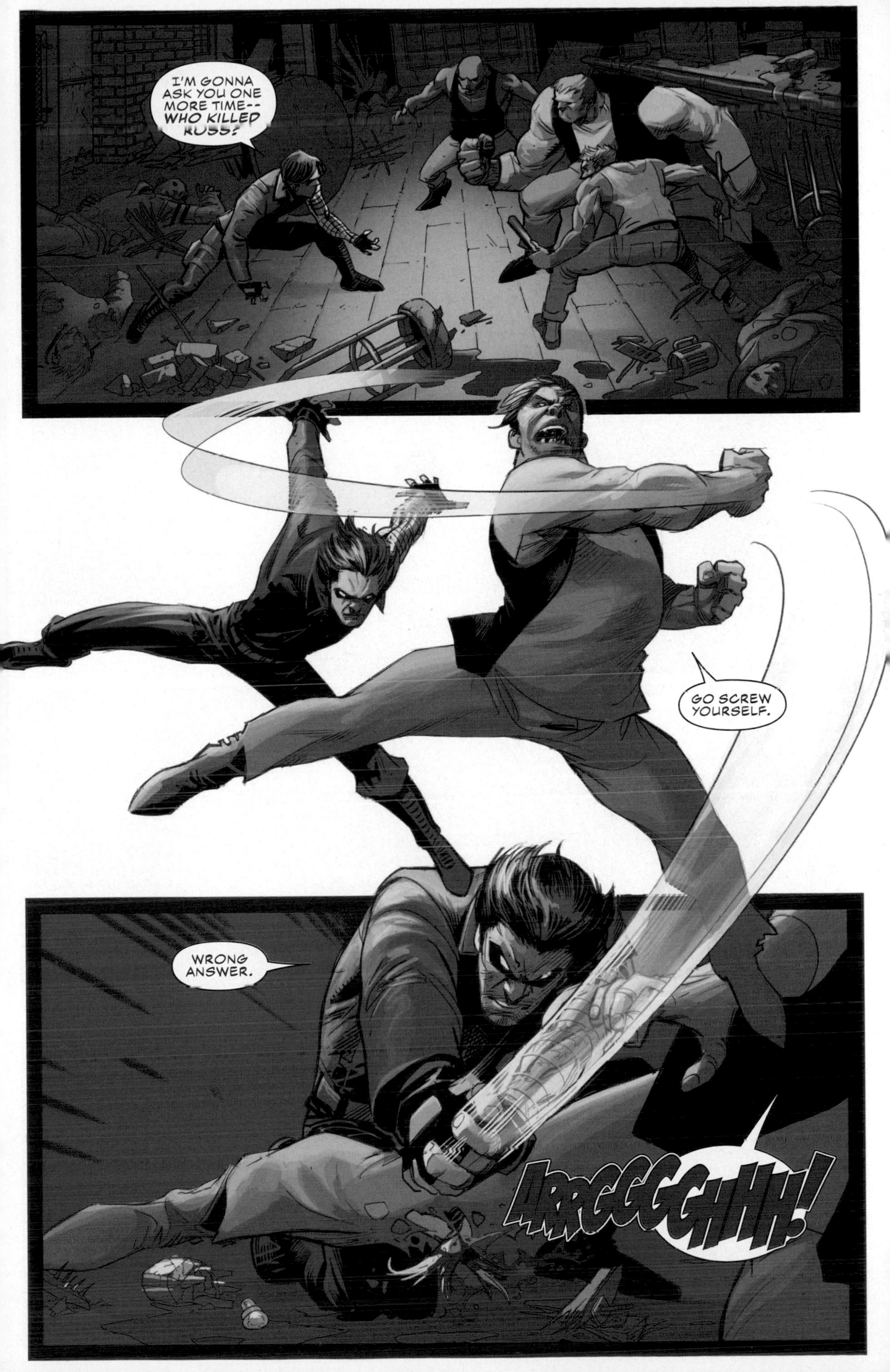
I'M GONNA ASK YOU ONE MORE TIME-- WHO KILLED RUSS?
GO SCREW YOURSELF.
WRONG ANSWER.
ARRGGGGHHH!

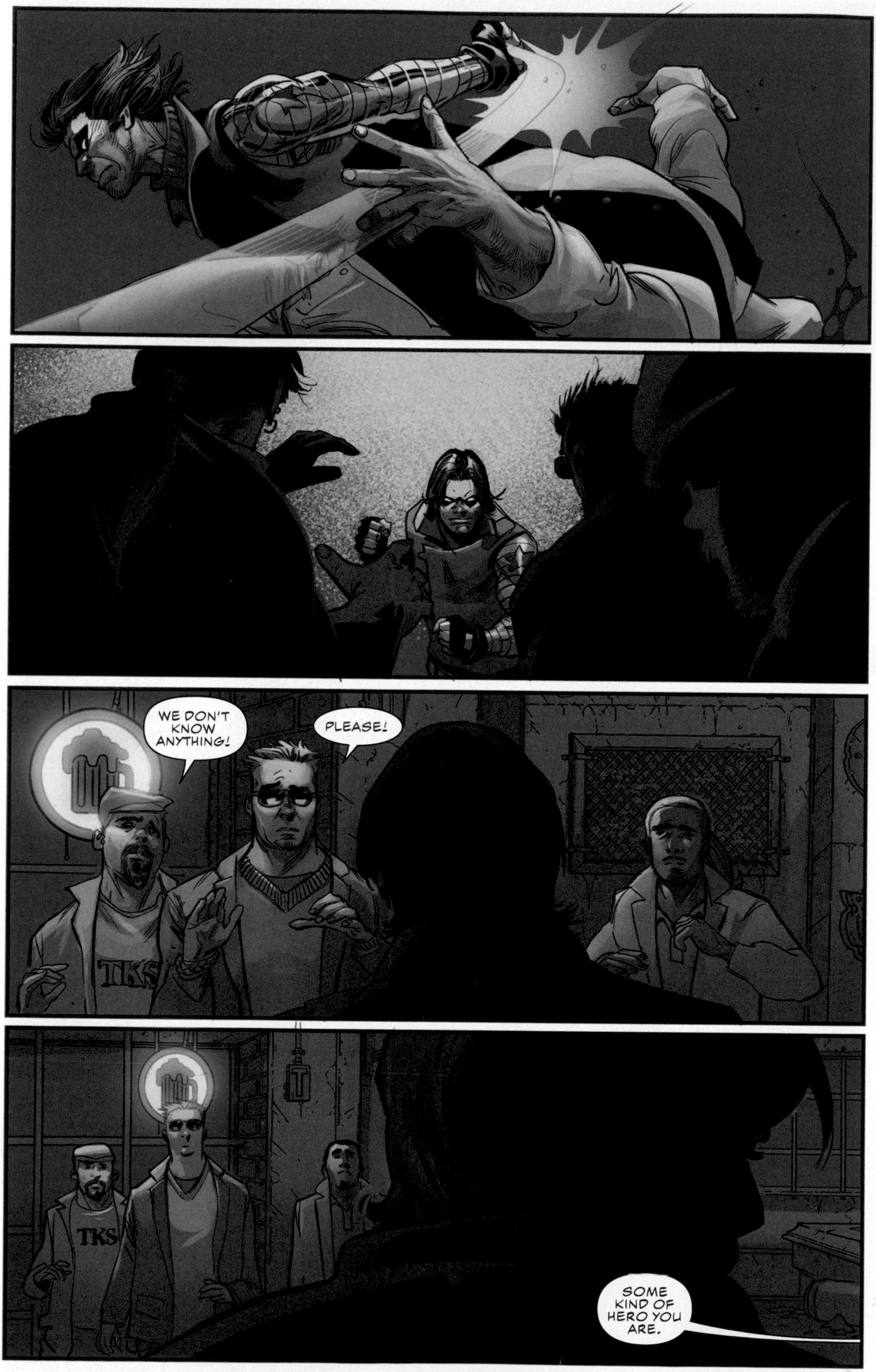
WE DON'T KNOW ANYTHING!
PLEASE!
TKS
TKS
SOME KIND OF HERO YOU ARE.

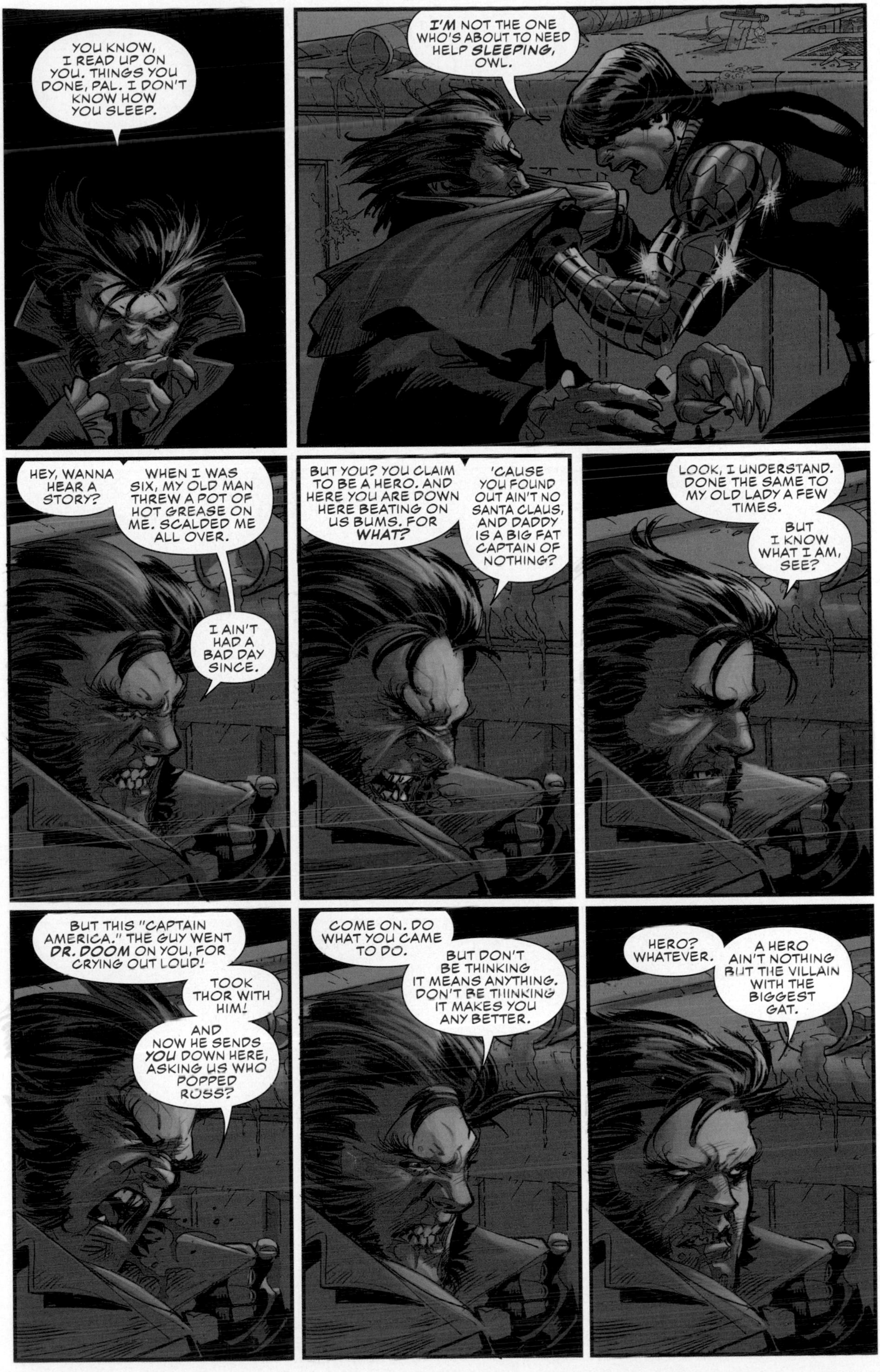
YOU KNOW, I READ UP ON YOU. THINGS YOU DONE, PAL. I DON'T KNOW HOW YOU SLEEP.
I'M NOT THE ONE WHO'S ABOUT TO NEED HELP SLEEPING, OWL.
HEY, WANNA HEAR A STORY?
WHEN I WAS SIX, MY OLD MAN THREW A POT OF HOT GREASE ON ME. SCALDED ME ALL OVER.
I AIN'T HAD A BAD DAY SINCE.
BUT YOU? YOU CLAIM TO BE A HERO. AND HERE YOU ARE DOWN HERE BEATING ON US BUMS. FOR WHAT?
'CAUSE YOU FOUND OUT AIN'T NO SANTA CLAUS, AND DADDY IS A BIG FAT CAPTAIN OF NOTHING?
LOOK, I UNDERSTAND. DONE THE SAME TO MY OLD LADY A FEW TIMES.
BUT I KNOW WHAT I AM, SEE?
BUT THIS "CAPTAIN AMERICA." THE GUY WENT DR. DOOM ON YOU, FOR CRYING OUT LOUD!
TOOK THOR WITH HIM!
AND NOW HE SENDS YOU DOWN HERE, ASKING US WHO POPPED ROSS?
COME ON. DO WHAT YOU CAME TO DO.
BUT DON'T BE THINKING IT MEANS ANYTHING. DON'T BE THINKING IT MAKES YOU ANY BETTER.
HERO? WHATEVER.
A HERO AIN'T NOTHING BUT THE VILLAIN WITH THE BIGGEST GAT.

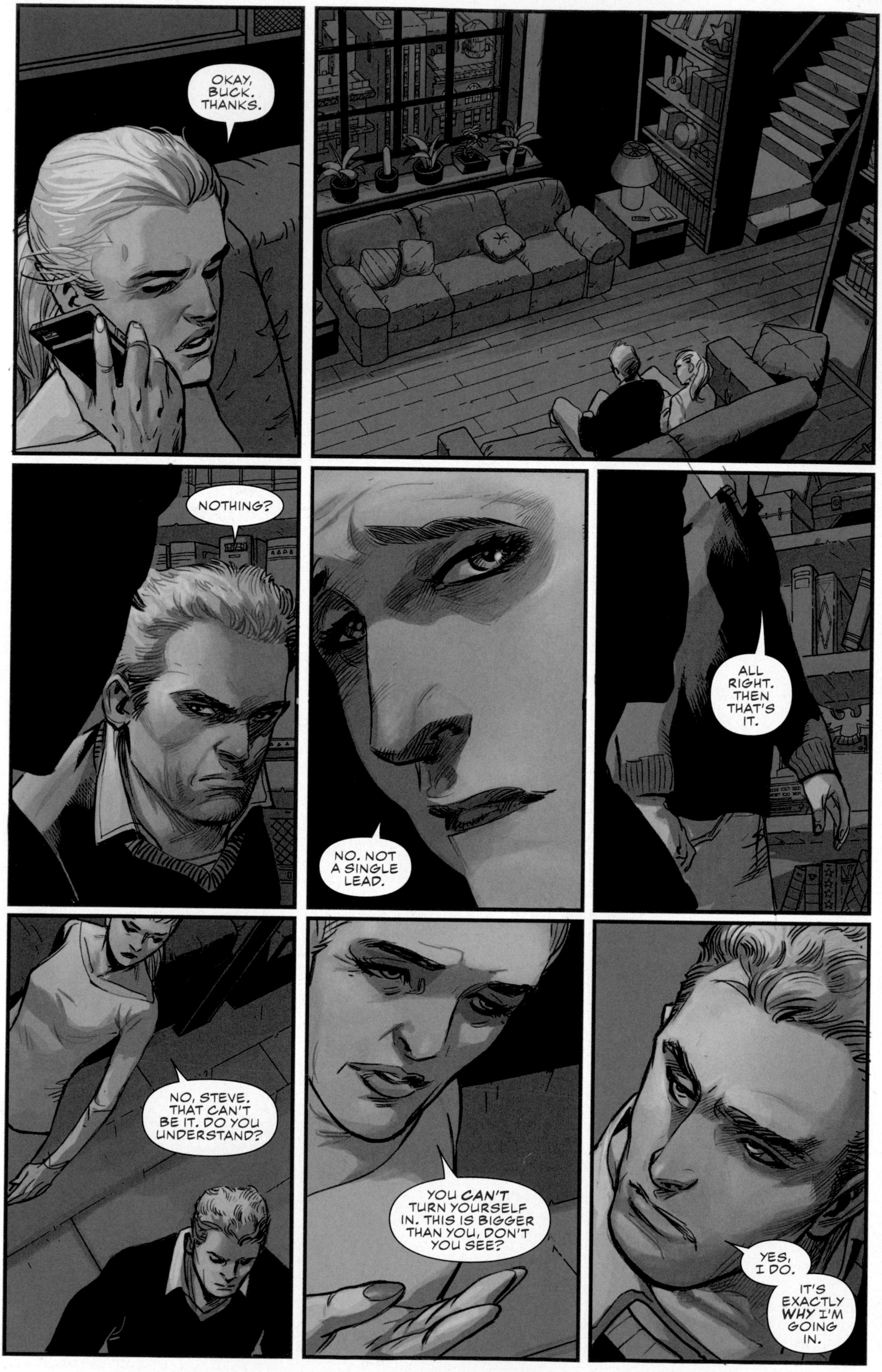
OKAY, BUCK. THANKS.
NOTHING?
NO. NOT A SINGLE LEAD.
ALL RIGHT. THEN THAT'S IT.
NO, STEVE. THAT CAN'T BE IT. DO YOU UNDERSTAND?
YOU CAN'T TURN YOURSELF IN. THIS IS BIGGER THAN YOU, DON'T YOU SEE?
YES, I DO.
IT'S EXACTLY WHY I'M GOING IN.

LOOK AT EVERYTHING THAT'S HAPPENED, SHARON, EVERYTHING DONE IN MY NAME.

FOR THE MILLIONTH TIME, THE SUPREME COMMANDER WAS NOT YOU!

YOU'RE RIGHT, BUT HE WAS CAPTAIN AMERICA.

AND THIS DIDN'T START WITH HYDRA.

IT GOES BACK TO THE REGISTRATION ACT.

TO MY DAYS AS NOMAD AND THEN THE CAPTAIN.

HOW CAN I CLAIM TO SERVE MY COUNTRY WHEN I CONSTANTLY OPPOSE IT?

HOW LONG CAN I CARRY THIS SHIELD AND FIGHT THE GOVERNMENT THAT ENTRUSTED ME WITH IT?

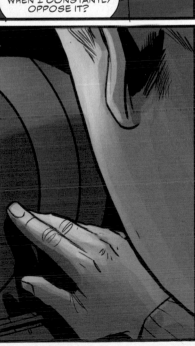

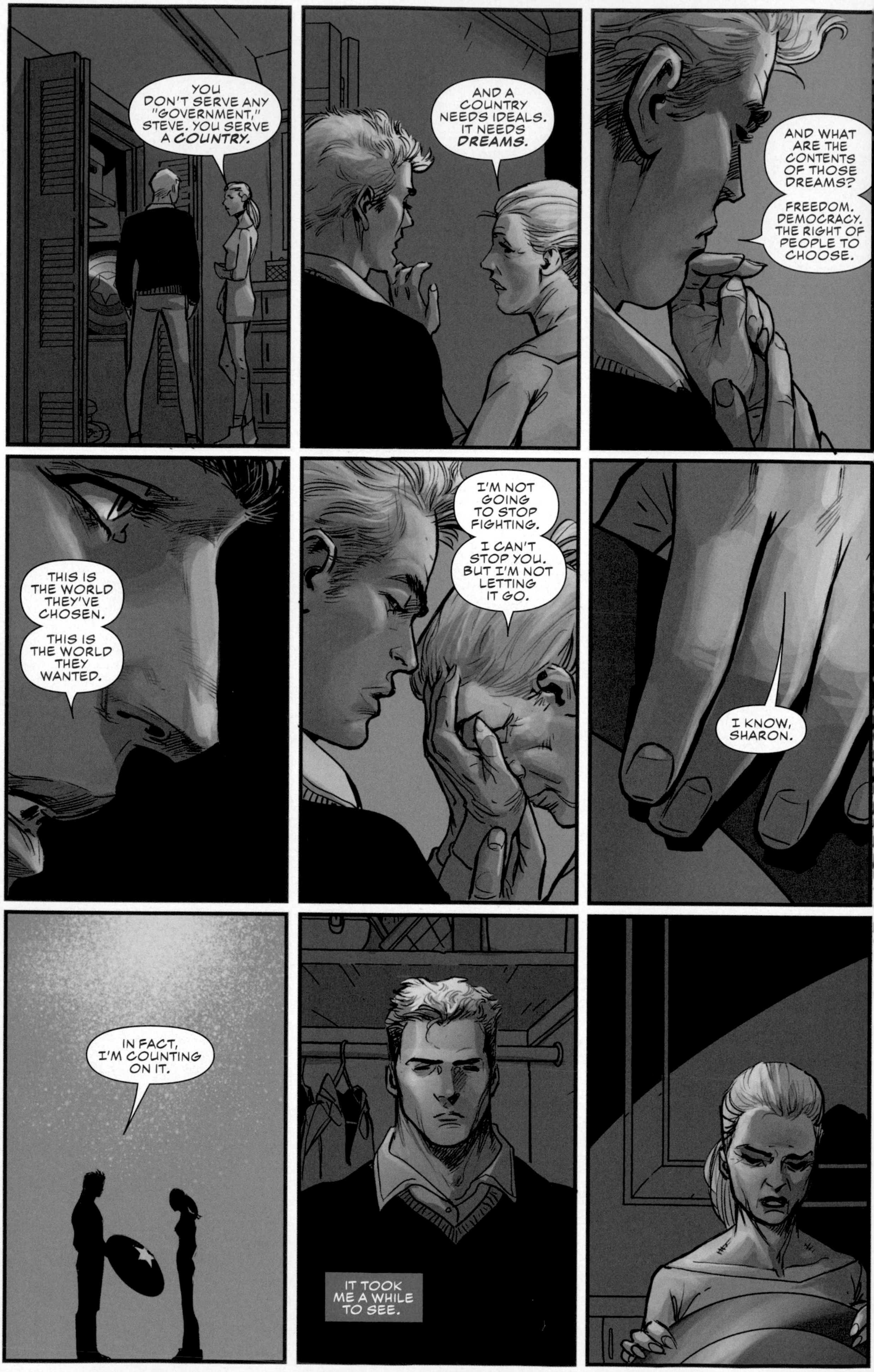
YOU DON'T SERVE ANY "GOVERNMENT," STEVE. YOU SERVE A COUNTRY.
AND A COUNTRY NEEDS IDEALS. IT NEEDS DREAMS.
AND WHAT ARE THE CONTENTS OF THOSE DREAMS?
FREEDOM. DEMOCRACY. THE RIGHT OF PEOPLE TO CHOOSE.
THIS IS THE WORLD THEY'VE CHOSEN.
THIS IS THE WORLD THEY WANTED.
I'M NOT GOING TO STOP FIGHTING.
I CAN'T STOP YOU. BUT I'M NOT LETTING IT GO.
I KNOW, SHARON.
IN FACT, I'M COUNTING ON IT.
IT TOOK ME A WHILE TO SEE.

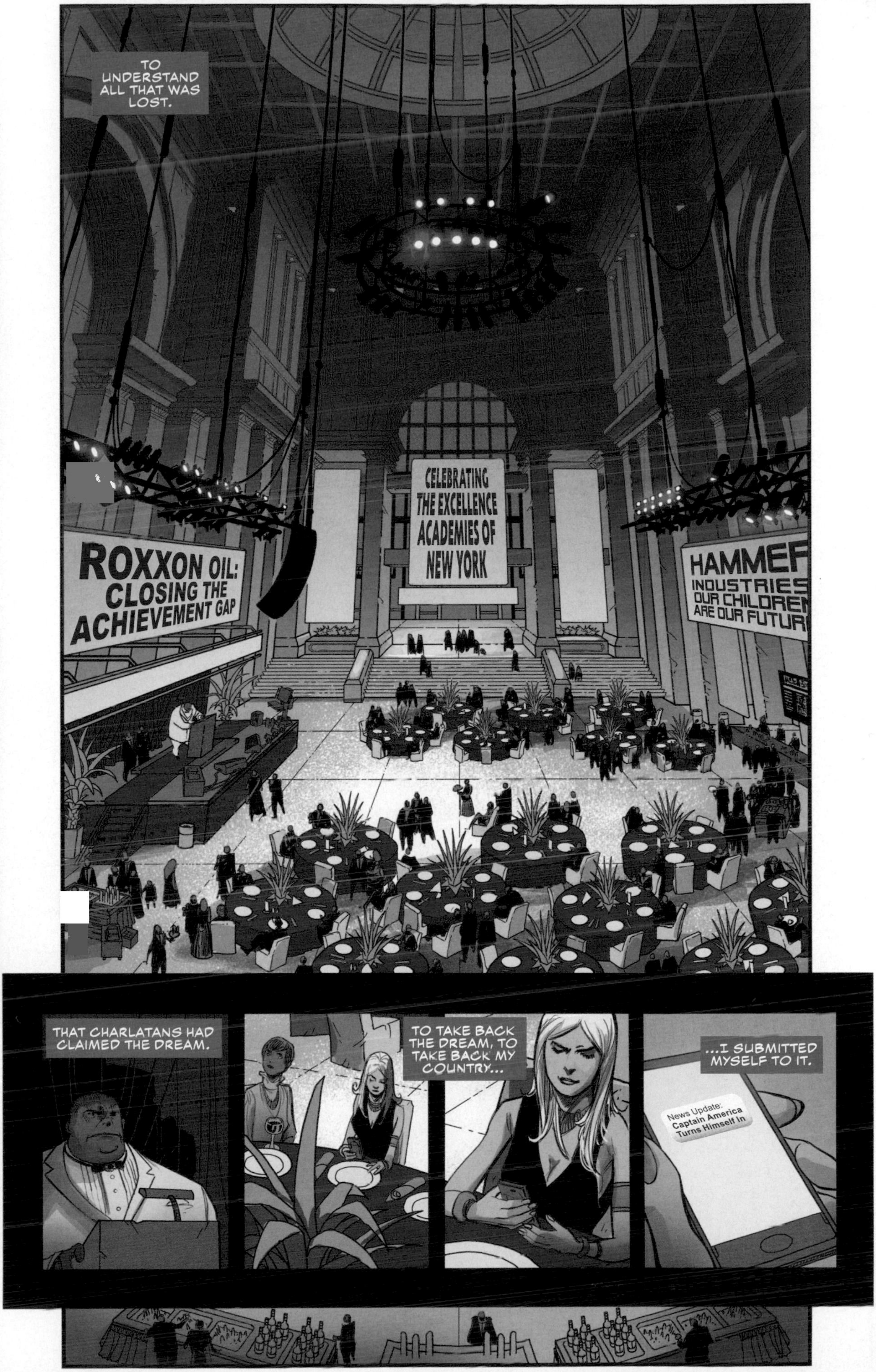

TO UNDERSTAND ALL THAT WAS LOST.
CELEBRATING THE EXCELLENCE ACADEMIES OF NEW YORK
ROXXON OIL: CLOSING THE ACHIEVEMENT GAP
HAMMER INDUSTRIES OUR CHILDREN ARE OUR FUTURE
THAT CHARLATANS HAD CLAIMED THE DREAM.
TO TAKE BACK THE DREAM, TO TAKE BACK MY COUNTRY...
...I SUBMITTED MYSELF TO IT.
News Update:
Captain America Turns Himself In

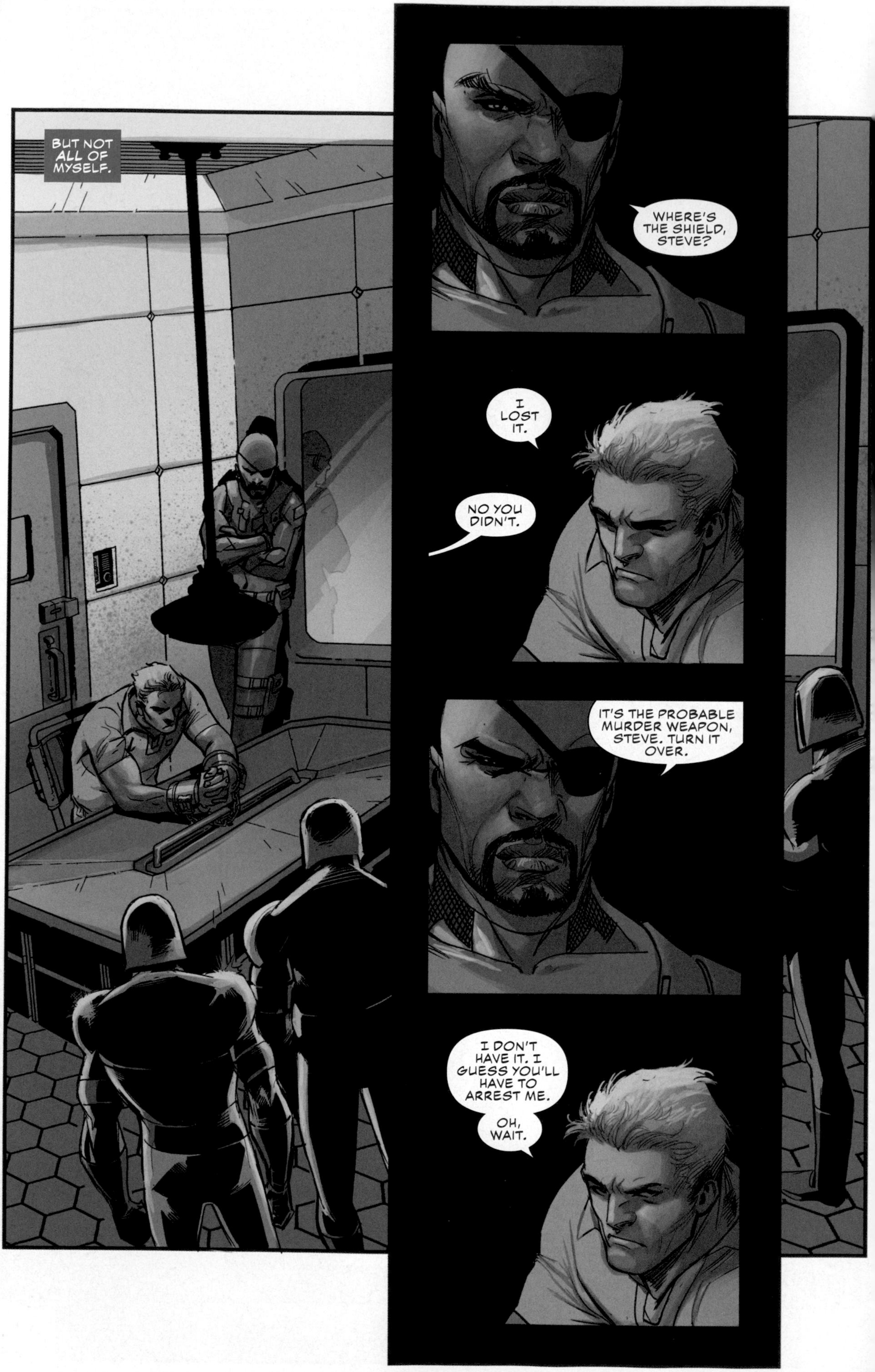
BUT NOT ALL OF MYSELF.
WHERE'S THE SHIELD, STEVE?
I LOST IT.
NO YOU DIDN'T.
IT'S THE PROBABLE MURDER WEAPON, STEVE. TURN IT OVER.
I DON'T HAVE IT. I GUESS YOU'LL HAVE TO ARREST ME.
OH, WAIT.

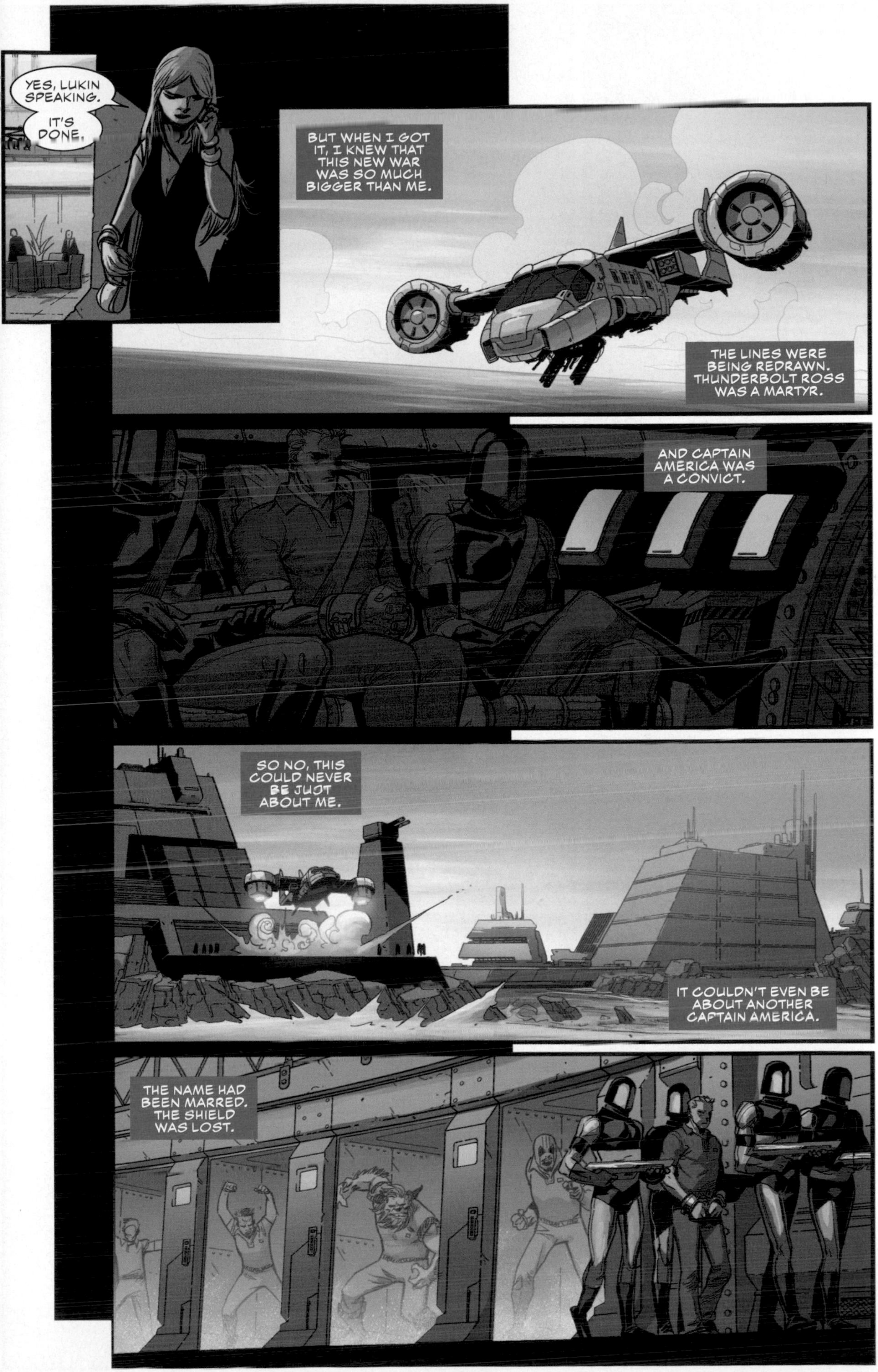
YES, LUKIN SPEAKING.
IT'S DONE.
BUT WHEN I GOT IT, I KNEW THAT THIS NEW WAR WAS SO MUCH BIGGER THAN ME.
THE LINES WERE BEING REDRAWN. THUNDERBOLT ROSS WAS A MARTYR.
AND CAPTAIN AMERICA WAS A CONVICT.
SO NO, THIS COULD NEVER BE JUST ABOUT ME.
IT COULDN'T EVEN BE ABOUT ANOTHER CAPTAIN AMERICA.
THE NAME HAD BEEN MARRED. THE SHIELD WAS LOST.

BUT BELIEVE IT OR NOT, THERE ARE THINGS IN THIS WORLD OLDER THAN CAPTAIN AMERICA.

AND WHAT I WAS, WHAT I REPRESENTED, WAS A NEED AS OLD AS HUMANITY ITSELF.

AND THE NEED FOR FREEDOM, LIBERTY AND THE PURSUIT OF HAPPINESS, WELL, IT IS FOREVER.

YOU SEE, THEY COULD KILL A DREAMER.

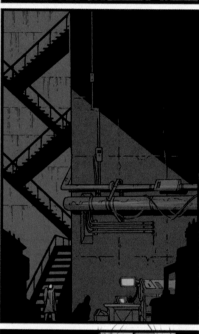

BUT THEY COULD NEVER KILL THE DREAM.

AETERNUM FILIAS, SISTERS.

AGAIN THE DRYAD SUMMONS US.

AGAIN THE ANCIENT SERPENT ARISES.

THEY COULD JAIL THE REVOLUTIONARY.

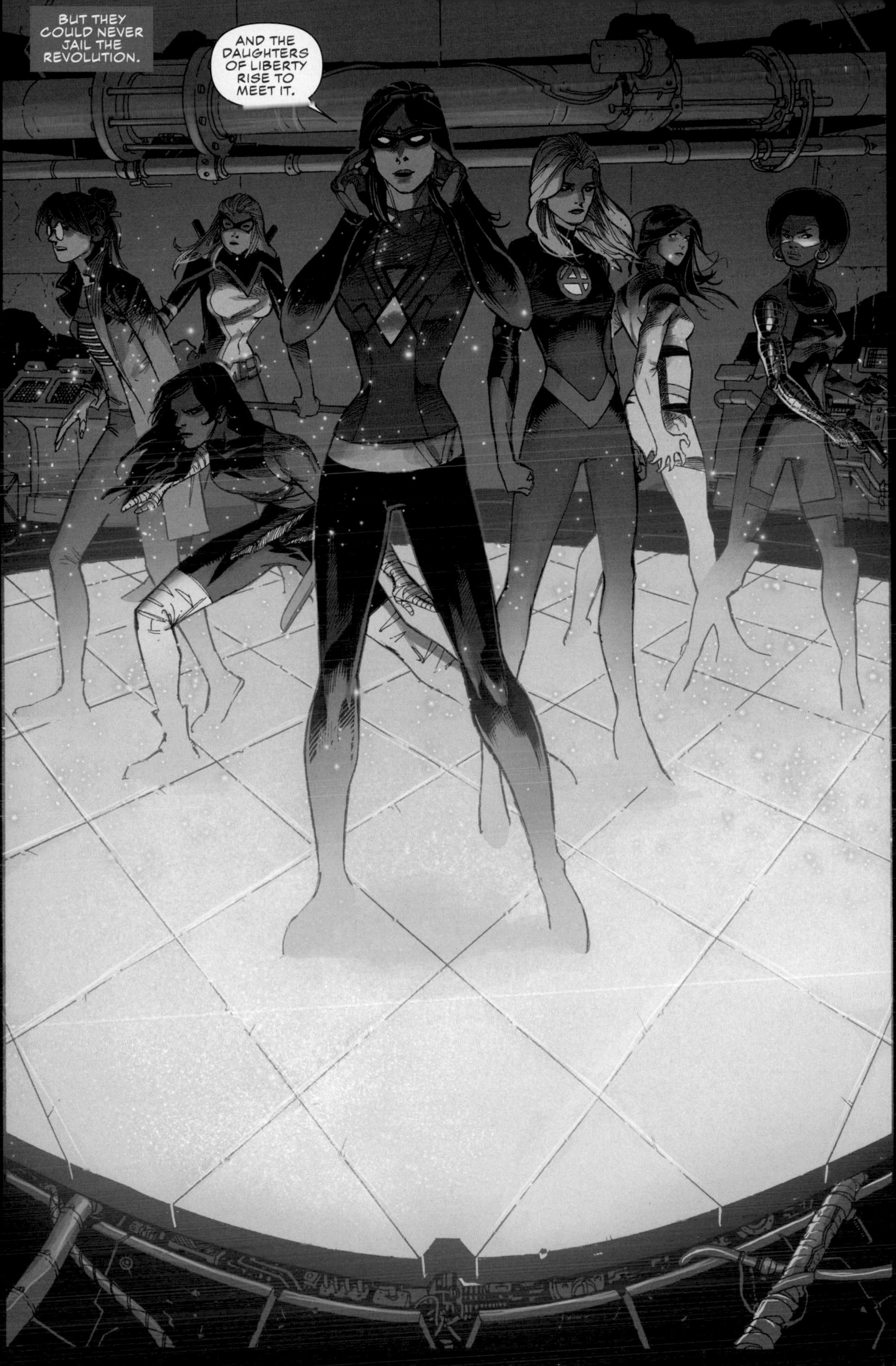
BUT THEY COULD NEVER JAIL THE REVOLUTION.
AND THE DAUGHTERS OF LIBERTY RISE TO MEET IT.

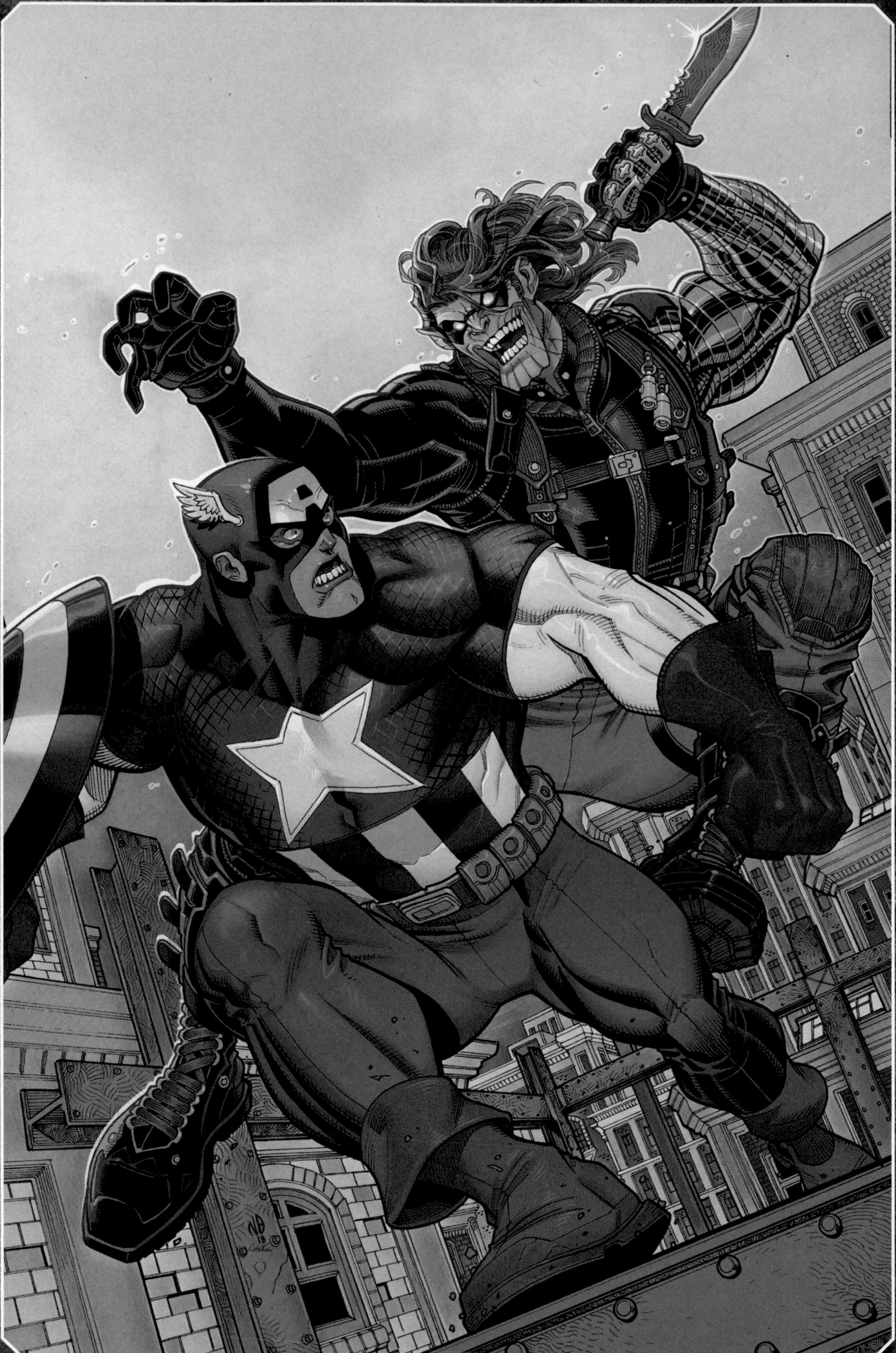

NICK BRADSHAW & JOHN RAUCH
8 SKRULLS VARIANT

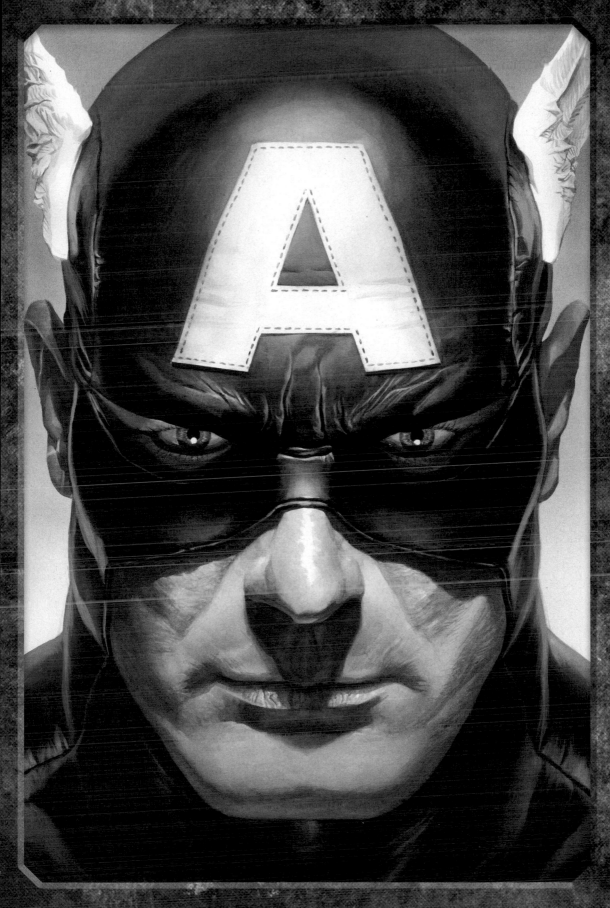

8

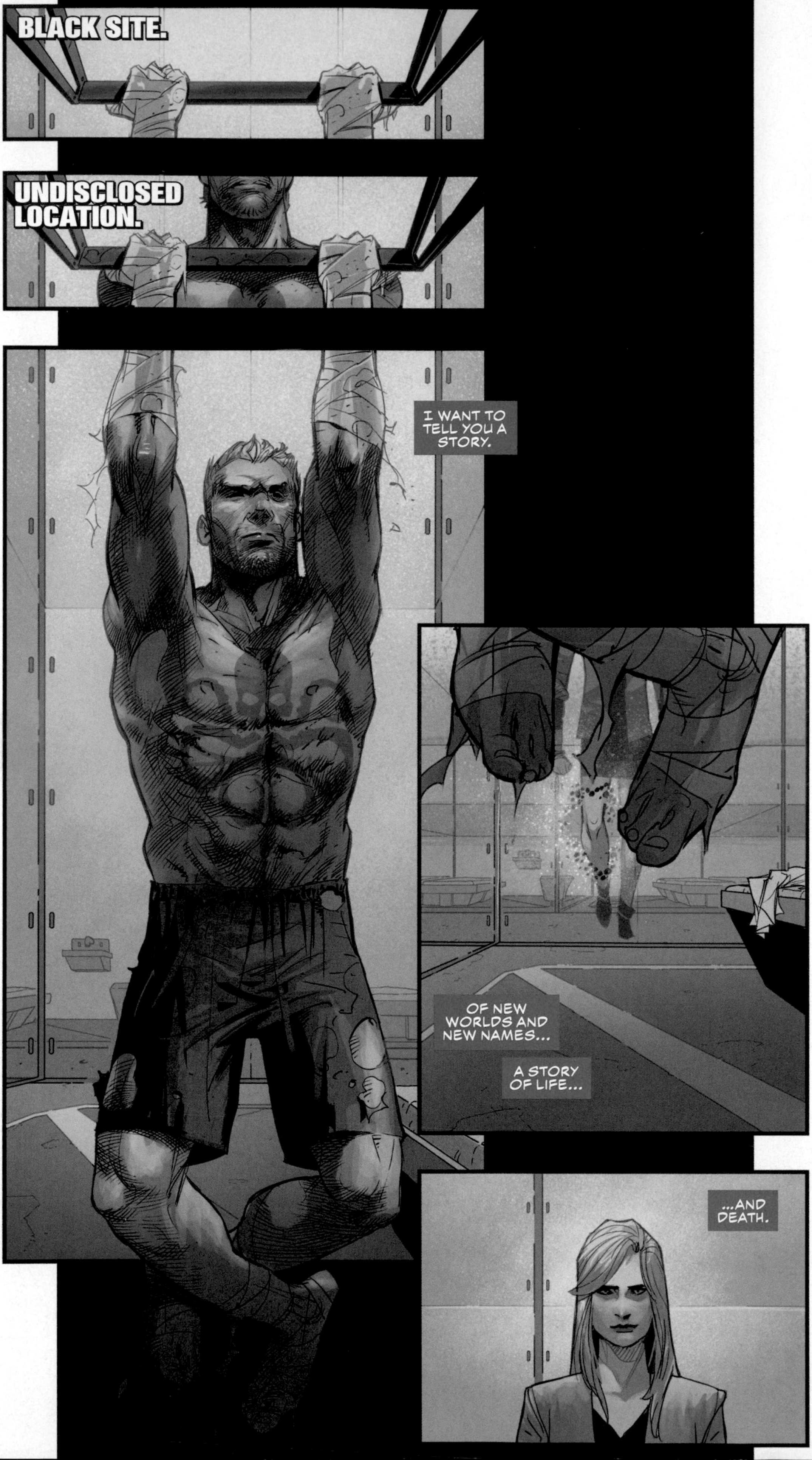
BLACK SITE.
UNDISCLOSED LOCATION.
I WANT TO TELL YOU A STORY.
OF NEW WORLDS AND NEW NAMES...
A STORY OF LIFE...
...AND DEATH.

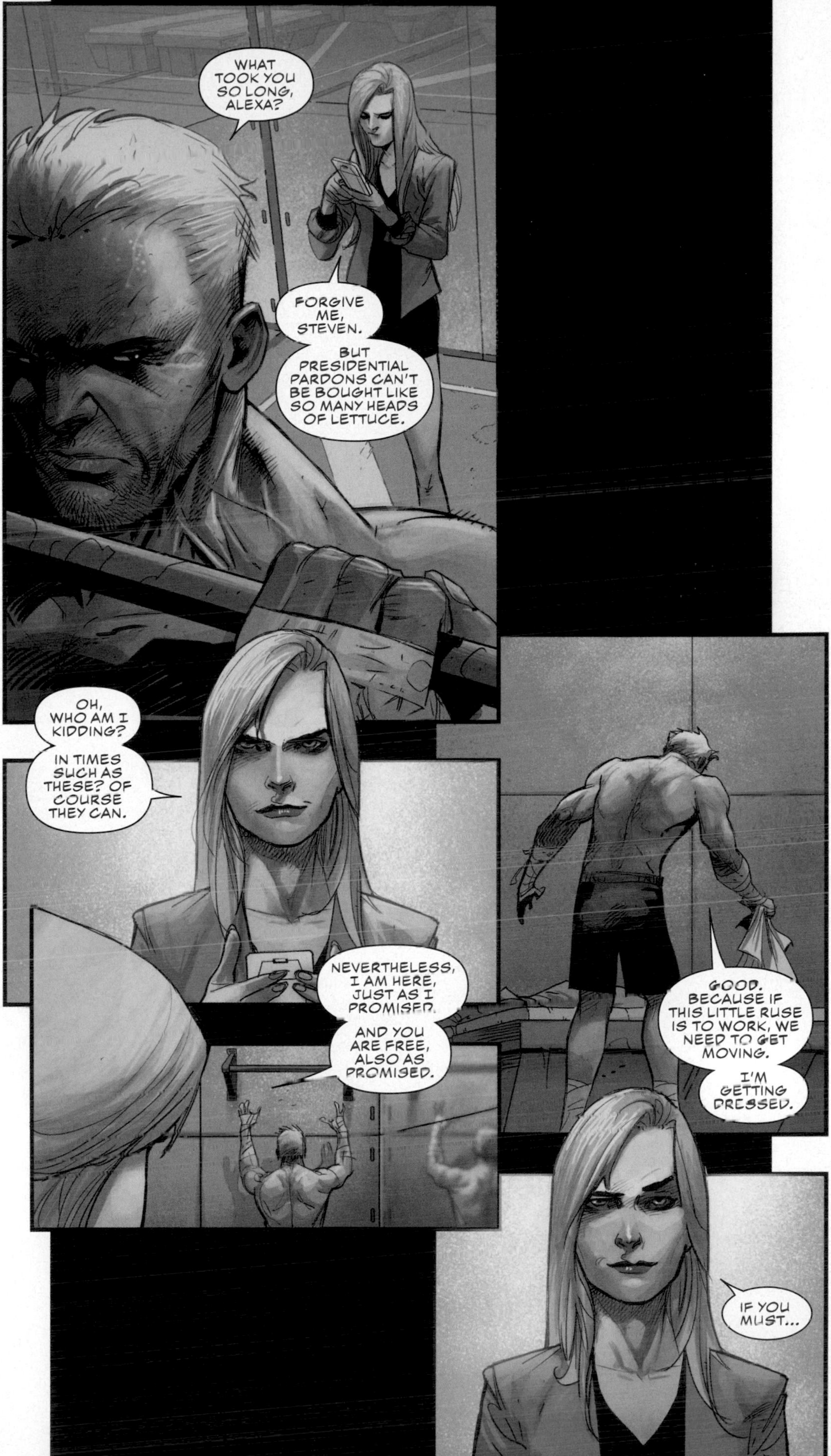
WHAT TOOK YOU SO LONG, ALEXA?
FORGIVE ME, STEVEN.
BUT PRESIDENTIAL PARDONS CAN'T BE BOUGHT LIKE SO MANY HEADS OF LETTUCE.
OH, WHO AM I KIDDING?
IN TIMES SUCH AS THESE? OF COURSE THEY CAN.
NEVERTHELESS, I AM HERE, JUST AS I PROMISED.
AND YOU ARE FREE, ALSO AS PROMISED.
GOOD. BECAUSE IF THIS LITTLE RUSE IS TO WORK, WE NEED TO GET MOVING.
I'M GETTING DRESSED.
IF YOU MUST...

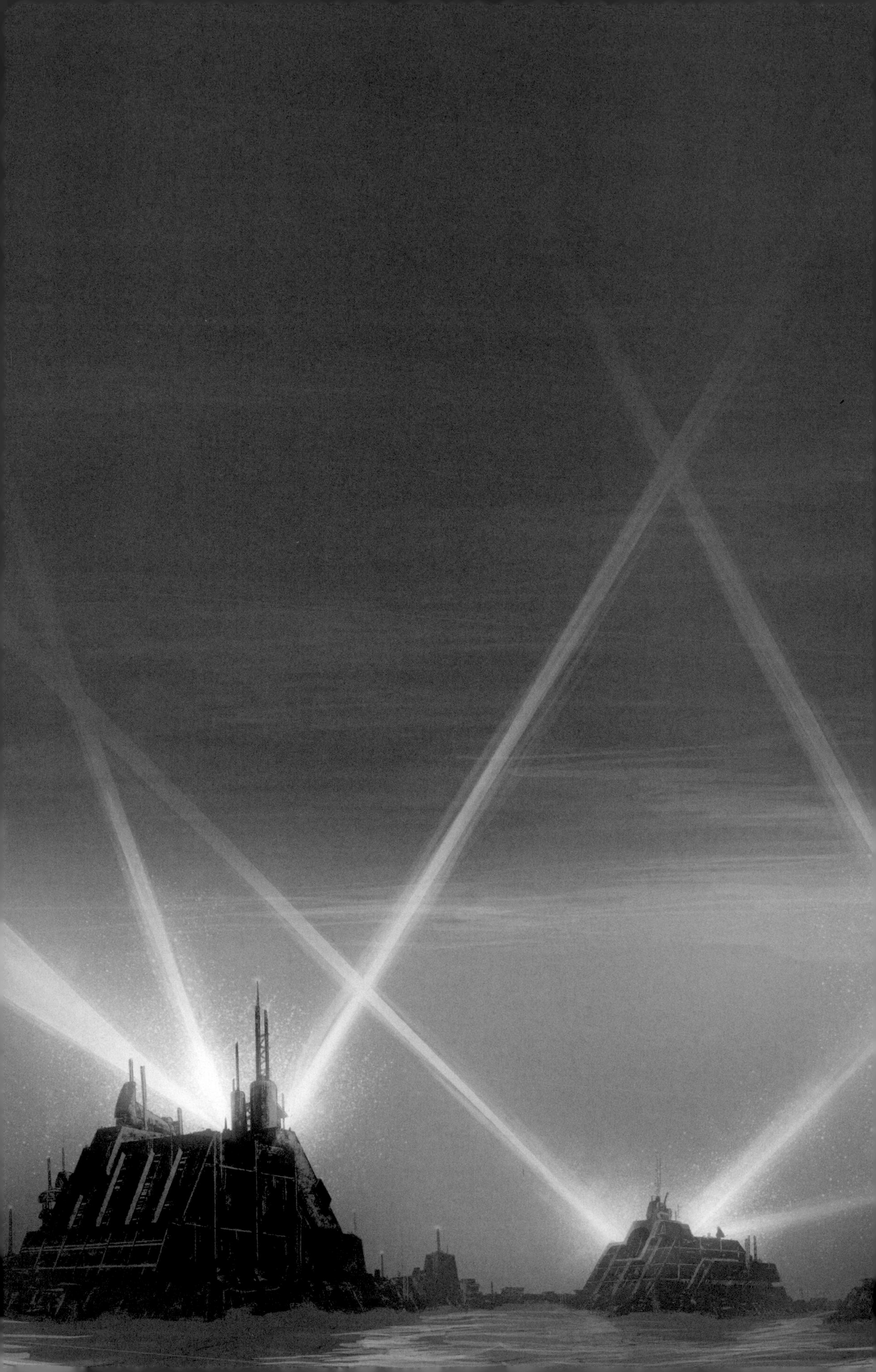

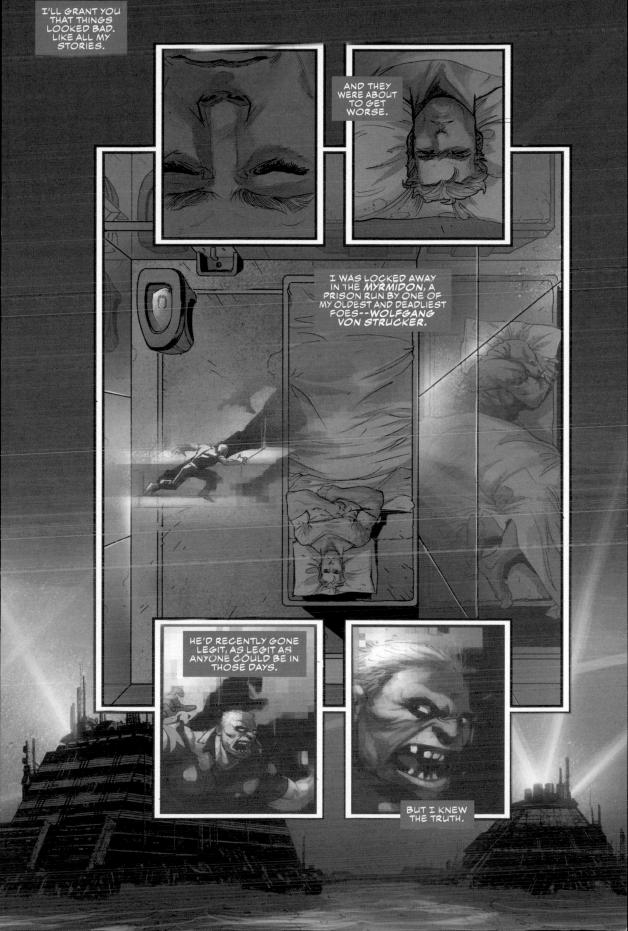

I'LL GRANT YOU THAT THINGS LOOKED BAD. LIKE ALL MY STORIES.

AND THEY WERE ABOUT TO GET WORSE.

I WAS LOCKED AWAY IN THE *MYRMIDON*, A PRISON RUN BY ONE OF MY OLDEST AND DEADLIEST FOES--WOLFGANG VON STRUCKER.

HE'D RECENTLY GONE LEGIT, AS LEGIT AS ANYONE COULD BE IN THOSE DAYS.

BUT I KNEW THE TRUTH.

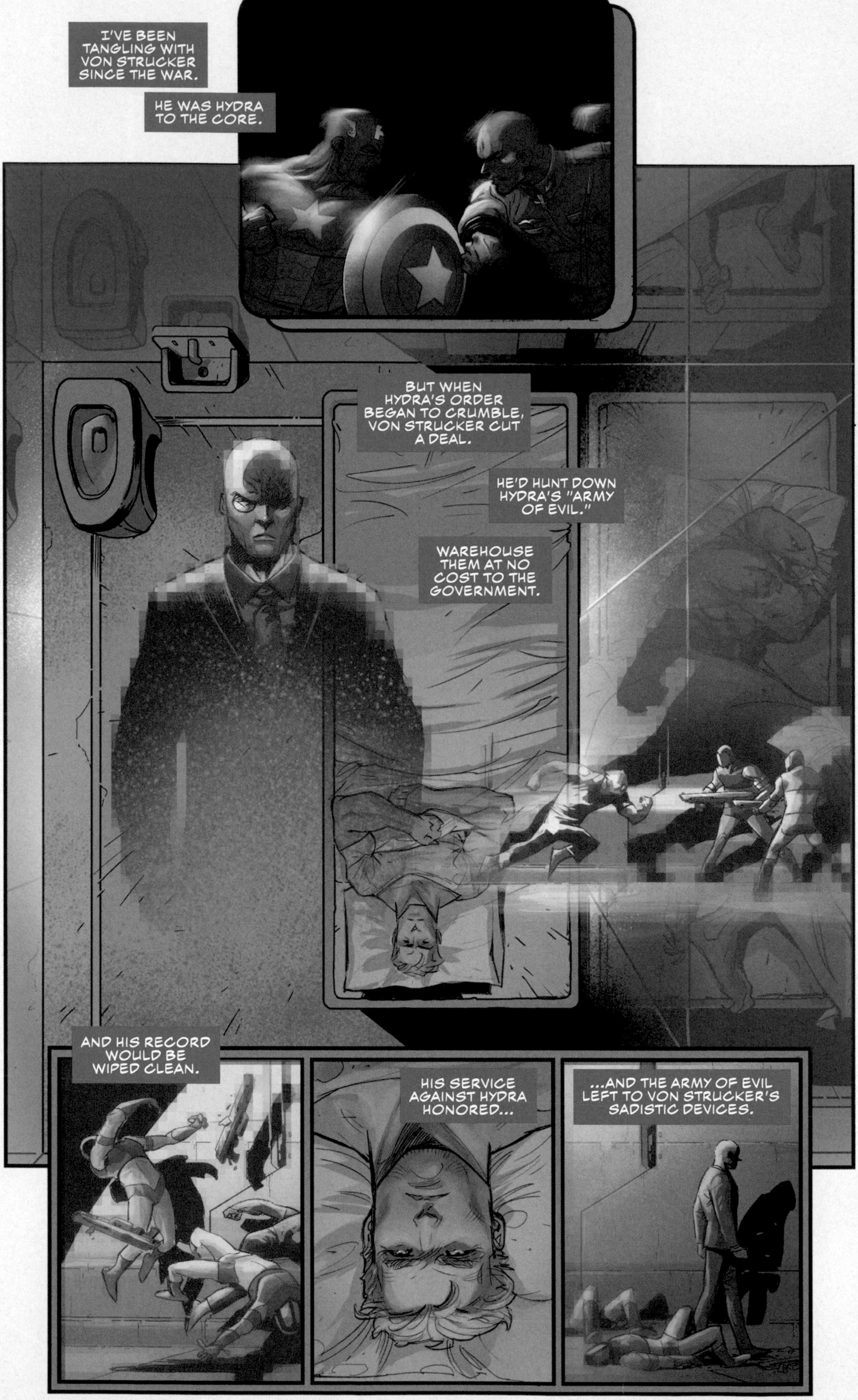
I'VE BEEN TANGLING WITH VON STRUCKER SINCE THE WAR.
HE WAS HYDRA TO THE CORE.
BUT WHEN HYDRA'S ORDER BEGAN TO CRUMBLE, VON STRUCKER CUT A DEAL.
HE'D HUNT DOWN HYDRA'S "ARMY OF EVIL."
WAREHOUSE THEM AT NO COST TO THE GOVERNMENT.
AND HIS RECORD WOULD BE WIPED CLEAN.
HIS SERVICE AGAINST HYDRA HONORED...
...AND THE ARMY OF EVIL LEFT TO VON STRUCKER'S SADISTIC DEVICES.

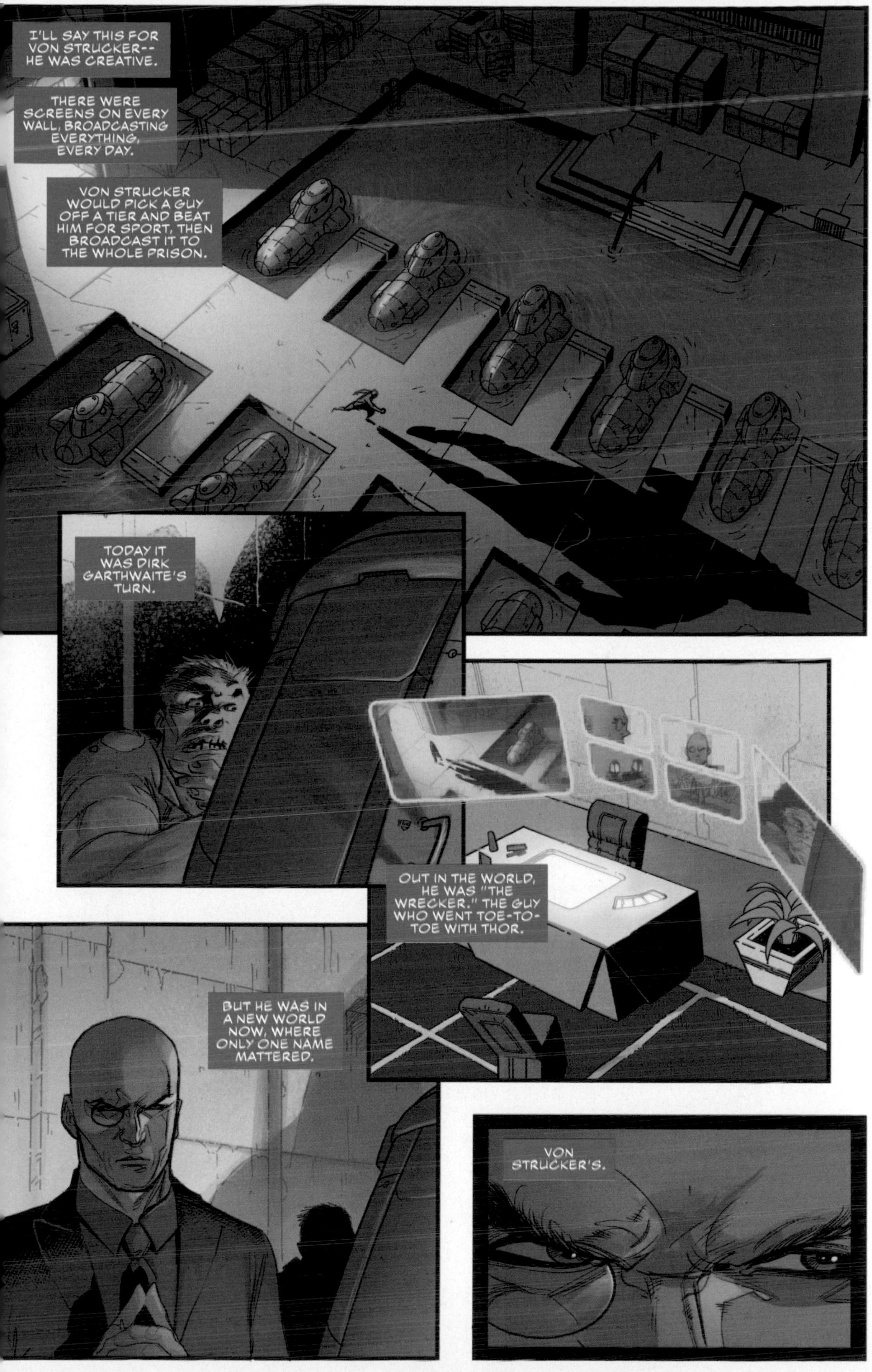
I'LL SAY THIS FOR VON STRUCKER-- HE WAS CREATIVE.
THERE WERE SCREENS ON EVERY WALL, BROADCASTING EVERYTHING, EVERY DAY.
VON STRUCKER WOULD PICK A GUY OFF A TIER AND BEAT HIM FOR SPORT, THEN BROADCAST IT TO THE WHOLE PRISON.
TODAY IT WAS DIRK GARTHWAITE'S TURN.
OUT IN THE WORLD, HE WAS "THE WRECKER." THE GUY WHO WENT TOE-TO-TOE WITH THOR.
BUT HE WAS IN A NEW WORLD NOW, WHERE ONLY ONE NAME MATTERED.
VON STRUCKER'S.

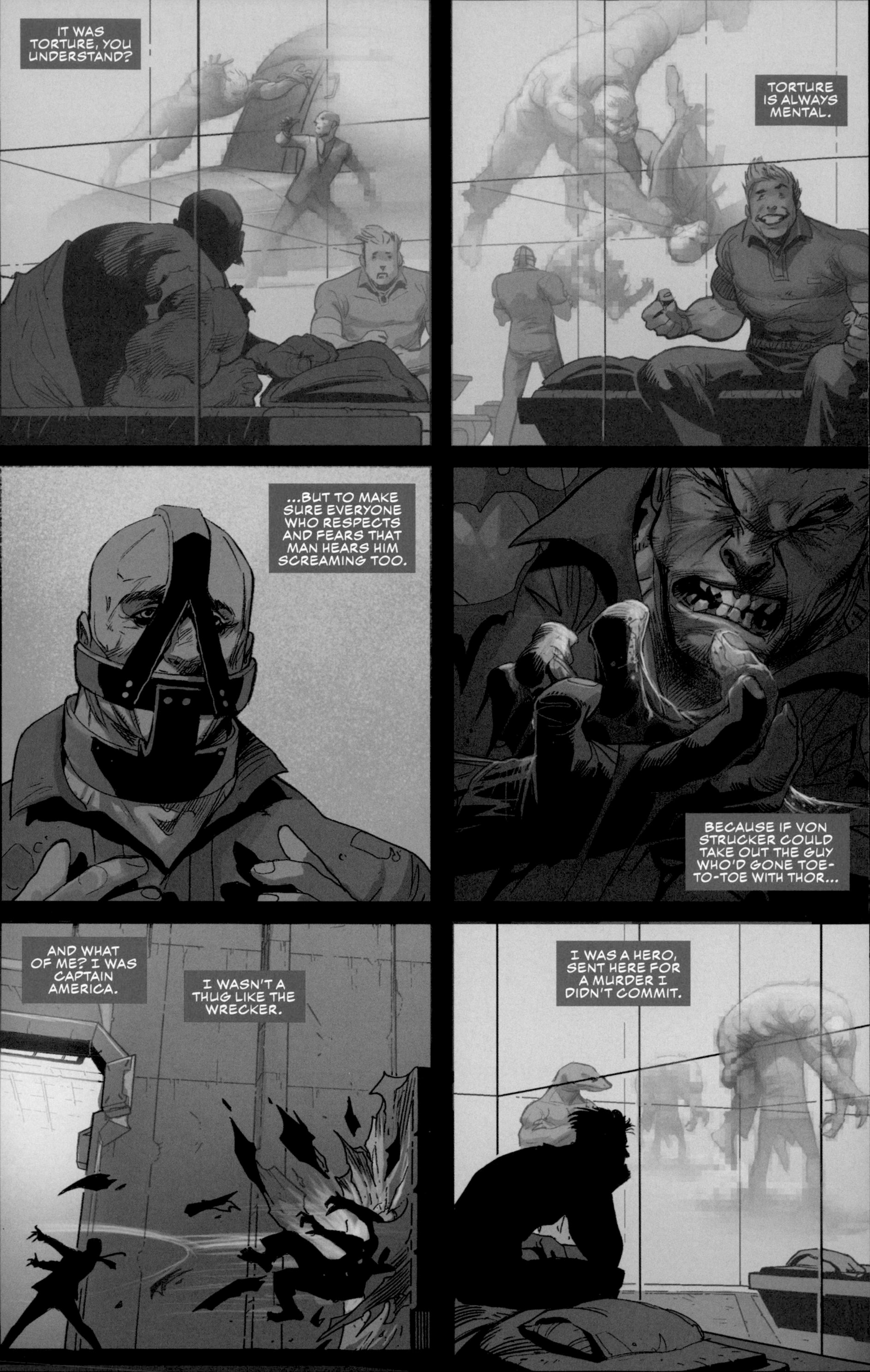
IT WAS TORTURE, YOU UNDERSTAND?
TORTURE IS ALWAYS MENTAL.
...BUT TO MAKE SURE EVERYONE WHO RESPECTS AND FEARS THAT MAN HEARS HIM SCREAMING TOO.
BECAUSE IF VON STRUCKER COULD TAKE OUT THE GUY WHO'D GONE TOE-TO-TOE WITH THOR...
AND WHAT OF ME? I WAS CAPTAIN AMERICA.
I WASN'T A THUG LIKE THE WRECKER.
I WAS A HERO, SENT HERE FOR A MURDER I DIDN'T COMMIT.

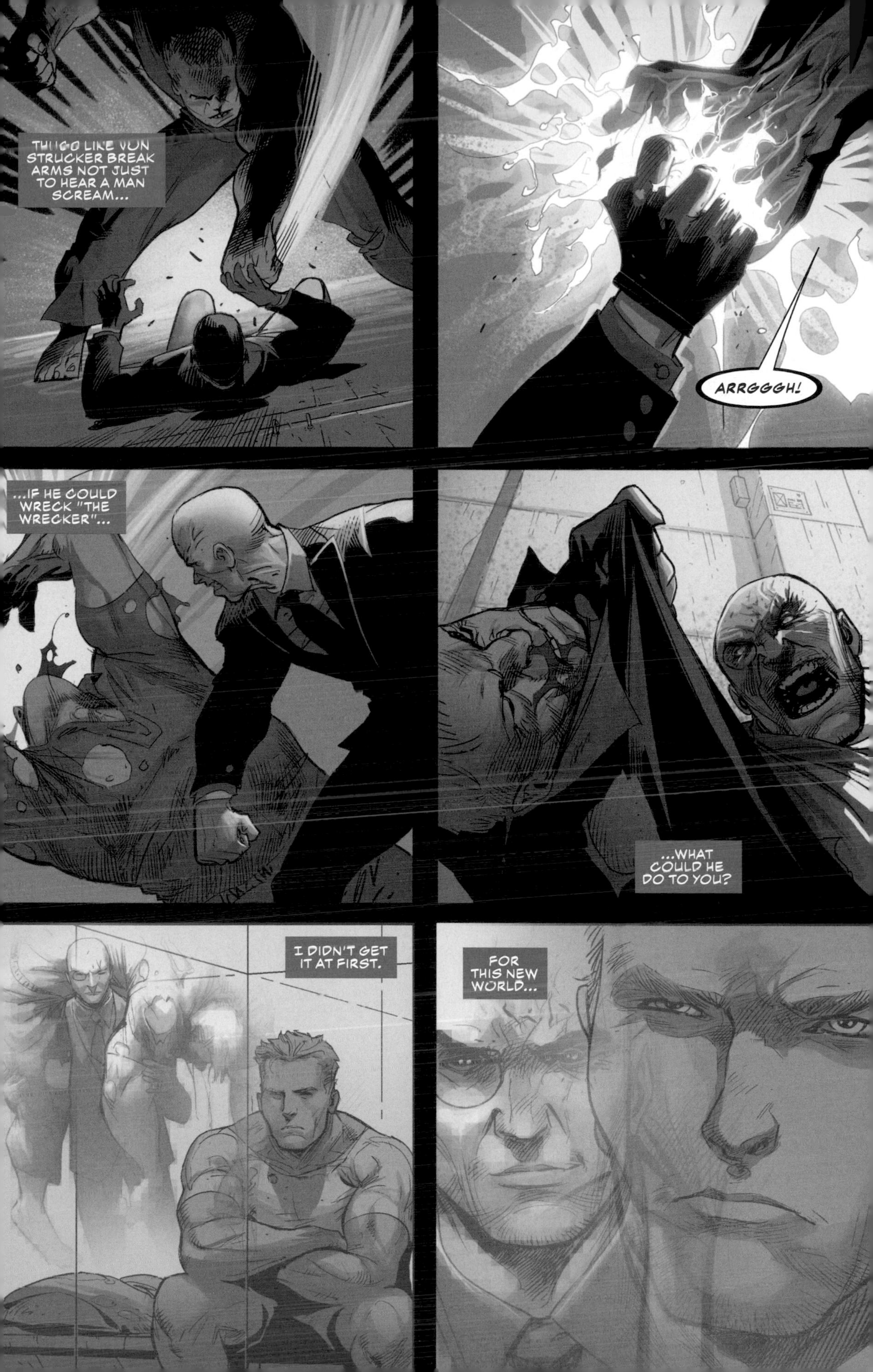
THUGS LIKE VON STRUCKER BREAK ARMS NOT JUST TO HEAR A MAN SCREAM...
ARRGGGH!
...IF HE COULD WRECK "THE WRECKER"...
...WHAT COULD HE DO TO YOU?
I DIDN'T GET IT AT FIRST.
FOR THIS NEW WORLD...

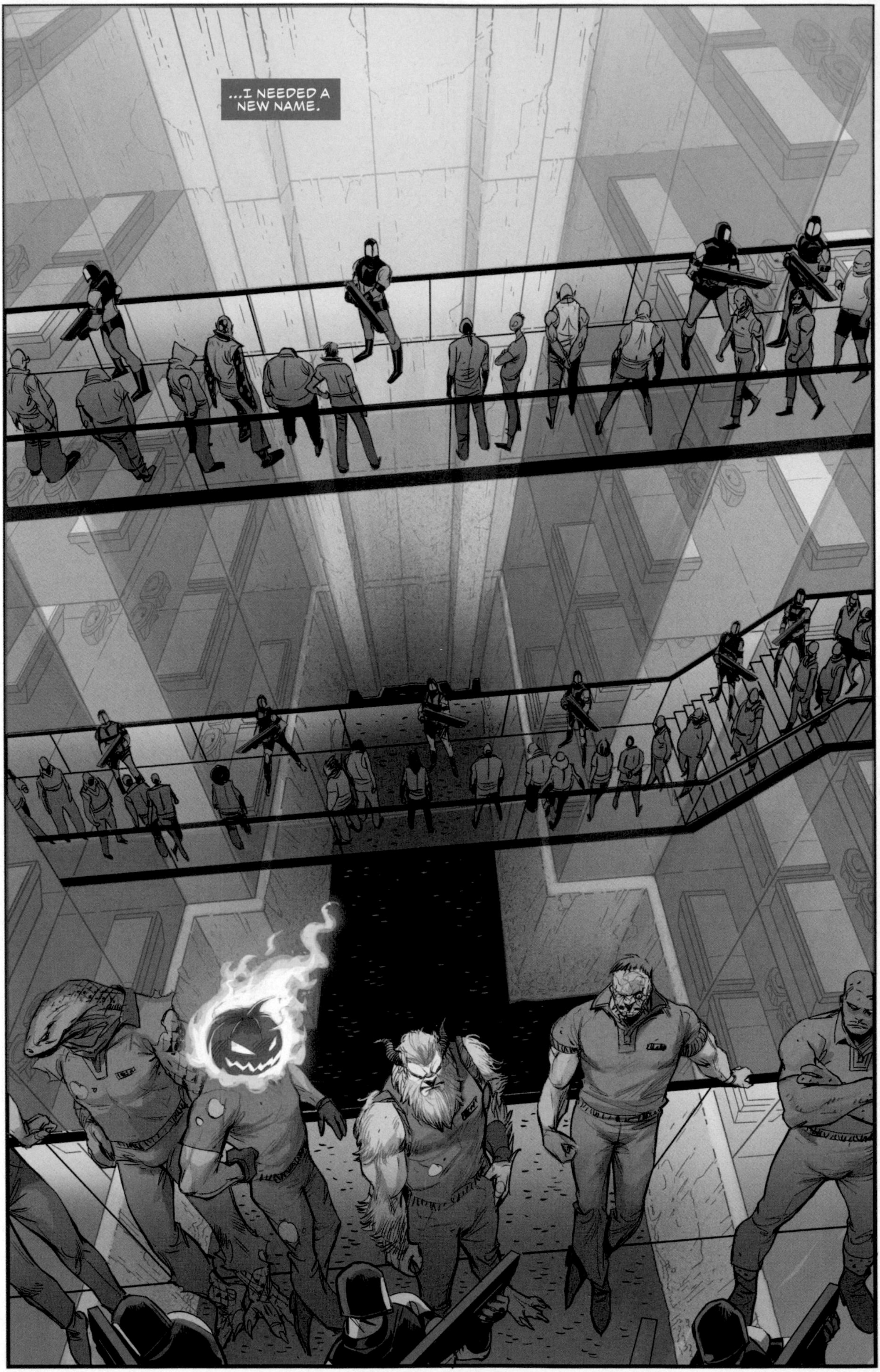
...I NEEDED A NEW NAME.

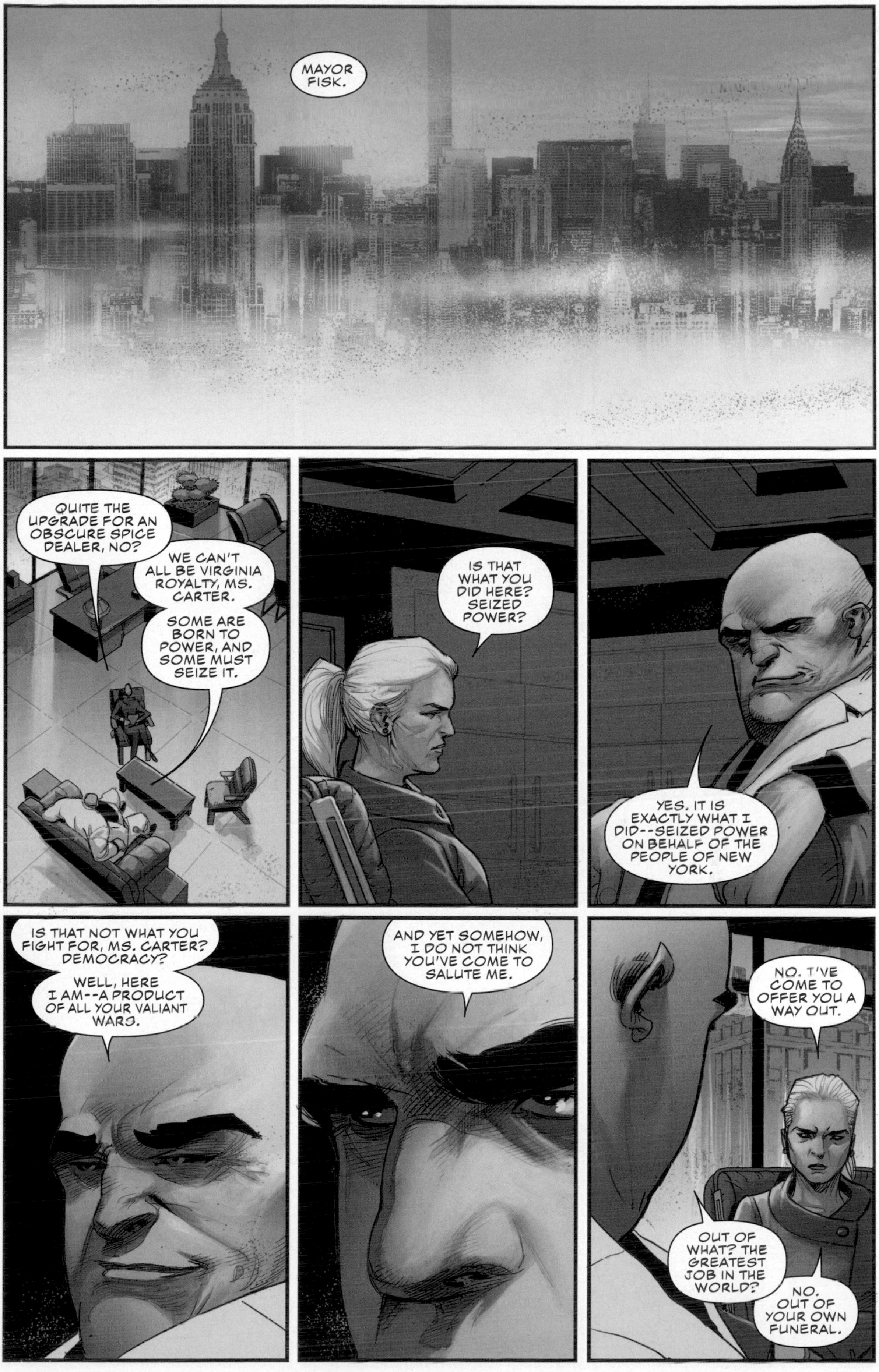
MAYOR FISK.
QUITE THE UPGRADE FOR AN OBSCURE SPICE DEALER, NO?
WE CAN'T ALL BE VIRGINIA ROYALTY, MS. CARTER.
SOME ARE BORN TO POWER, AND SOME MUST SEIZE IT.
IS THAT WHAT YOU DID HERE? SEIZED POWER?
YES. IT IS EXACTLY WHAT I DID--SEIZED POWER ON BEHALF OF THE PEOPLE OF NEW YORK.
IS THAT NOT WHAT YOU FIGHT FOR, MS. CARTER? DEMOCRACY?
WELL, HERE I AM--A PRODUCT OF ALL YOUR VALIANT WARS.
AND YET SOMEHOW, I DO NOT THINK YOU'VE COME TO SALUTE ME.
NO. I'VE COME TO OFFER YOU A WAY OUT.
OUT OF WHAT? THE GREATEST JOB IN THE WORLD?
NO. OUT OF YOUR OWN FUNERAL.

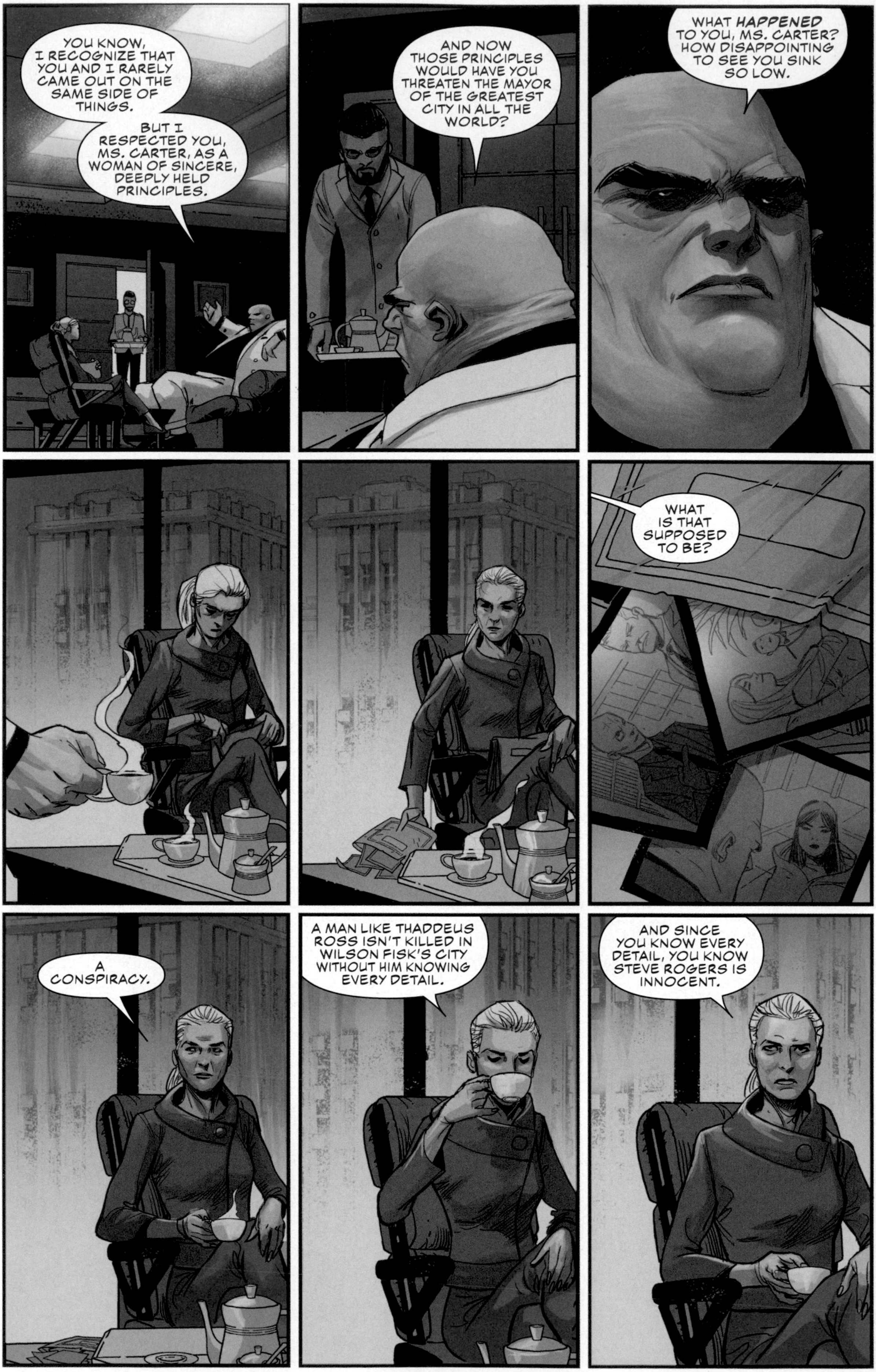
YOU KNOW, I RECOGNIZE THAT YOU AND I RARELY CAME OUT ON THE SAME SIDE OF THINGS.
BUT I RESPECTED YOU, MS. CARTER, AS A WOMAN OF SINCERE, DEEPLY HELD PRINCIPLES.
AND NOW THOSE PRINCIPLES WOULD HAVE YOU THREATEN THE MAYOR OF THE GREATEST CITY IN ALL THE WORLD?
WHAT *HAPPENED* TO YOU, MS. CARTER? HOW DISAPPOINTING TO SEE YOU SINK SO LOW.
WHAT IS THAT SUPPOSED TO BE?
A CONSPIRACY.
A MAN LIKE THADDEUS ROSS ISN'T KILLED IN WILSON FISK'S CITY WITHOUT HIM KNOWING EVERY DETAIL.
AND SINCE YOU KNOW EVERY DETAIL, YOU KNOW STEVE ROGERS IS INNOCENT.

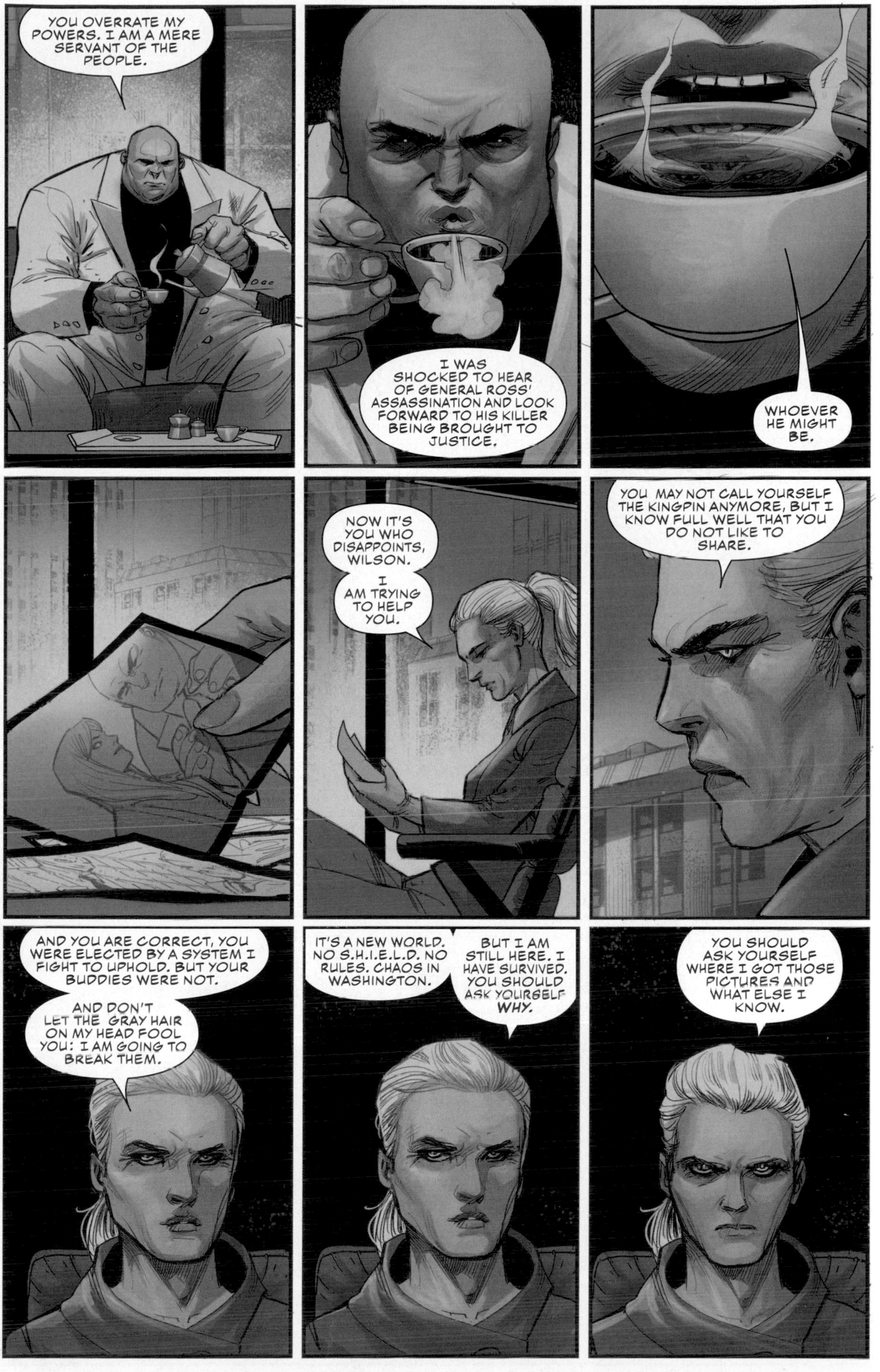
YOU OVERRATE MY POWERS. I AM A MERE SERVANT OF THE PEOPLE.
I WAS SHOCKED TO HEAR OF GENERAL ROSS' ASSASSINATION AND LOOK FORWARD TO HIS KILLER BEING BROUGHT TO JUSTICE.
WHOEVER HE MIGHT BE.
NOW IT'S YOU WHO DISAPPOINTS, WILSON.
I AM TRYING TO HELP YOU.
YOU MAY NOT CALL YOURSELF THE KINGPIN ANYMORE, BUT I KNOW FULL WELL THAT YOU DO NOT LIKE TO SHARE.
AND YOU ARE CORRECT, YOU WERE ELECTED BY A SYSTEM I FIGHT TO UPHOLD. BUT YOUR BUDDIES WERE NOT.
AND DON'T LET THE GRAY HAIR ON MY HEAD FOOL YOU: I AM GOING TO BREAK THEM.
IT'S A NEW WORLD. NO S.H.I.E.L.D. NO RULES. CHAOS IN WASHINGTON.
BUT I AM STILL HERE. I HAVE SURVIVED. YOU SHOULD ASK YOURSELF WHY.
YOU SHOULD ASK YOURSELF WHERE I GOT THOSE PICTURES AND WHAT ELSE I KNOW.

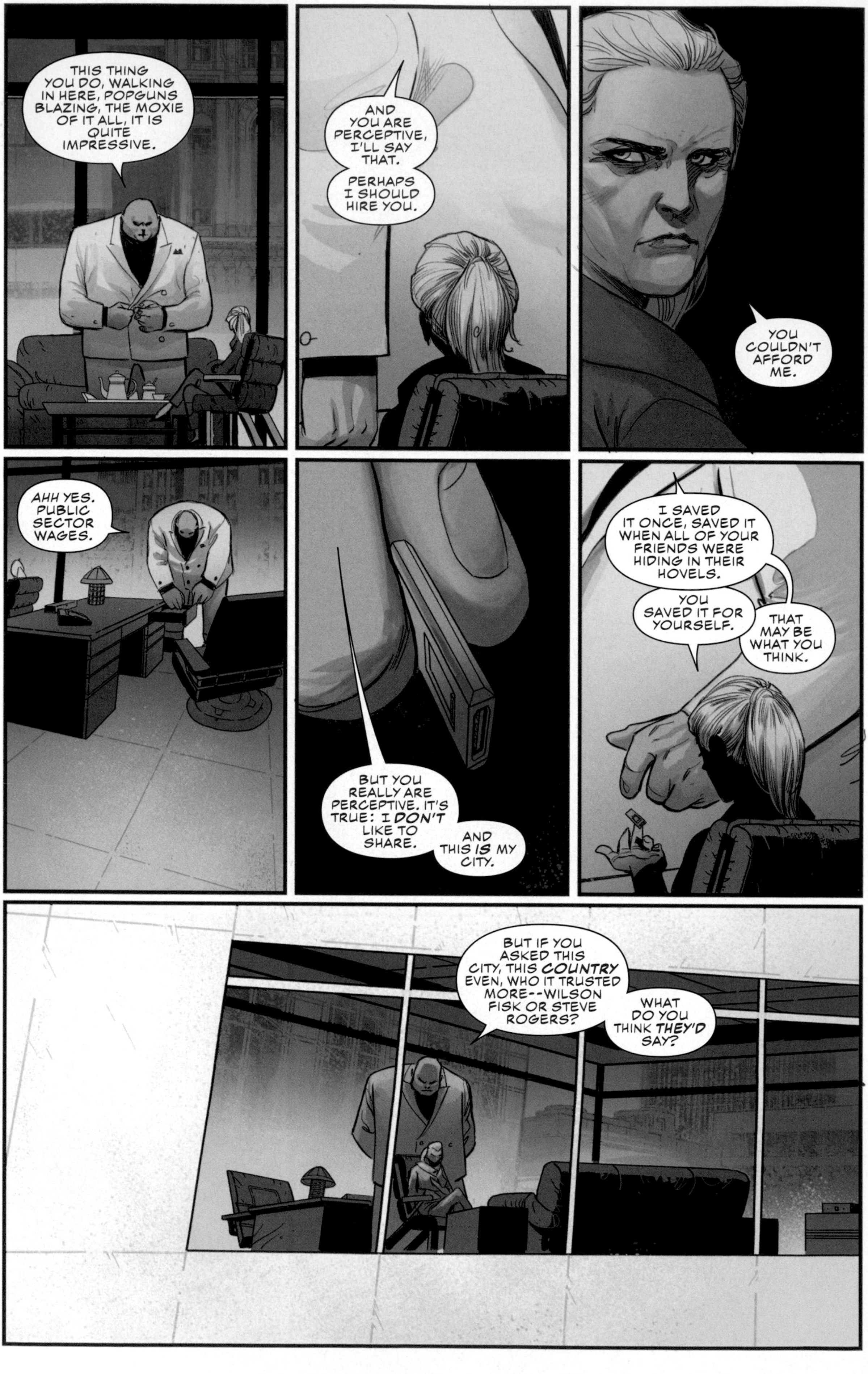
THIS THING YOU DO, WALKING IN HERE, POPGUNS BLAZING, THE MOXIE OF IT ALL, IT IS QUITE IMPRESSIVE.
AND YOU ARE PERCEPTIVE, I'LL SAY THAT.
PERHAPS I SHOULD HIRE YOU.
YOU COULDN'T AFFORD ME.
AHH YES. PUBLIC SECTOR WAGES.
BUT YOU REALLY ARE PERCEPTIVE. IT'S TRUE: I *DON'T* LIKE TO SHARE.
AND THIS *IS* MY CITY.
I SAVED IT ONCE, SAVED IT WHEN ALL OF YOUR FRIENDS WERE HIDING IN THEIR HOVELS.
YOU SAVED IT FOR YOURSELF.
THAT MAY BE WHAT YOU THINK.
BUT IF YOU ASKED THIS CITY, THIS *COUNTRY* EVEN, WHO IT TRUSTED MORE--WILSON FISK OR STEVE ROGERS?
WHAT DO YOU THINK *THEY'D* SAY?

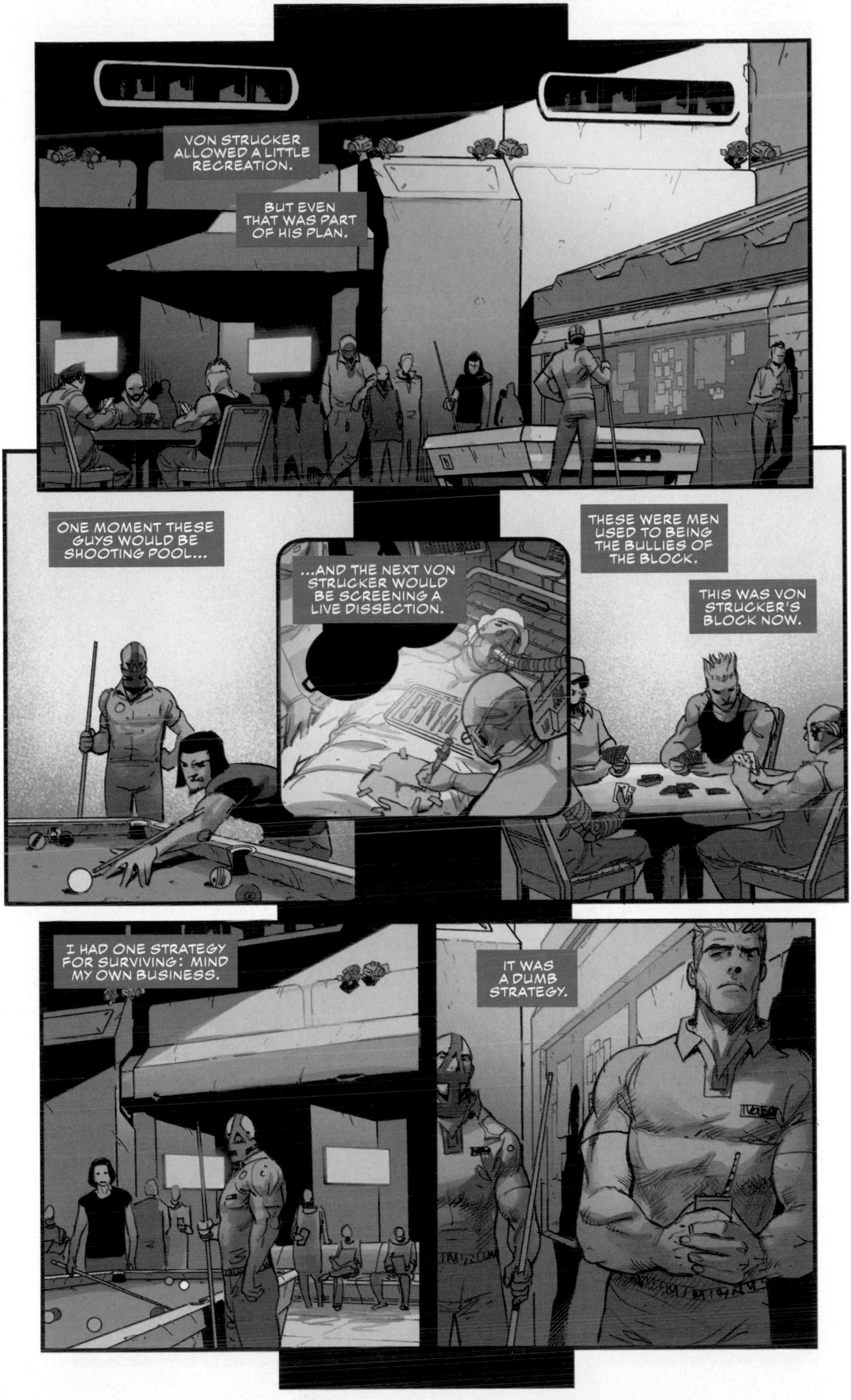
VON STRUCKER ALLOWED A LITTLE RECREATION.
BUT EVEN THAT WAS PART OF HIS PLAN.
ONE MOMENT THESE GUYS WOULD BE SHOOTING POOL...
...AND THE NEXT VON STRUCKER WOULD BE SCREENING A LIVE DISSECTION.
THESE WERE MEN USED TO BEING THE BULLIES OF THE BLOCK.
THIS WAS VON STRUCKER'S BLOCK NOW.
I HAD ONE STRATEGY FOR SURVIVING: MIND MY OWN BUSINESS.
IT WAS A DUMB STRATEGY.

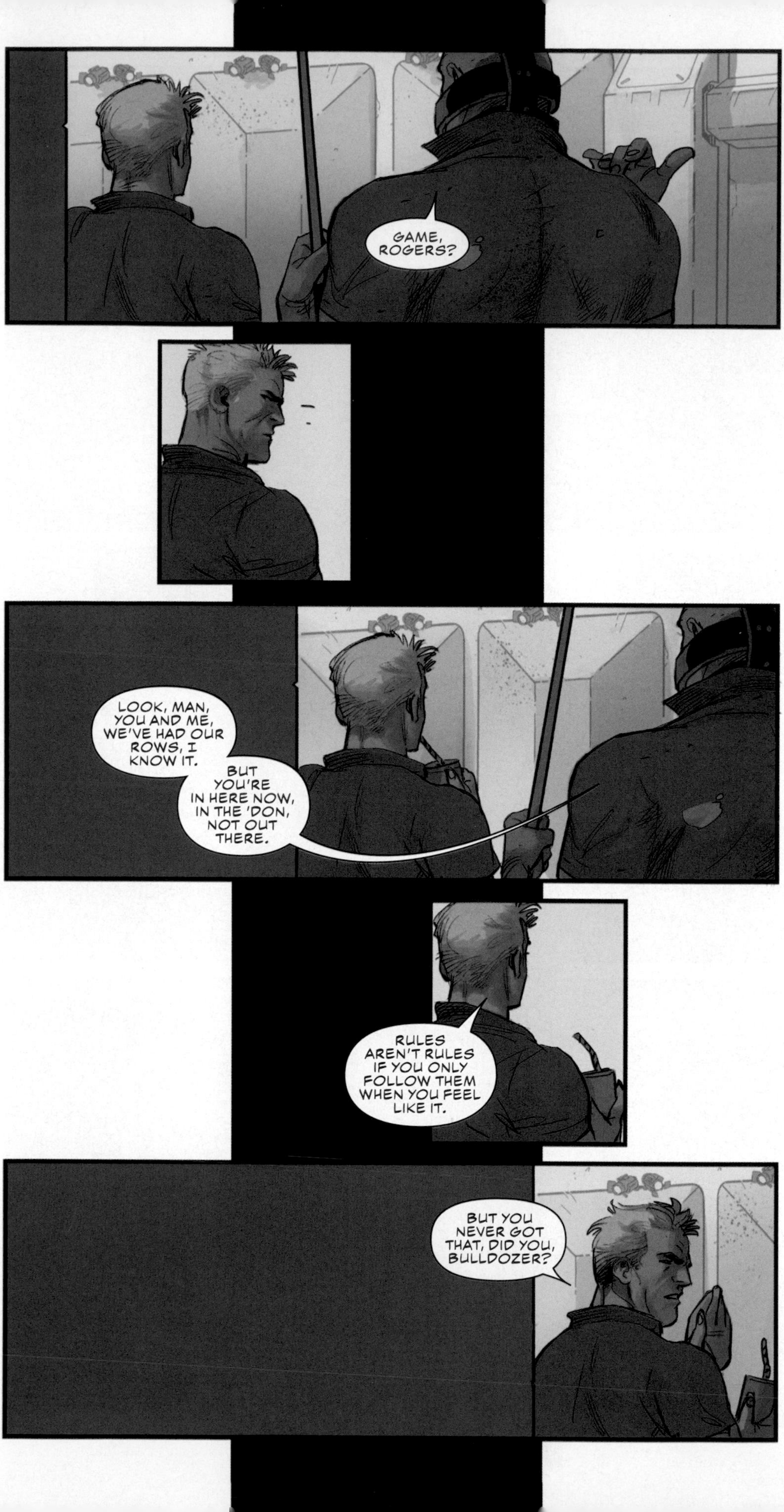
GAME, ROGERS?
LOOK, MAN, YOU AND ME, WE'VE HAD OUR ROWS, I KNOW IT.
BUT YOU'RE IN HERE NOW, IN THE 'DON, NOT OUT THERE.
RULES AREN'T RULES IF YOU ONLY FOLLOW THEM WHEN YOU FEEL LIKE IT.
BUT YOU NEVER GOT THAT, DID YOU, BULLDOZER?

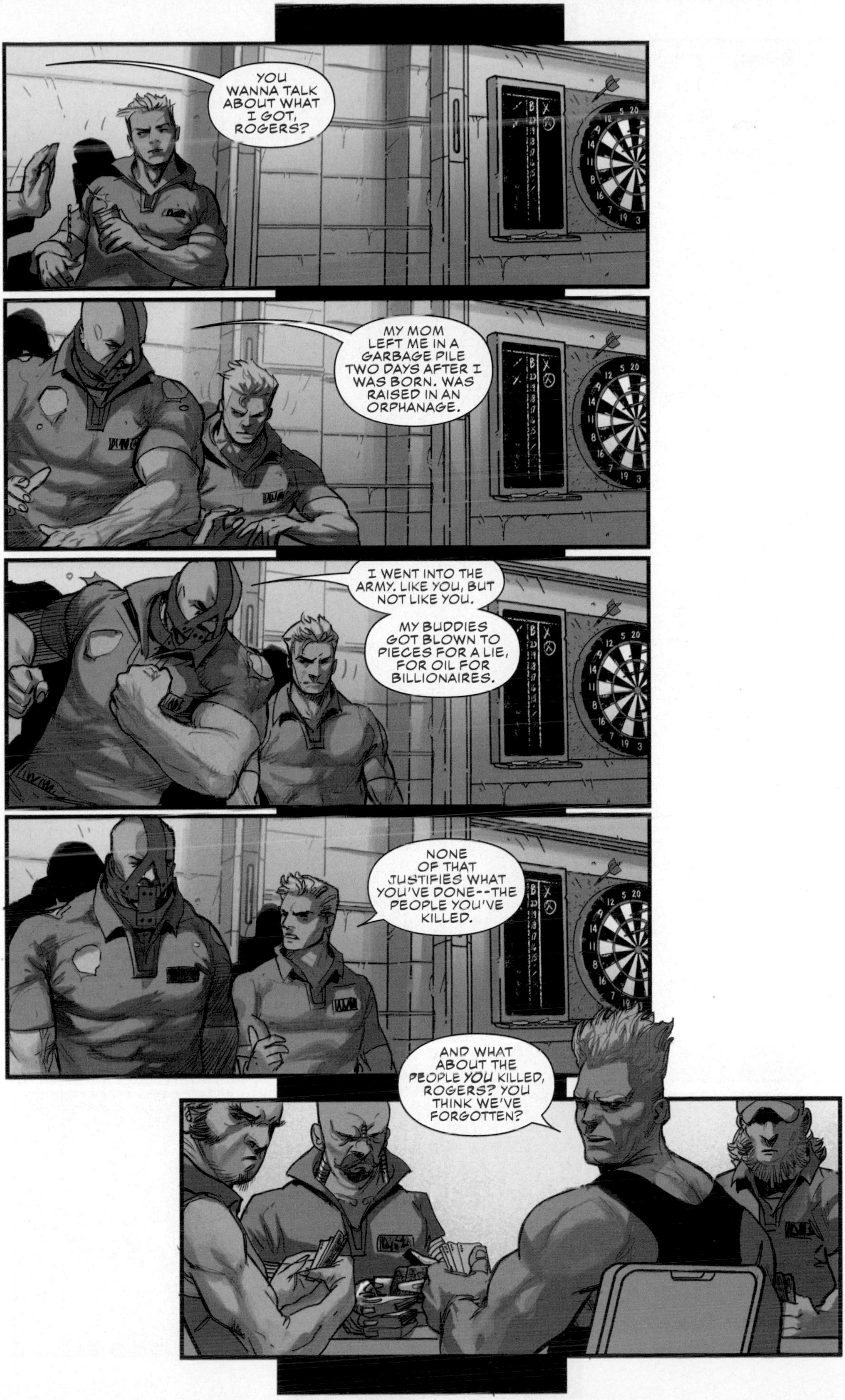
YOU WANNA TALK ABOUT WHAT I GOT, ROGERS?
MY MOM LEFT ME IN A GARBAGE PILE TWO DAYS AFTER I WAS BORN. WAS RAISED IN AN ORPHANAGE.
I WENT INTO THE ARMY. LIKE YOU, BUT NOT LIKE YOU.
MY BUDDIES GOT BLOWN TO PIECES FOR A LIE, FOR OIL FOR BILLIONAIRES.
NONE OF THAT JUSTIFIES WHAT YOU'VE DONE--THE PEOPLE YOU'VE KILLED.
AND WHAT ABOUT THE PEOPLE *YOU* KILLED, ROGERS? YOU THINK WE'VE FORGOTTEN?

I DIDN'T KILL ROSS.

STOP TELLING ON YOURSELF. THIS AIN'T ABOUT ROSS, MR. "SUPREME COMMANDER."

PILEDRIVER, YOU KNOW FULL WELL THAT WASN'T...

YEAH, I'VE HEARD THAT LINE. NOT SO SURE. BUT LET'S SAY IT WASN'T, SPARKY.

YOU'RE CAPTAIN AMERICA. YOU MADE THE WORLD FEEL LIKE THERE WAS A GUY THEY COULD TRUST MORE THAN JESUS.

HOW MANY PEOPLE YOU THINK DIED ON THAT LIE?

INSPIRING PEOPLE ISN'T MURDER.

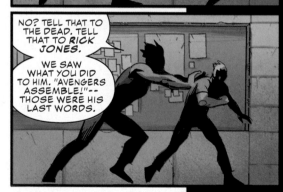

NO? TELL THAT TO THE DEAD. TELL THAT TO RICK JONES.

WE SAW WHAT YOU DID TO HIM. "AVENGERS ASSEMBLE!"-- THOSE WERE HIS LAST WORDS.

AND NOBODY CAME. WHAT A CROCK!

HE WAS KILLED BY A LIE, JUST LIKE BULLDOZER'S BUDDIES.

YOUR LIE.

SO YEAH, IT STARTED OFF BAD.

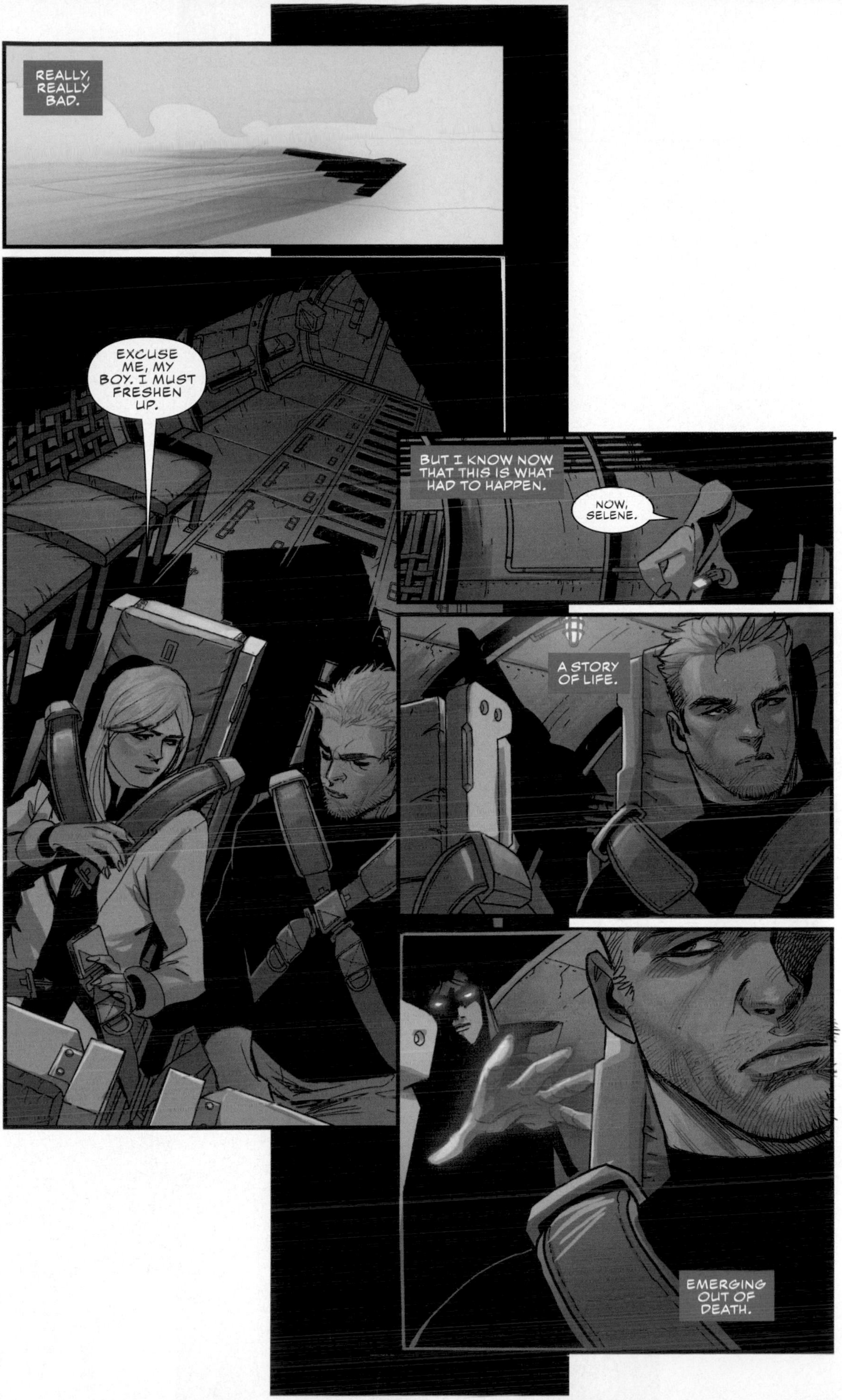
REALLY, REALLY BAD.
EXCUSE ME, MY BOY. I MUST FRESHEN UP.
BUT I KNOW NOW THAT THIS IS WHAT HAD TO HAPPEN.
NOW, SELENE.
A STORY OF LIFE.
EMERGING OUT OF DEATH.

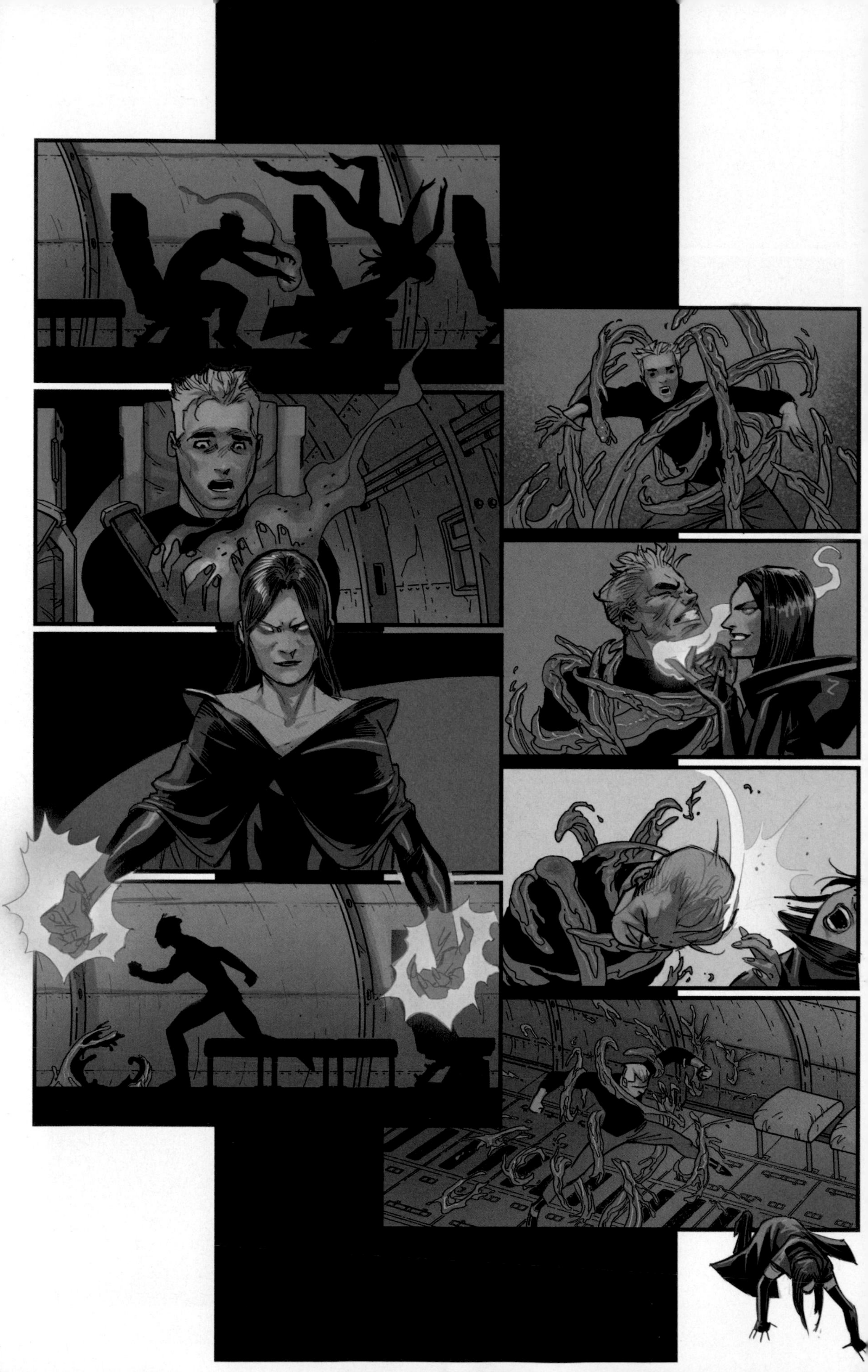

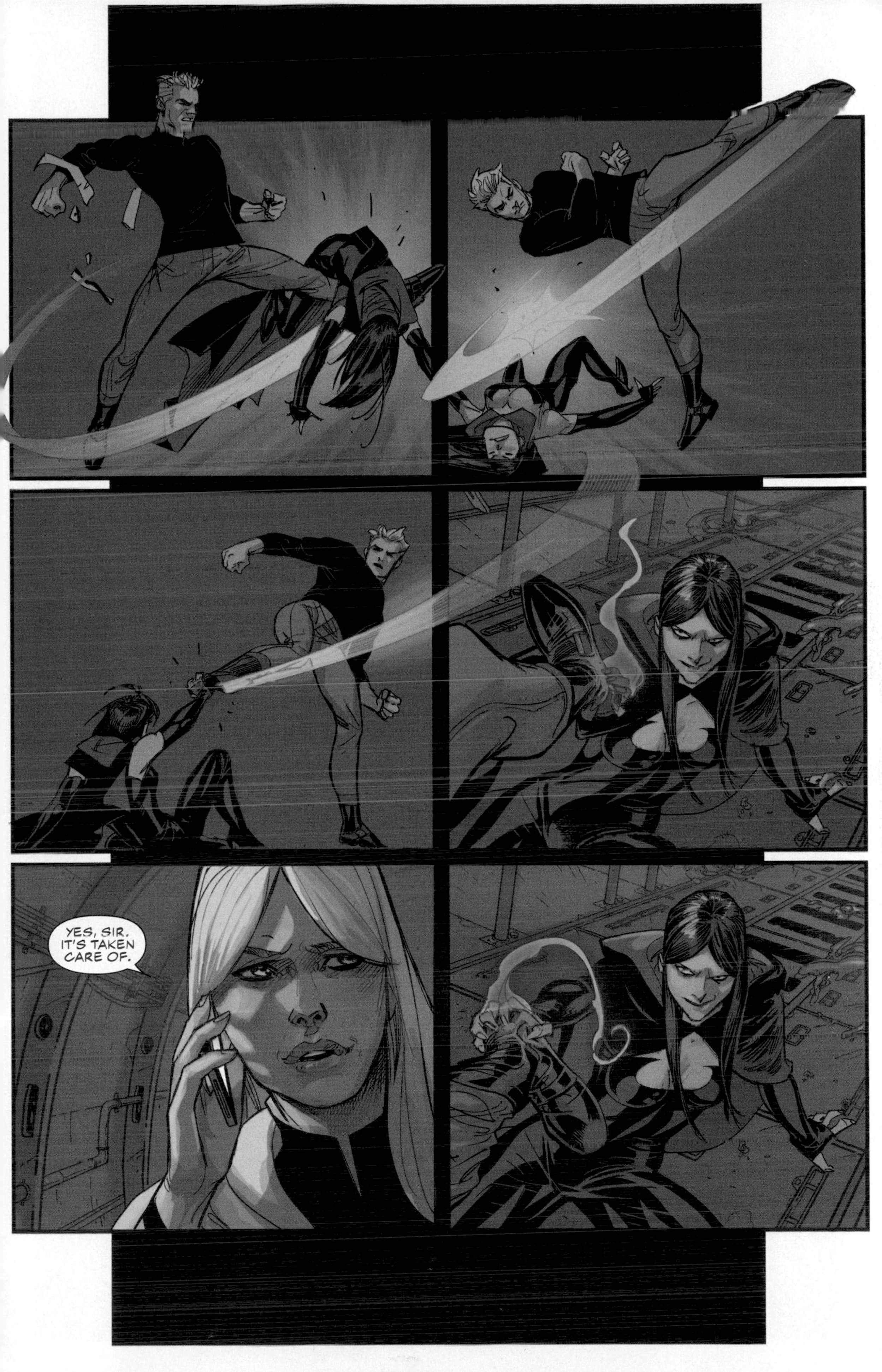
YES, SIR. IT'S TAKEN CARE OF.

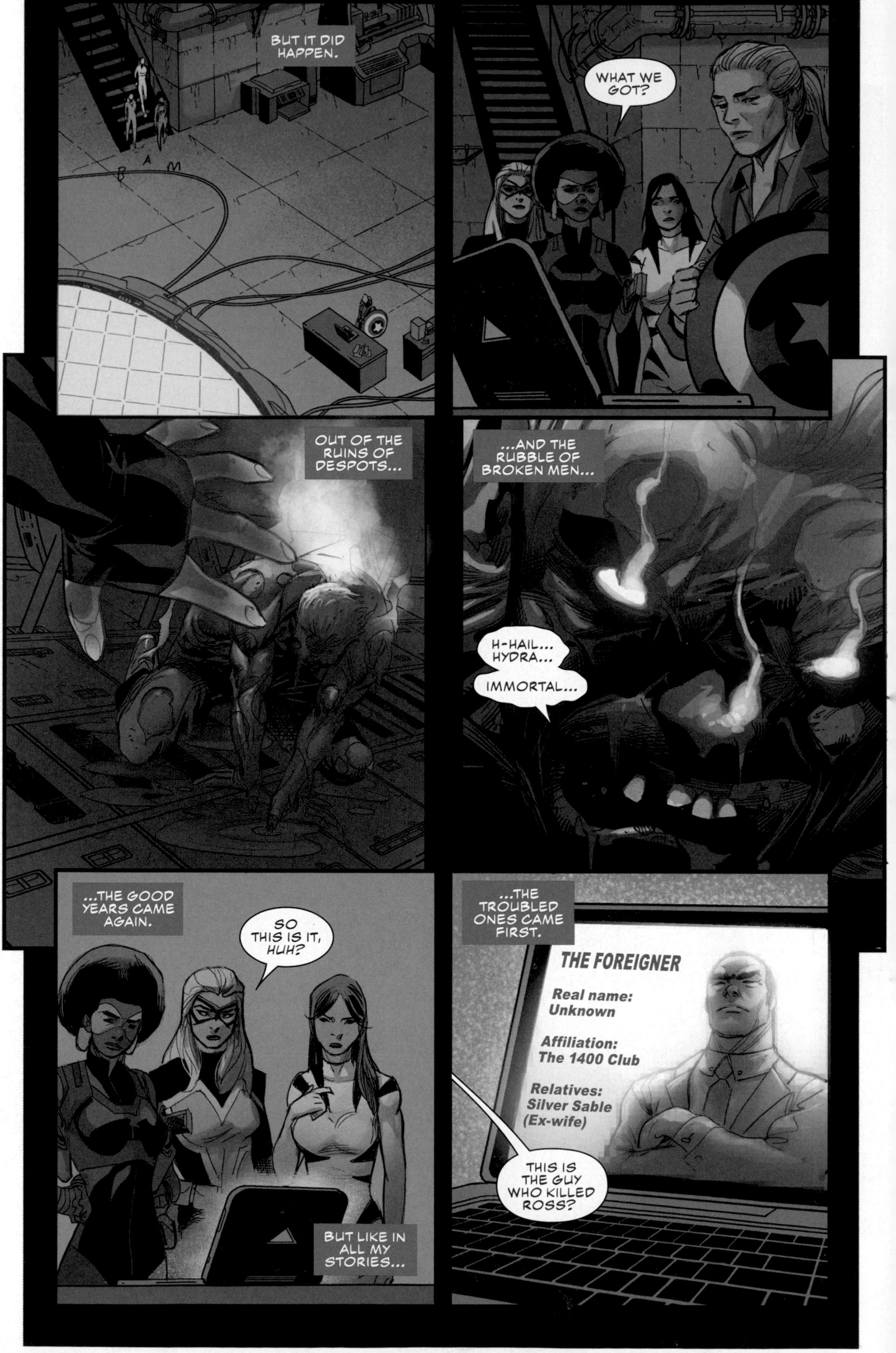
BUT IT DID HAPPEN.
B A M
WHAT WE GOT?
OUT OF THE RUINS OF DESPOTS...
...AND THE RUBBLE OF BROKEN MEN...
H-HAIL... HYDRA...
IMMORTAL...
...THE GOOD YEARS CAME AGAIN.
SO THIS IS IT, HUH?
BUT LIKE IN ALL MY STORIES...
...THE TROUBLED ONES CAME FIRST.
THE FOREIGNER
Real name: Unknown
Affiliation: The 1400 Club
Relatives: Silver Sable (Ex-wife)
THIS IS THE GUY WHO KILLED ROSS?

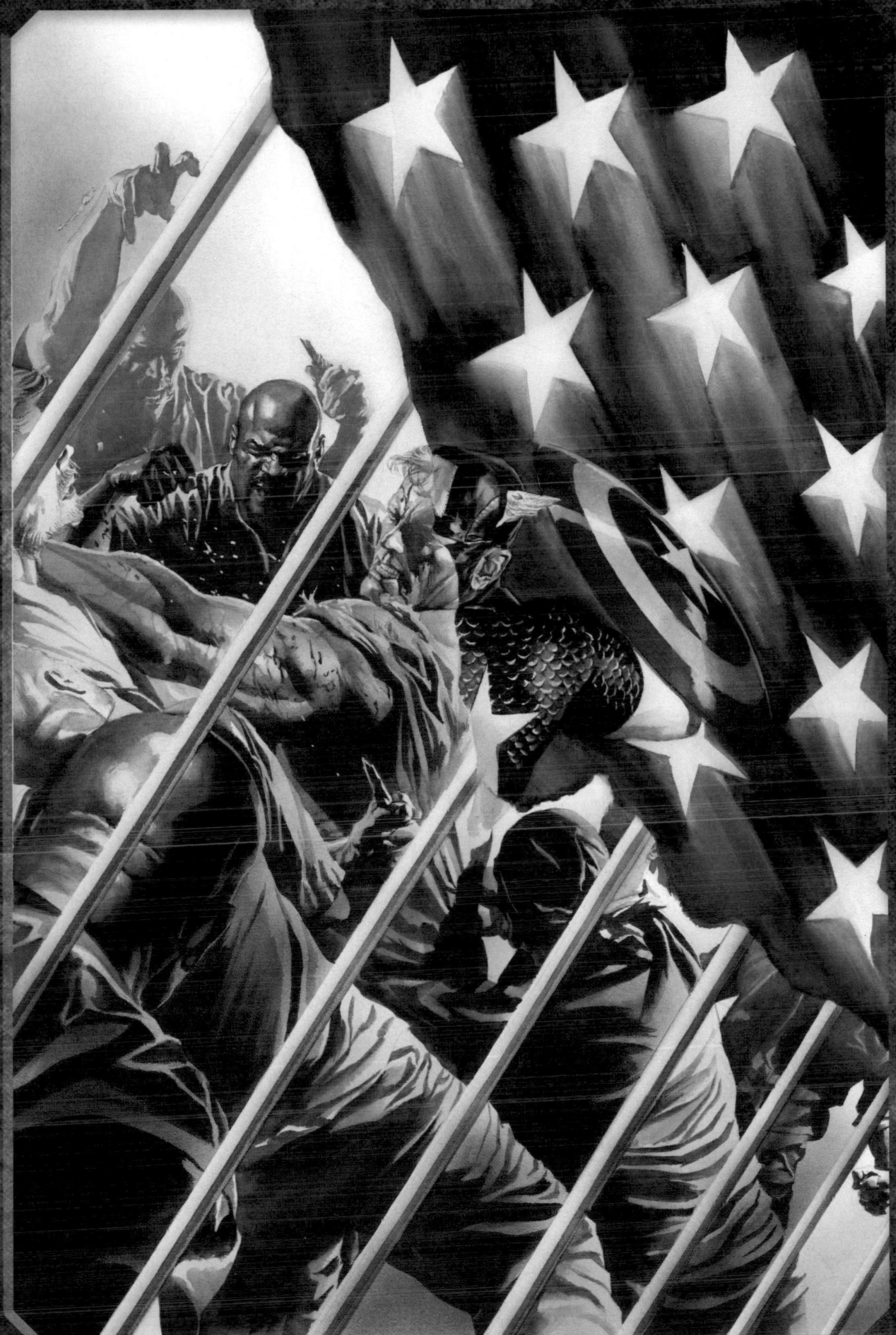

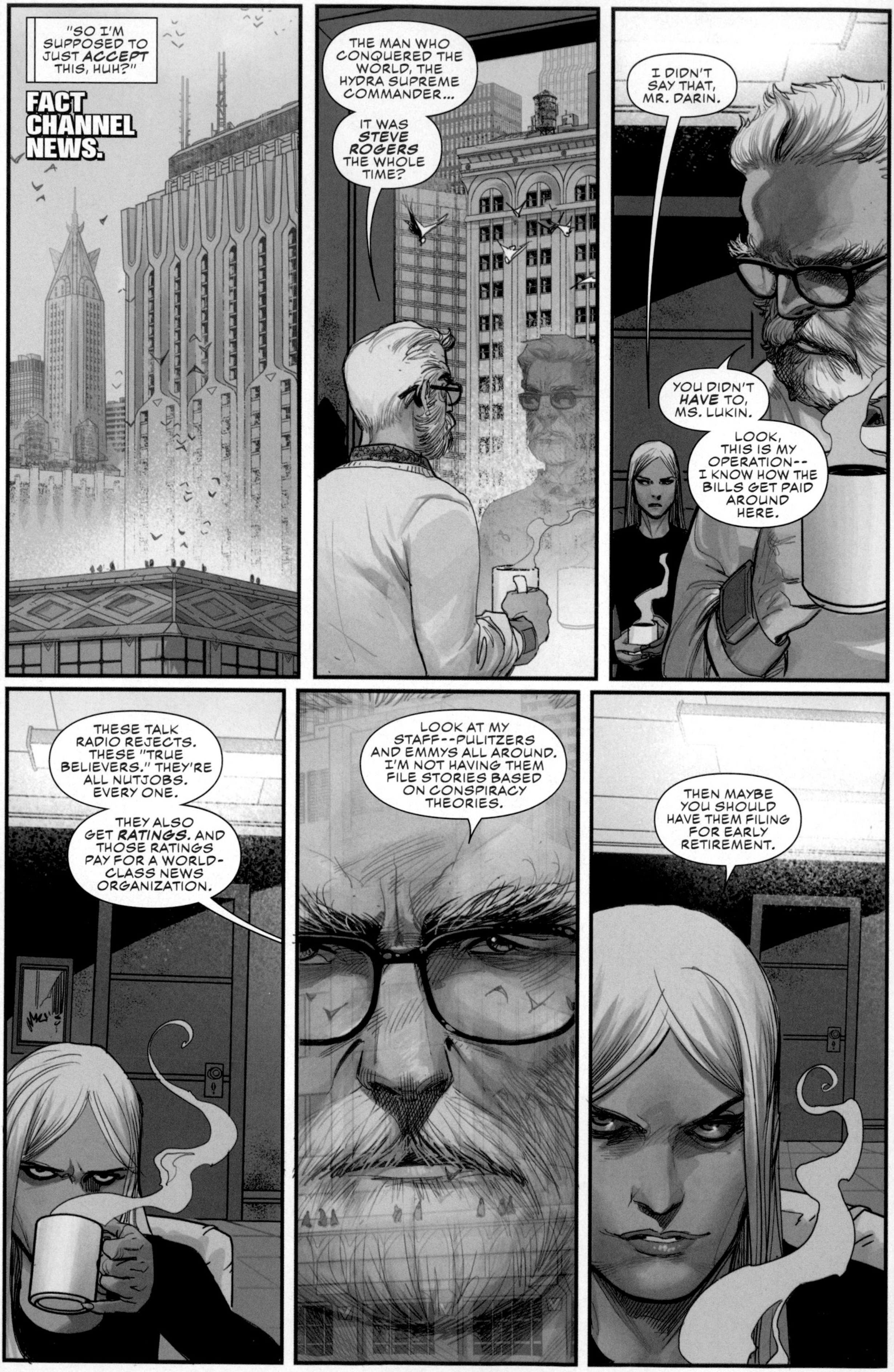
"SO I'M SUPPOSED TO JUST ACCEPT THIS, HUH?"
FACT CHANNEL NEWS.
THE MAN WHO CONQUERED THE WORLD, THE HYDRA SUPREME COMMANDER...
IT WAS STEVE ROGERS THE WHOLE TIME?
I DIDN'T SAY THAT, MR. DARIN.
YOU DIDN'T HAVE TO, MS. LUKIN.
LOOK, THIS IS MY OPERATION-- I KNOW HOW THE BILLS GET PAID AROUND HERE.
THESE TALK RADIO REJECTS. THESE "TRUE BELIEVERS." THEY'RE ALL NUTJOBS. EVERY ONE.
THEY ALSO GET RATINGS. AND THOSE RATINGS PAY FOR A WORLD-CLASS NEWS ORGANIZATION.
LOOK AT MY STAFF--PULITZERS AND EMMYS ALL AROUND. I'M NOT HAVING THEM FILE STORIES BASED ON CONSPIRACY THEORIES.
THEN MAYBE YOU SHOULD HAVE THEM FILING FOR EARLY RETIREMENT.

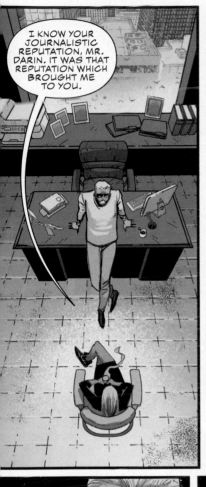

I KNOW YOUR JOURNALISTIC REPUTATION, MR. DARIN. IT WAS THAT REPUTATION WHICH BROUGHT ME TO YOU.

THIS IS NOT ABOUT "THEORY." THIS IS ABOUT A *REAL* CONSPIRACY THAT *REALLY* HAPPENED.

I SAW TOO MANY OF MY COUNTRYMEN SLAUGHTERED. I WILL NOT LET IT HAPPEN AGAIN.

AND SO, I AM TELLING YOU THAT THERE IS SOMETHING VERY *WRONG* WITH THE OFFICIAL STORY.

SOMETHING THAT THREATENS US ALL.

AND IF YOU CAN'T *SEE* THAT, PERHAPS I'LL TRY ONE OF YOUR COMPETITORS.

ALL YOU'RE GIVING ME ARE RUMORS AND HEARSAY. WHAT DO YOU SUPPOSE I SHOULD DO?

YOUR JOB.

YOU'RE A REPORTER, MR. DARIN.

REPORT.

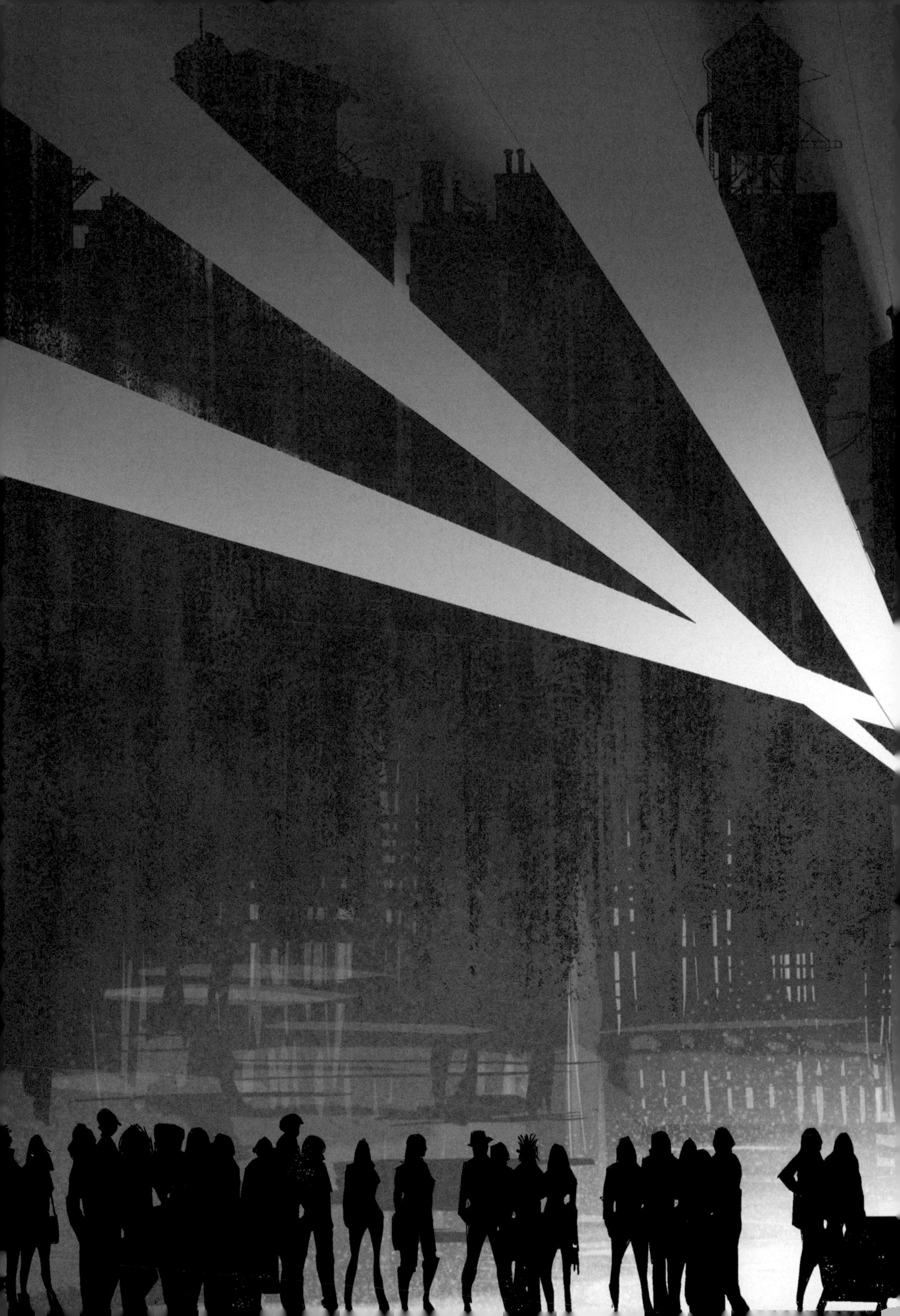

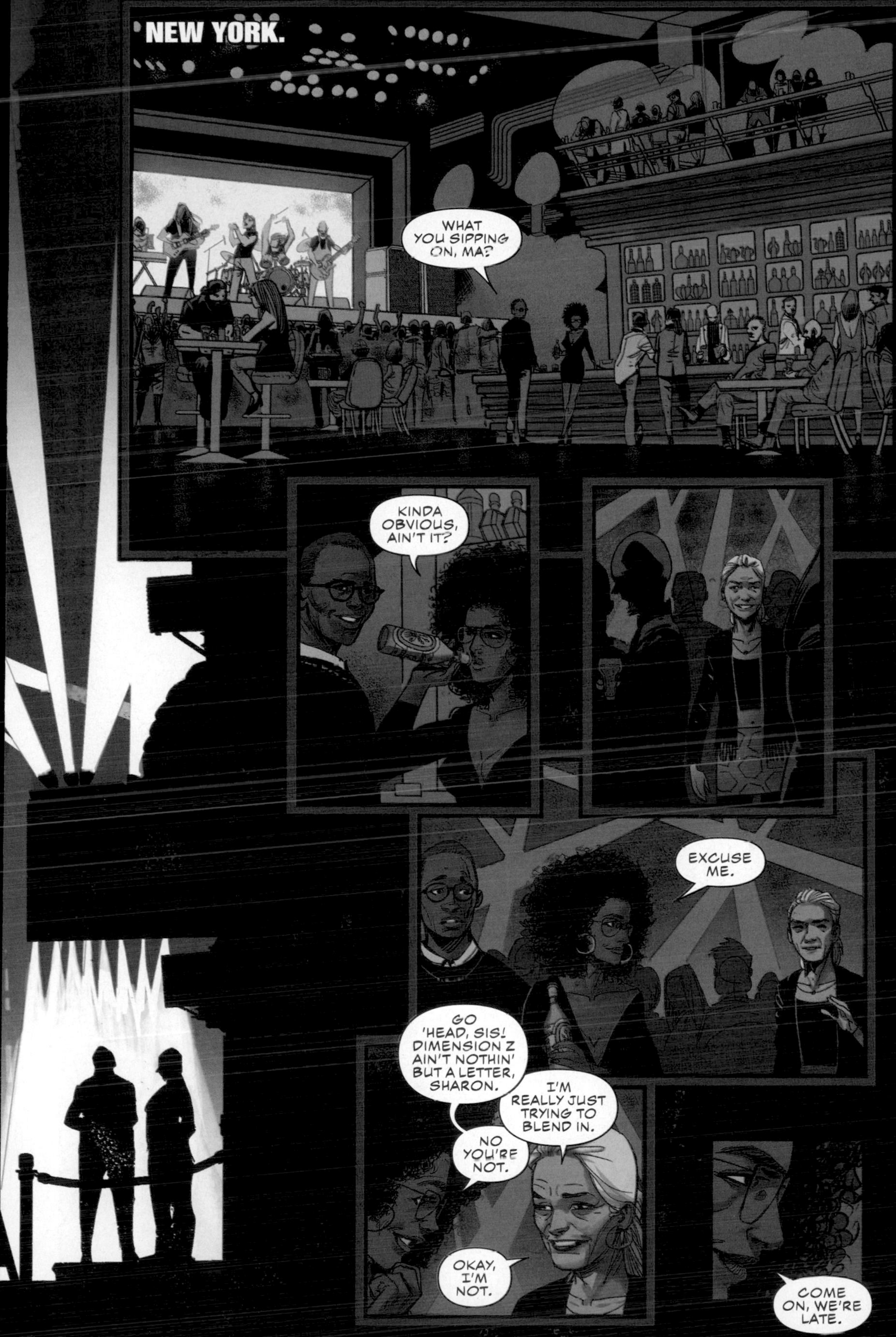
NEW YORK.
WHAT YOU SIPPING ON, MA?
KINDA OBVIOUS, AIN'T IT?
EXCUSE ME.
GO 'HEAD, SIS! DIMENSION Z AIN'T NOTHIN' BUT A LETTER, SHARON.
I'M REALLY JUST TRYING TO BLEND IN.
NO YOU'RE NOT.
OKAY, I'M NOT.
COME ON, WE'RE LATE.

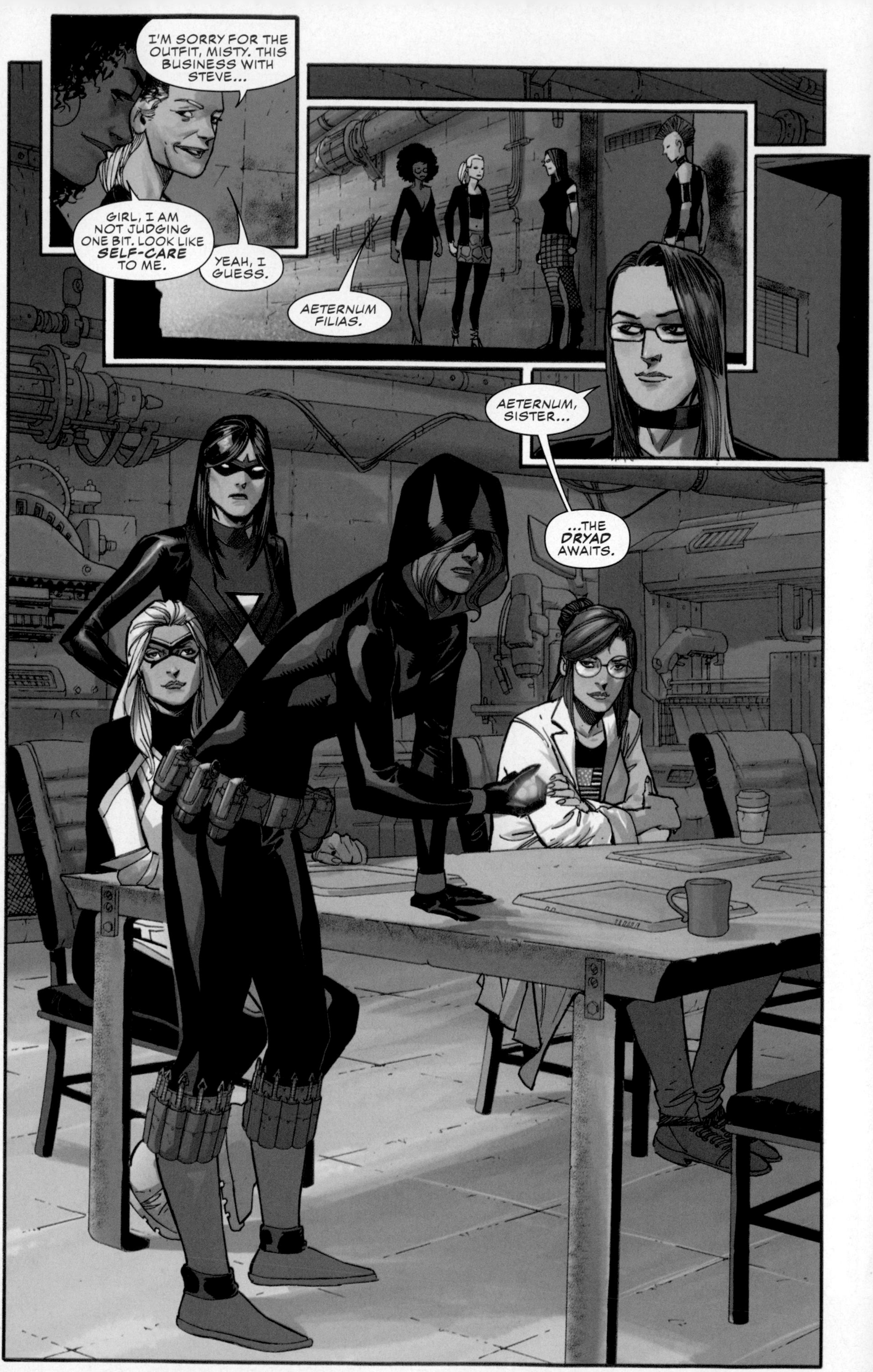
I'M SORRY FOR THE OUTFIT, MISTY. THIS BUSINESS WITH STEVE...
GIRL, I AM NOT JUDGING ONE BIT. LOOK LIKE SELF-CARE TO ME.
YEAH, I GUESS.
AETERNUM FILIAS.
AETERNUM, SISTER...
...THE DRYAD AWAITS.

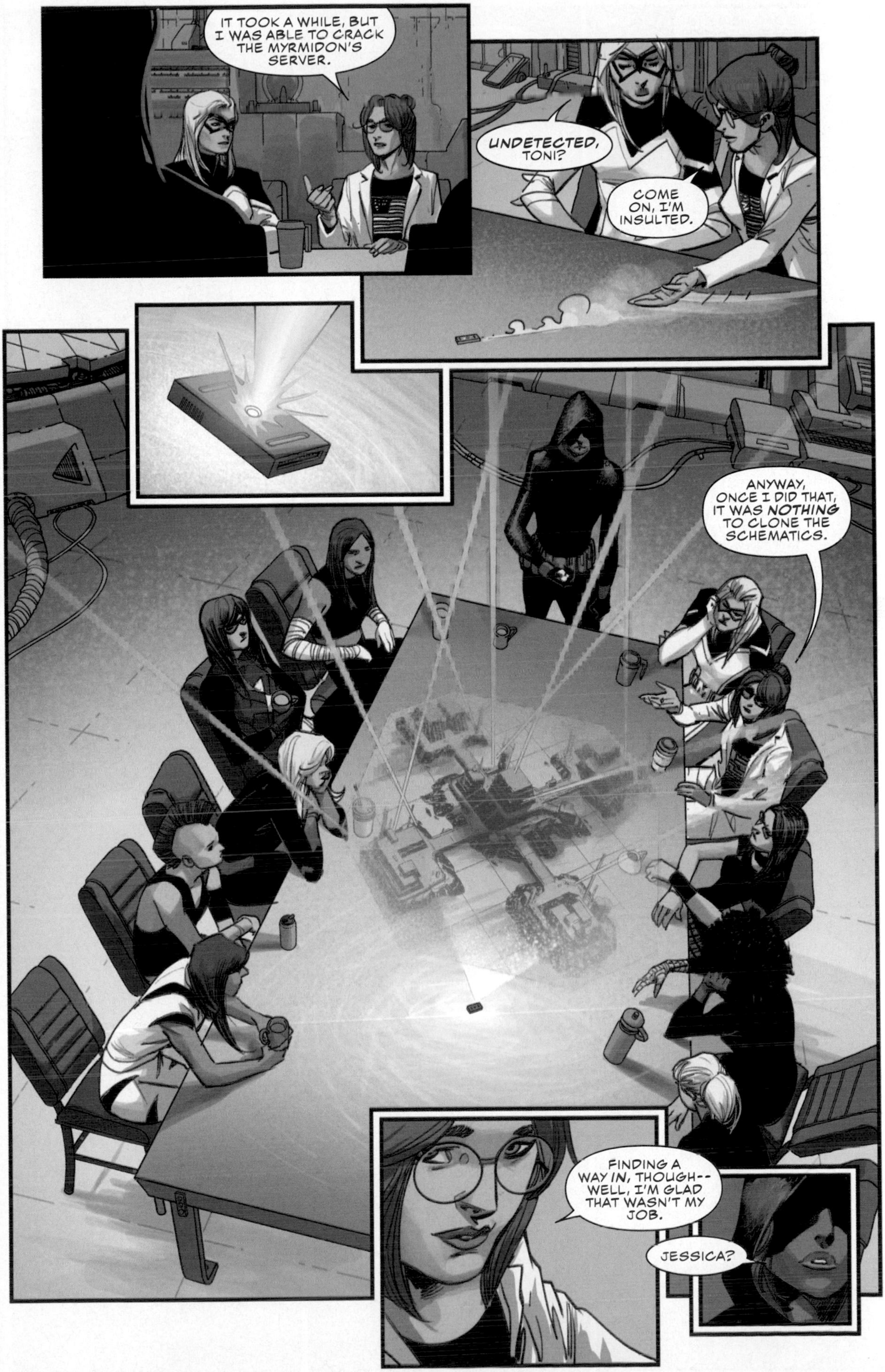
IT TOOK A WHILE, BUT I WAS ABLE TO CRACK THE MYRMIDON'S SERVER.
UNDETECTED, TONI?
COME ON, I'M INSULTED.
ANYWAY, ONCE I DID THAT, IT WAS NOTHING TO CLONE THE SCHEMATICS.
FINDING A WAY IN, THOUGH-- WELL, I'M GLAD THAT WASN'T MY JOB.
JESSICA?

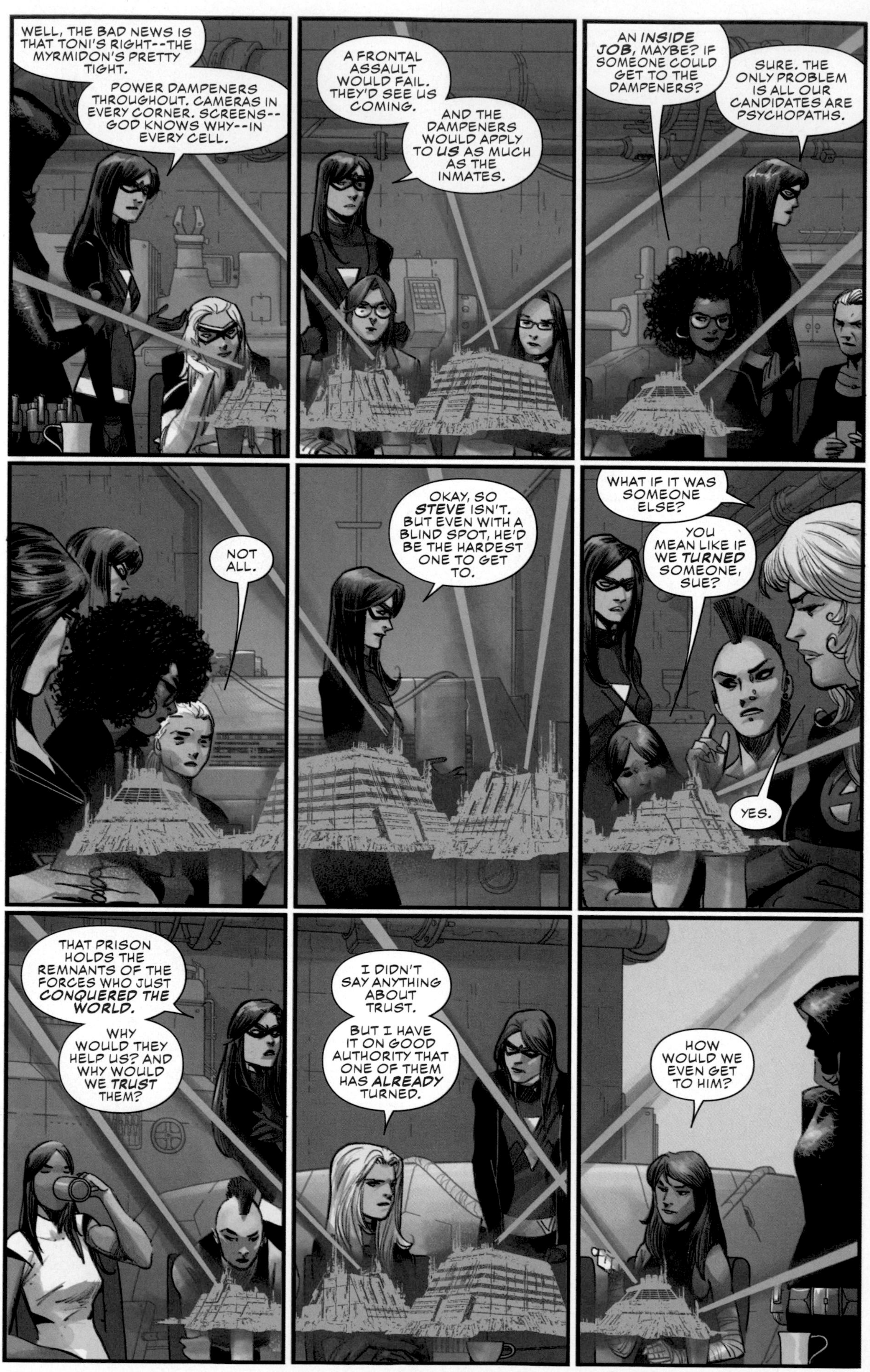
WELL, THE BAD NEWS IS THAT TONI'S RIGHT--THE MYRMIDON'S PRETTY TIGHT.
POWER DAMPENERS THROUGHOUT. CAMERAS IN EVERY CORNER. SCREENS--GOD KNOWS WHY--IN EVERY CELL.
A FRONTAL ASSAULT WOULD FAIL. THEY'D SEE US COMING.
AND THE DAMPENERS WOULD APPLY TO US AS MUCH AS THE INMATES.
AN INSIDE JOB, MAYBE? IF SOMEONE COULD GET TO THE DAMPENERS?
SURE. THE ONLY PROBLEM IS ALL OUR CANDIDATES ARE PSYCHOPATHS.
NOT ALL.
OKAY, SO STEVE ISN'T. BUT EVEN WITH A BLIND SPOT, HE'D BE THE HARDEST ONE TO GET TO.
WHAT IF IT WAS SOMEONE ELSE?
YOU MEAN LIKE IF WE TURNED SOMEONE, SUE?
YES.
THAT PRISON HOLDS THE REMNANTS OF THE FORCES WHO JUST CONQUERED THE WORLD.
WHY WOULD THEY HELP US? AND WHY WOULD WE TRUST THEM?
I DIDN'T SAY ANYTHING ABOUT TRUST.
BUT I HAVE IT ON GOOD AUTHORITY THAT ONE OF THEM HAS ALREADY TURNED.
HOW WOULD WE EVEN GET TO HIM?

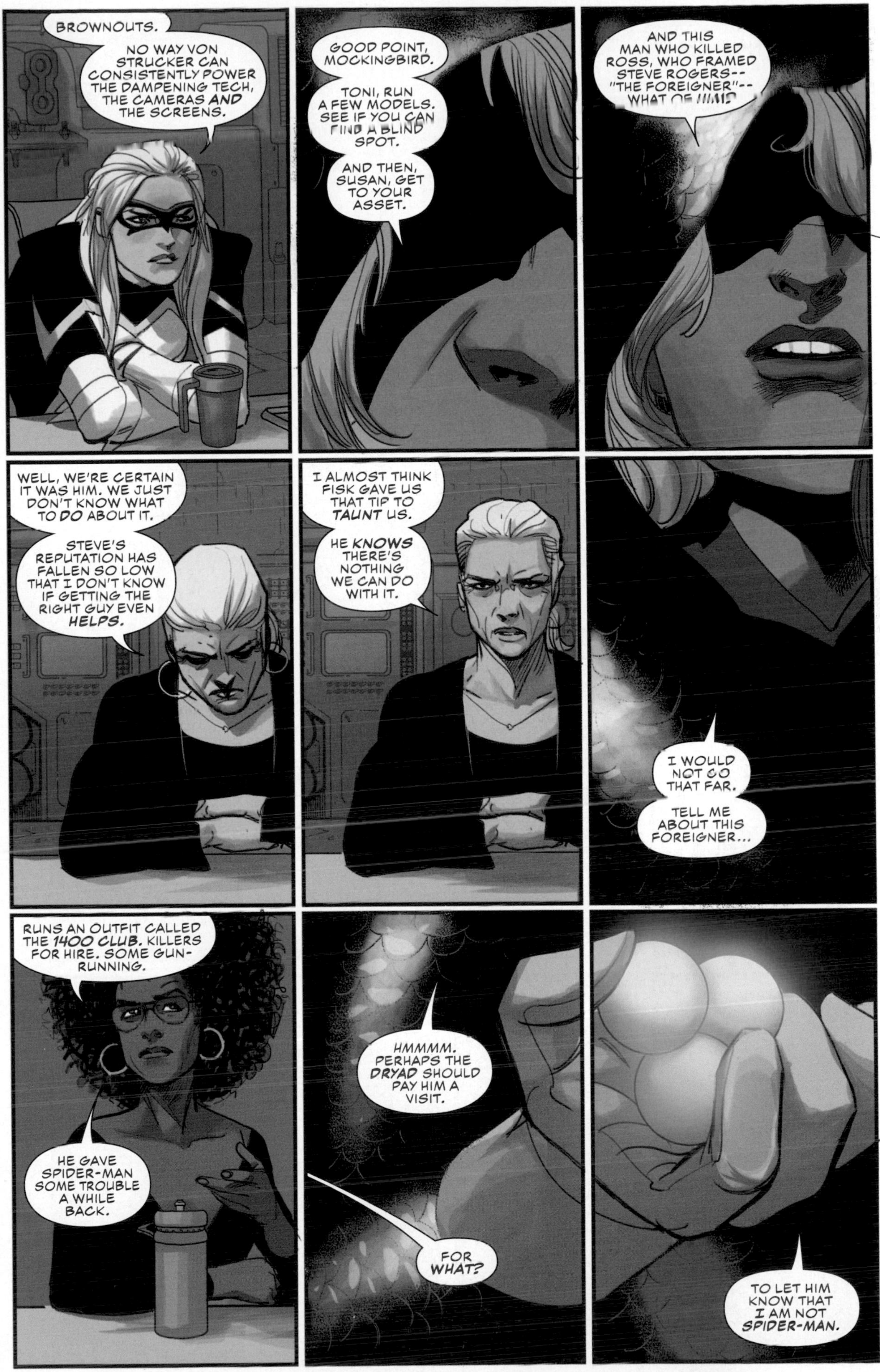
BROWNOUTS.
NO WAY VON STRUCKER CAN CONSISTENTLY POWER THE DAMPENING TECH, THE CAMERAS AND THE SCREENS.
GOOD POINT, MOCKINGBIRD.
TONI, RUN A FEW MODELS. SEE IF YOU CAN FIND A BLIND SPOT.
AND THEN, SUSAN, GET TO YOUR ASSET.
AND THIS MAN WHO KILLED ROSS, WHO FRAMED STEVE ROGERS-- "THE FOREIGNER"-- WHAT OF
WELL, WE'RE CERTAIN IT WAS HIM. WE JUST DON'T KNOW WHAT TO DO ABOUT IT.
STEVE'S REPUTATION HAS FALLEN SO LOW THAT I DON'T KNOW IF GETTING THE RIGHT GUY EVEN HELPS.
I ALMOST THINK FISK GAVE US THAT TIP TO TAUNT US.
HE KNOWS THERE'S NOTHING WE CAN DO WITH IT.
I WOULD NOT GO THAT FAR.
TELL ME ABOUT THIS FOREIGNER...
RUNS AN OUTFIT CALLED THE 1400 CLUB. KILLERS FOR HIRE. SOME GUN-RUNNING.
HE GAVE SPIDER-MAN SOME TROUBLE A WHILE BACK.
HMMMM. PERHAPS THE DRYAD SHOULD PAY HIM A VISIT.
FOR WHAT?
TO LET HIM KNOW THAT I AM NOT SPIDER-MAN.

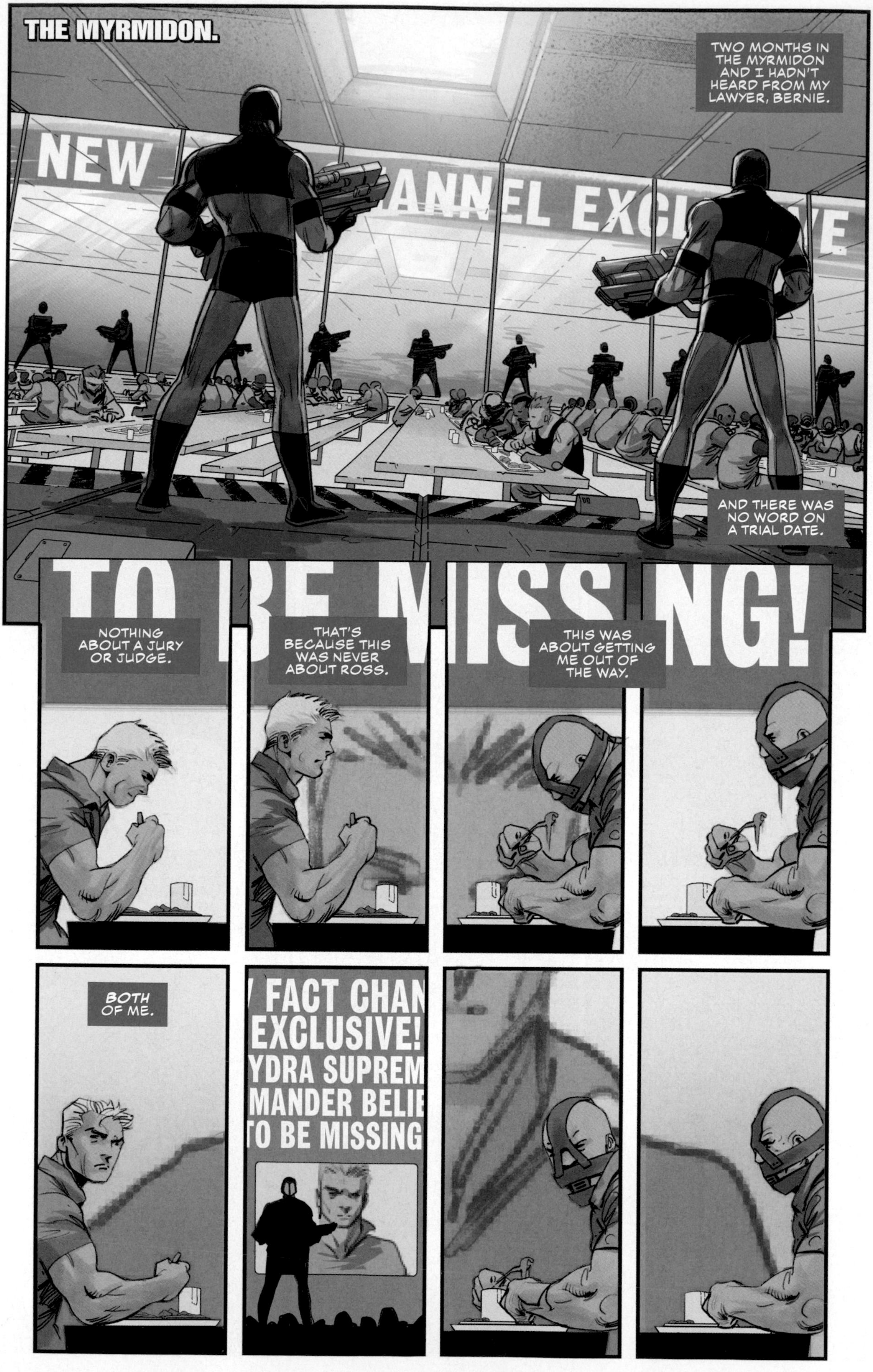
THE MYRMIDON.
TWO MONTHS IN THE MYRMIDON AND I HADN'T HEARD FROM MY LAWYER, BERNIE.
NEW
ANNEL EXCL
AND THERE WAS NO WORD ON A TRIAL DATE.
NG!
NOTHING ABOUT A JURY OR JUDGE.
THAT'S BECAUSE THIS WAS NEVER ABOUT ROSS.
THIS WAS ABOUT GETTING ME OUT OF THE WAY.
BOTH OF ME.
FACT CHAN
EXCLUSIVE!
YDRA SUPREM
MANDER BELIE
TO BE MISSING

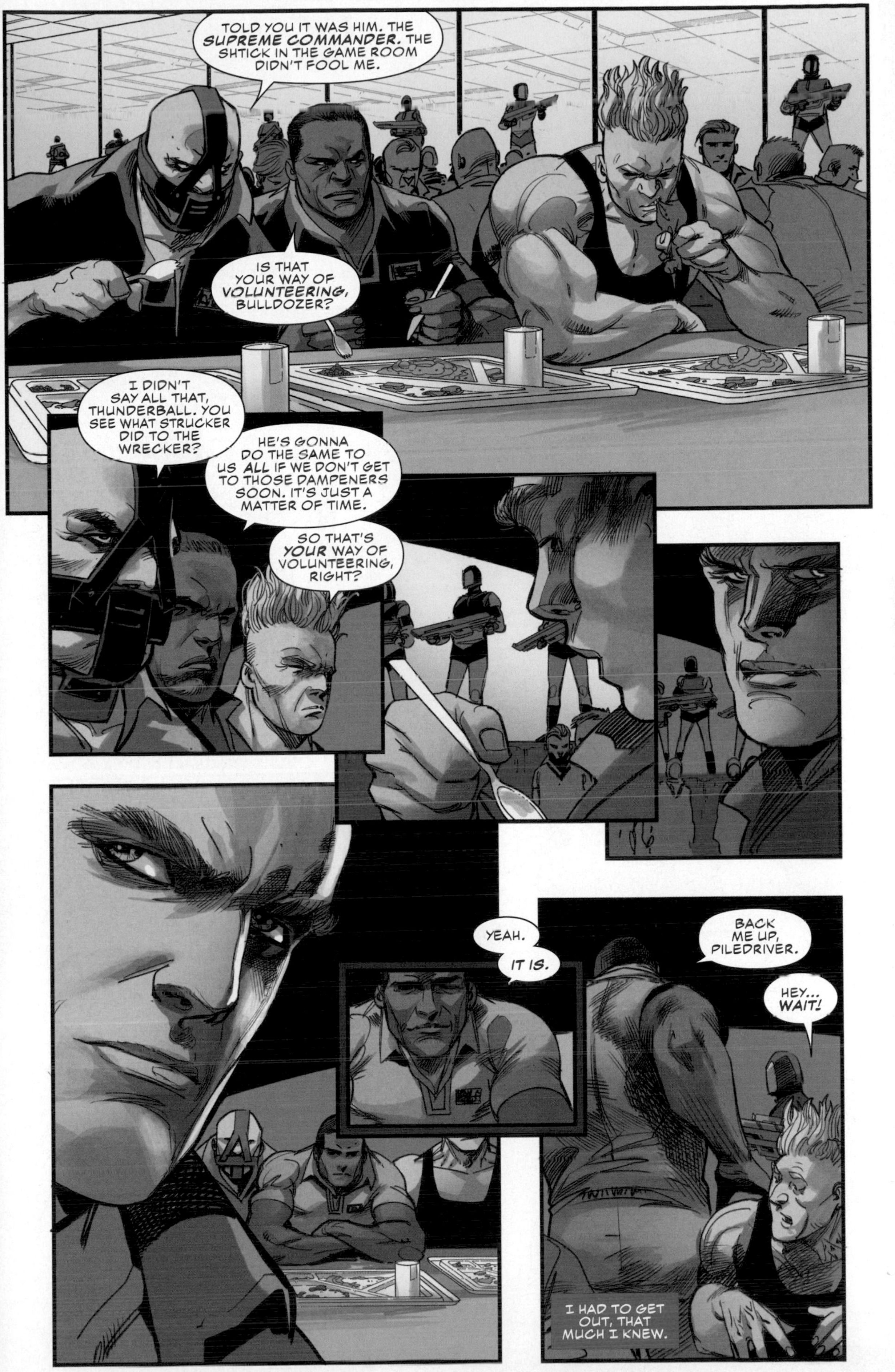

TOLD YOU IT WAS HIM. THE SUPREME COMMANDER. THE SHTICK IN THE GAME ROOM DIDN'T FOOL ME.
IS THAT YOUR WAY OF VOLUNTEERING, BULLDOZER?
I DIDN'T SAY ALL THAT, THUNDERBALL. YOU SEE WHAT STRUCKER DID TO THE WRECKER?
HE'S GONNA DO THE SAME TO US ALL IF WE DON'T GET TO THOSE DAMPENERS SOON. IT'S JUST A MATTER OF TIME.
SO THAT'S YOUR WAY OF VOLUNTEERING, RIGHT?
YEAH.
IT IS.
BACK ME UP, PILEDRIVER.
HEY... WAIT!
I HAD TO GET OUT, THAT MUCH I KNEW.

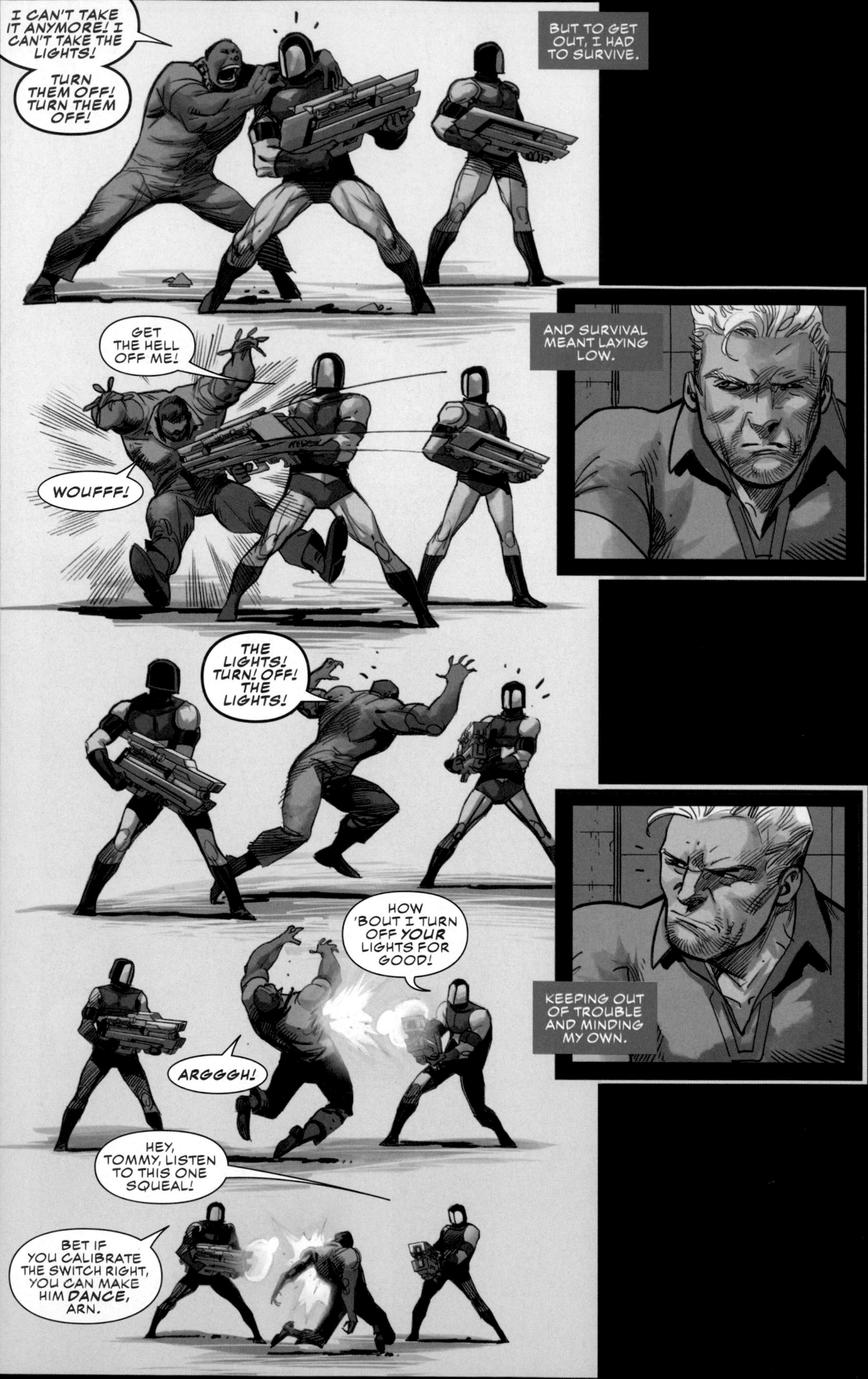
I CAN'T TAKE IT ANYMORE! I CAN'T TAKE THE LIGHTS!
TURN THEM OFF! TURN THEM OFF!
BUT TO GET OUT, I HAD TO SURVIVE.
GET THE HELL OFF ME!
WOUFFF!
AND SURVIVAL MEANT LAYING LOW.
THE LIGHTS! TURN! OFF! THE LIGHTS!
HOW 'BOUT I TURN OFF YOUR LIGHTS FOR GOOD!
ARGGGH!
KEEPING OUT OF TROUBLE AND MINDING MY OWN.
HEY, TOMMY, LISTEN TO THIS ONE SQUEAL!
BET IF YOU CALIBRATE THE SWITCH RIGHT, YOU CAN MAKE HIM DANCE, ARN.

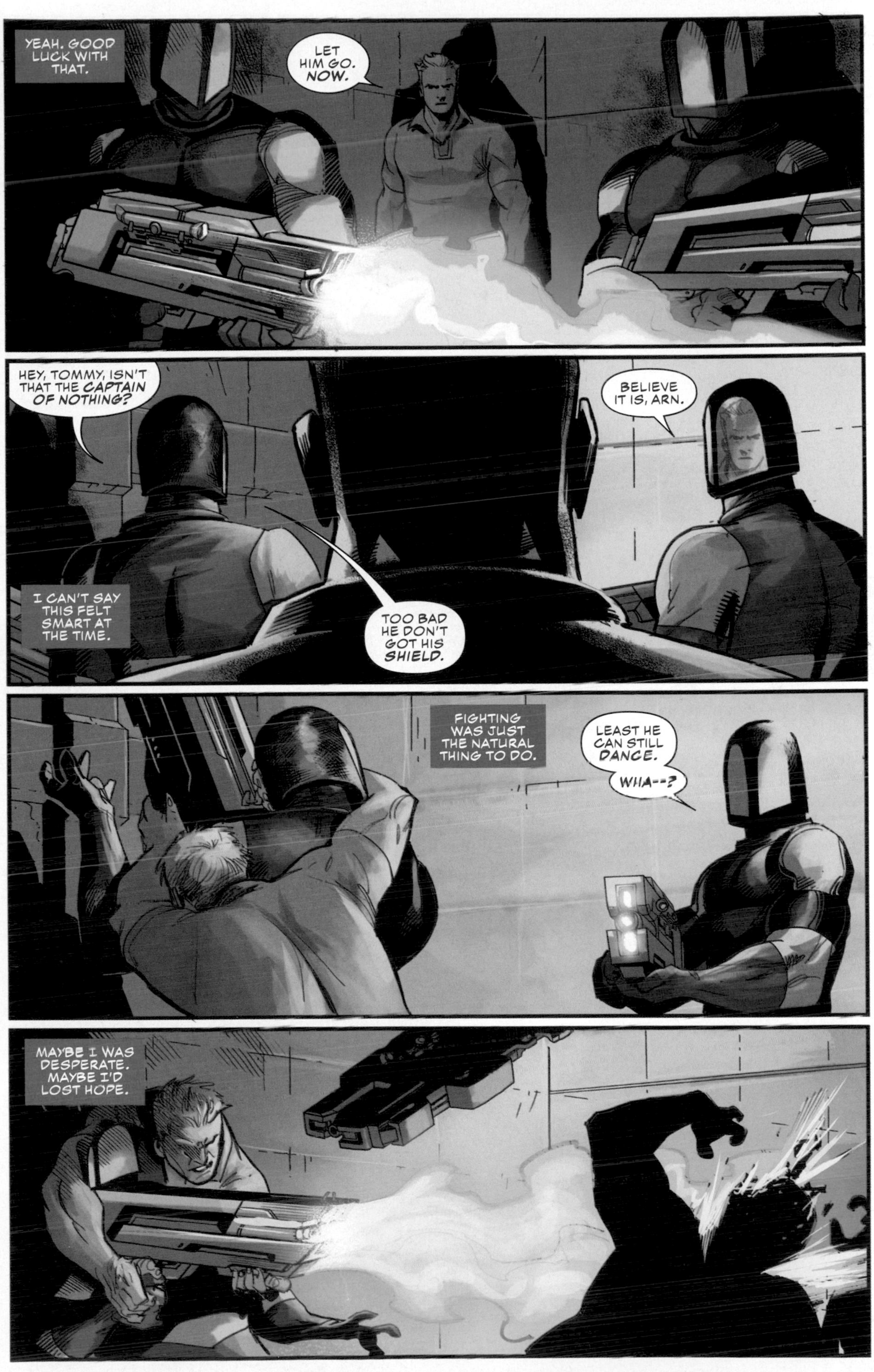
YEAH. GOOD LUCK WITH THAT.
LET HIM GO. NOW.
HEY, TOMMY, ISN'T THAT THE CAPTAIN OF NOTHING?
BELIEVE IT IS, ARN.
I CAN'T SAY THIS FELT SMART AT THE TIME.
TOO BAD HE DON'T GOT HIS SHIELD.
FIGHTING WAS JUST THE NATURAL THING TO DO.
LEAST HE CAN STILL DANCE.
WHA--?
MAYBE I WAS DESPERATE. MAYBE I'D LOST HOPE.

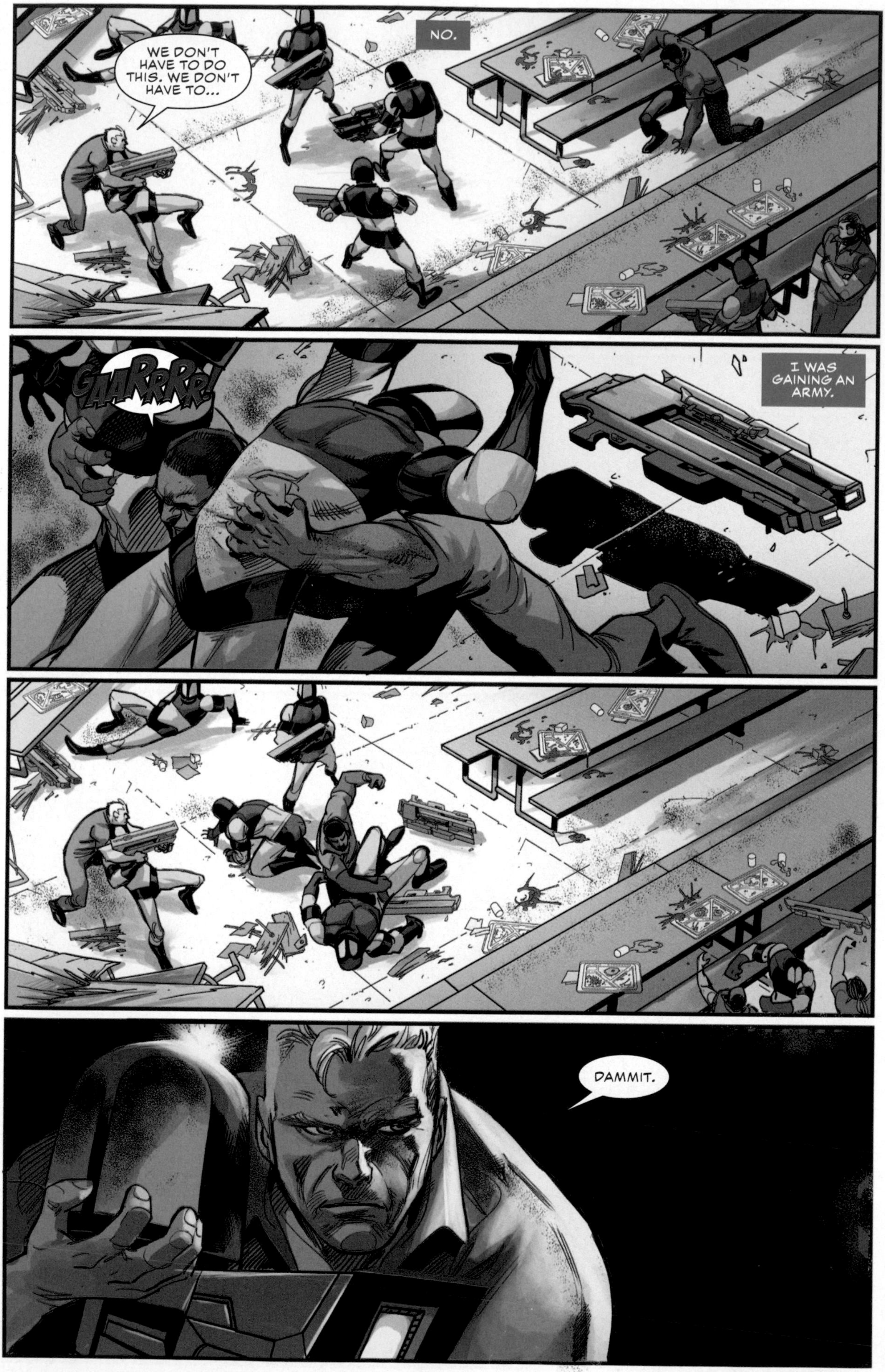
NO.
WE DON'T HAVE TO DO THIS. WE DON'T HAVE TO...
GAARRRR!
I WAS GAINING AN ARMY.
DAMMIT.

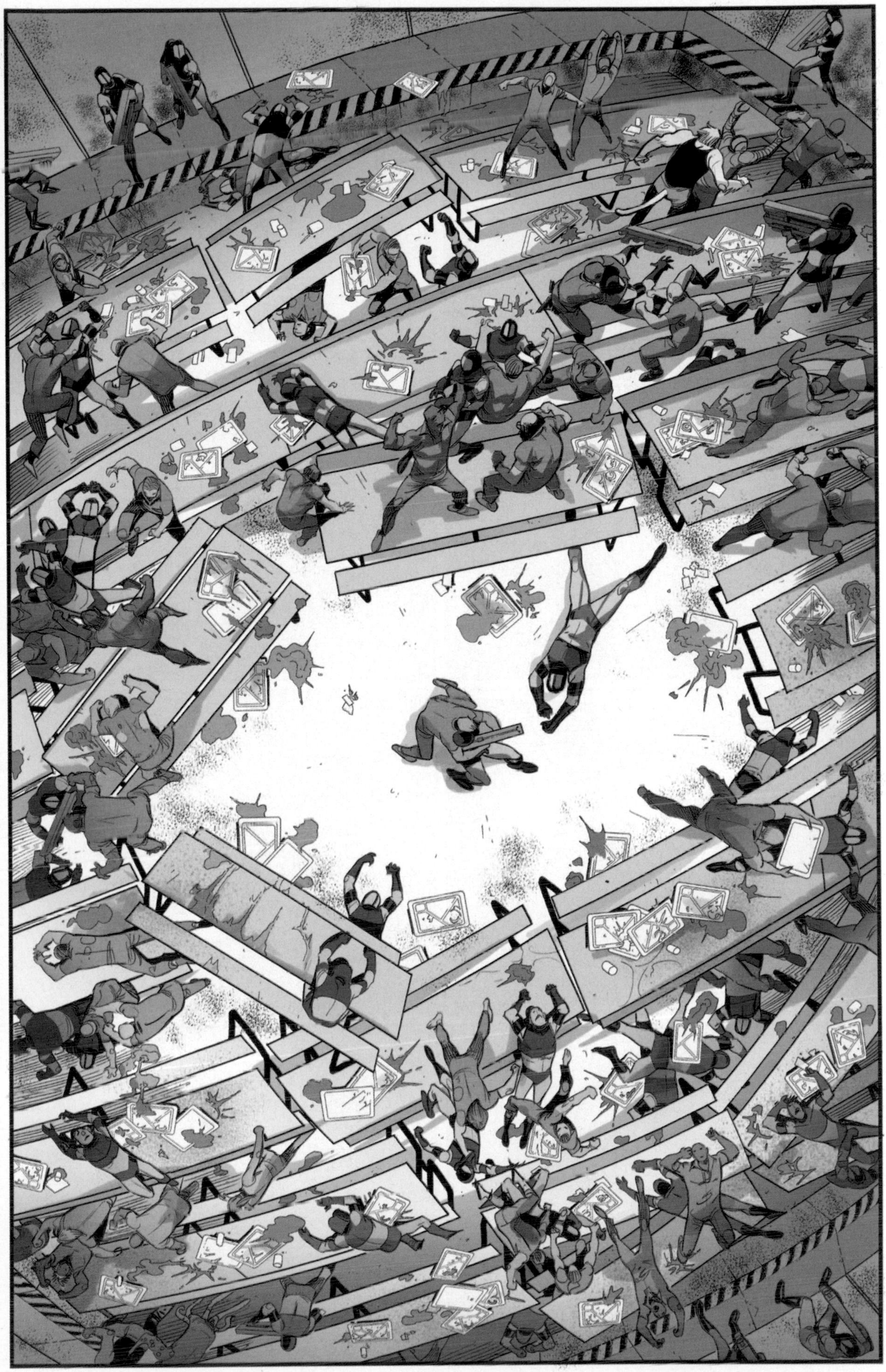

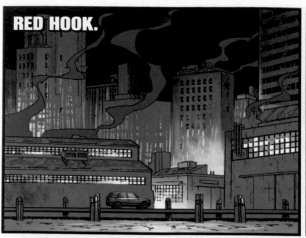

RED HOOK.

MEANWHILE, ON THE OUTSIDE, SHARON HAD AN ARMY OF HER OWN.

TRACKING THE FOREIGNER AND HIS 1400 CLUB.

THESE GUYS WERE PROFESSIONAL ASSASSINS.

GOOD ENOUGH TO MURDER ROSS AND MAKE IT LOOK LIKE IT WAS ME.

A CONFESSION WAS OUT OF THE QUESTION.

BUT A DOSE OF THEIR OWN MEDICINE...

A PAYBACK IN KIND...

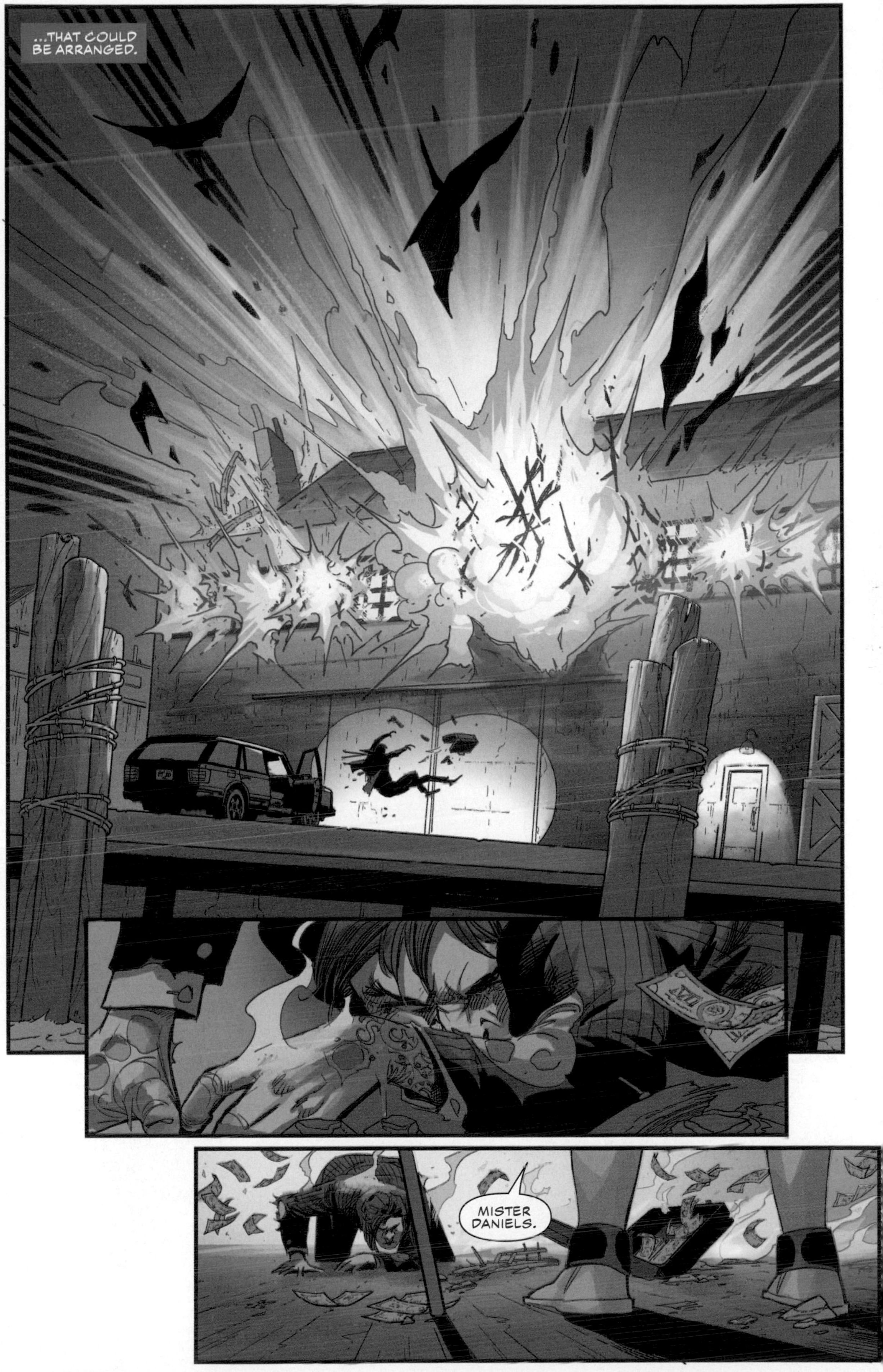
...THAT COULD BE ARRANGED.
MISTER DANIELS.

YOU CAN CALL HER THE DRYAD.
AND YOU REALLY SHOULD PAY ATTENTION.
BECAUSE RIGHT NOW, SHE'S THE WHOLE HOPE OF THE FREE WORLD.

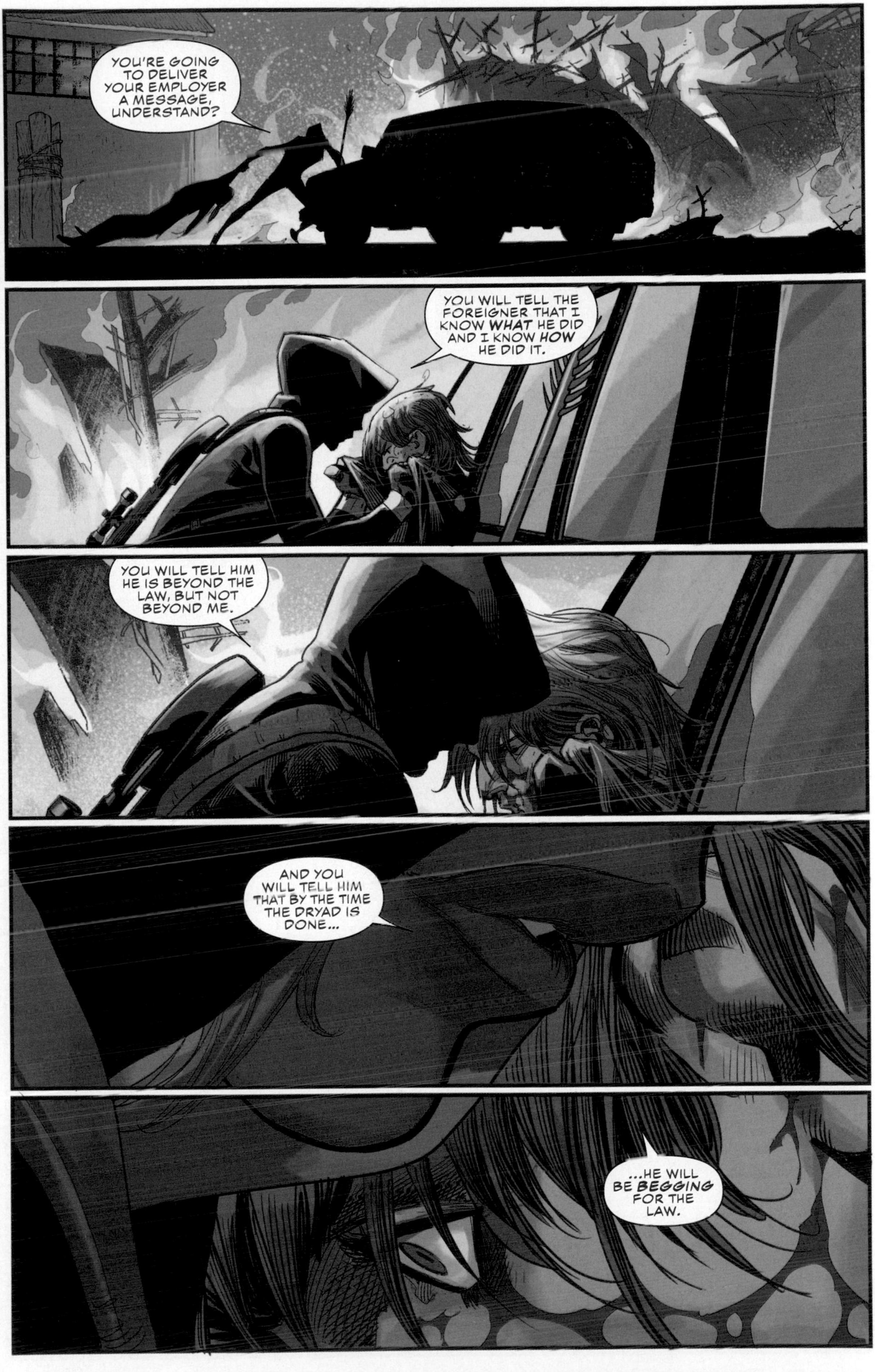
YOU'RE GOING TO DELIVER YOUR EMPLOYER A MESSAGE, UNDERSTAND?
YOU WILL TELL THE FOREIGNER THAT I KNOW WHAT HE DID AND I KNOW HOW HE DID IT.
YOU WILL TELL HIM HE IS BEYOND THE LAW, BUT NOT BEYOND ME.
AND YOU WILL TELL HIM THAT BY THE TIME THE DRYAD IS DONE...
...HE WILL BE BEGGING FOR THE LAW.

THE MYRMIDON.

BUT IT'S LIKE I SAID...

WHILE I WAS WAITING ON SHARON AND THIS DRYAD...

...I STILL HAD TO SURVIVE.

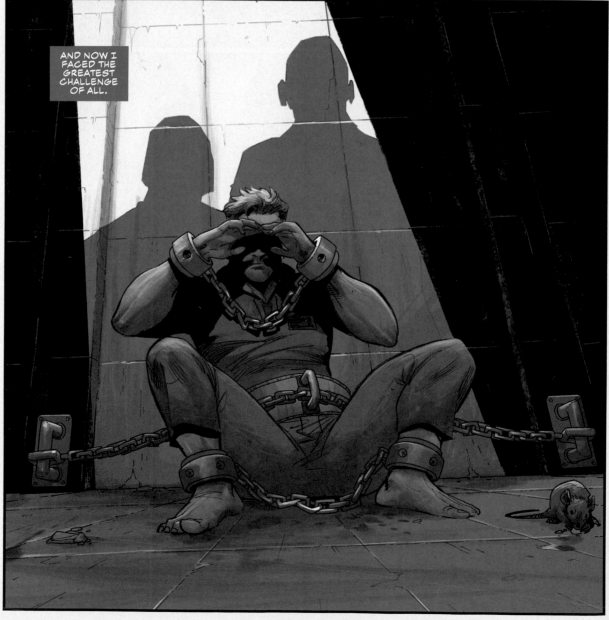

AND NOW I FACED THE GREATEST CHALLENGE OF ALL.

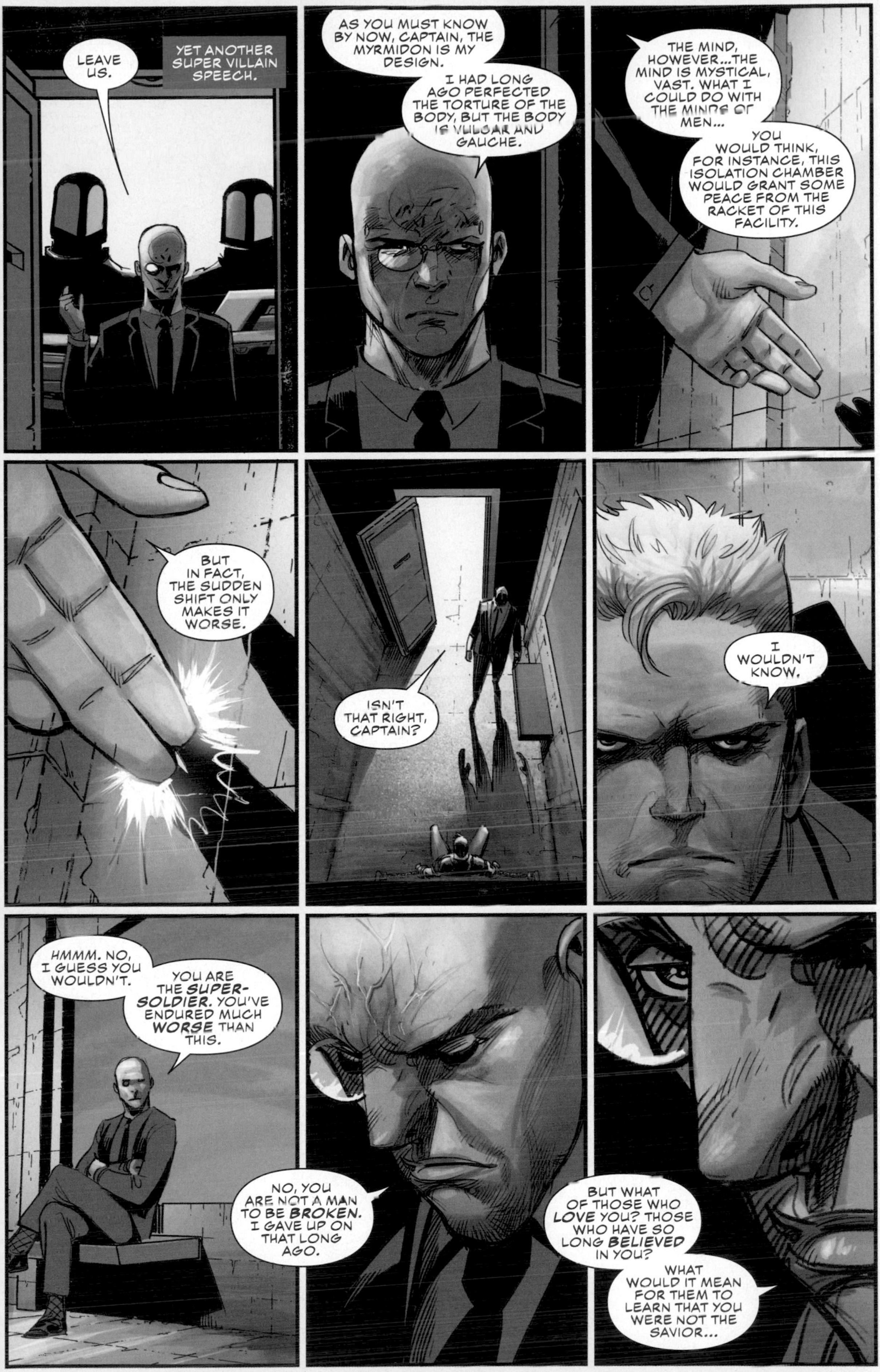

YET ANOTHER SUPER VILLAIN SPEECH.
LEAVE US.
AS YOU MUST KNOW BY NOW, CAPTAIN, THE MYRMIDON IS MY DESIGN.
I HAD LONG AGO PERFECTED THE TORTURE OF THE BODY, BUT THE BODY IS VULGAR AND GAUCHE.
THE MIND, HOWEVER...THE MIND IS MYSTICAL, VAST. WHAT I COULD DO WITH THE MINDS OF MEN...
YOU WOULD THINK, FOR INSTANCE, THIS ISOLATION CHAMBER WOULD GRANT SOME PEACE FROM THE RACKET OF THIS FACILITY.
BUT IN FACT, THE SUDDEN SHIFT ONLY MAKES IT WORSE.
ISN'T THAT RIGHT, CAPTAIN?
I WOULDN'T KNOW.
HMMM. NO, I GUESS YOU WOULDN'T.
YOU ARE THE SUPER-SOLDIER. YOU'VE ENDURED MUCH WORSE THAN THIS.
NO, YOU ARE NOT A MAN TO BE BROKEN. I GAVE UP ON THAT LONG AGO.
BUT WHAT OF THOSE WHO LOVE YOU? THOSE WHO HAVE SO LONG BELIEVED IN YOU?
WHAT WOULD IT MEAN FOR THEM TO LEARN THAT YOU WERE NOT THE SAVIOR...

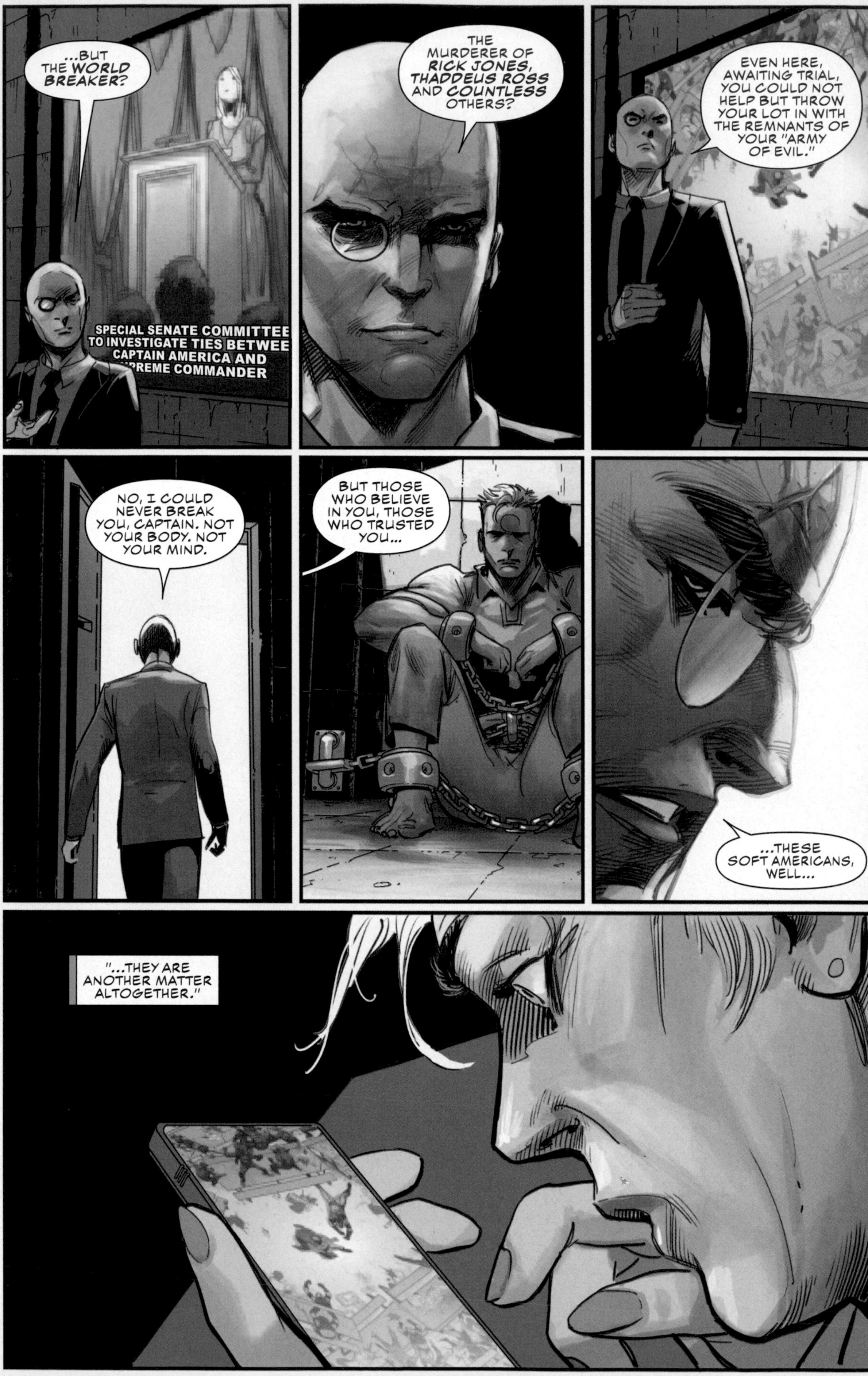
...BUT THE WORLD BREAKER?
SPECIAL SENATE COMMITTEE TO INVESTIGATE TIES BETWEE CAPTAIN AMERICA AND PREME COMMANDER
THE MURDERER OF RICK JONES, THADDEUS ROSS AND COUNTLESS OTHERS?
EVEN HERE, AWAITING TRIAL, YOU COULD NOT HELP BUT THROW YOUR LOT IN WITH THE REMNANTS OF YOUR "ARMY OF EVIL."
NO, I COULD NEVER BREAK YOU, CAPTAIN. NOT YOUR BODY. NOT YOUR MIND.
BUT THOSE WHO BELIEVE IN YOU, THOSE WHO TRUSTED YOU...
...THESE SOFT AMERICANS, WELL...
"...THEY ARE ANOTHER MATTER ALTOGETHER."

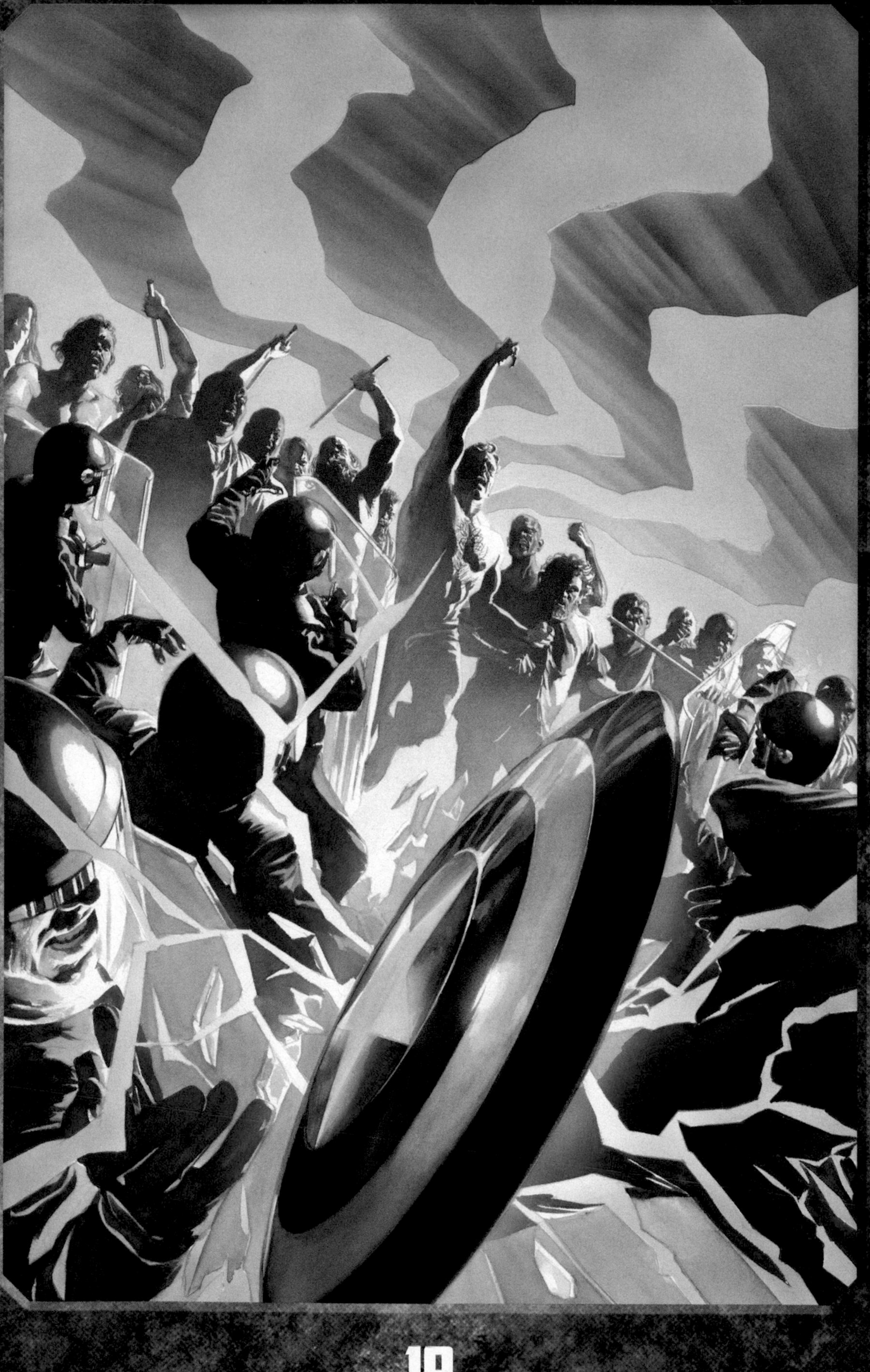

10

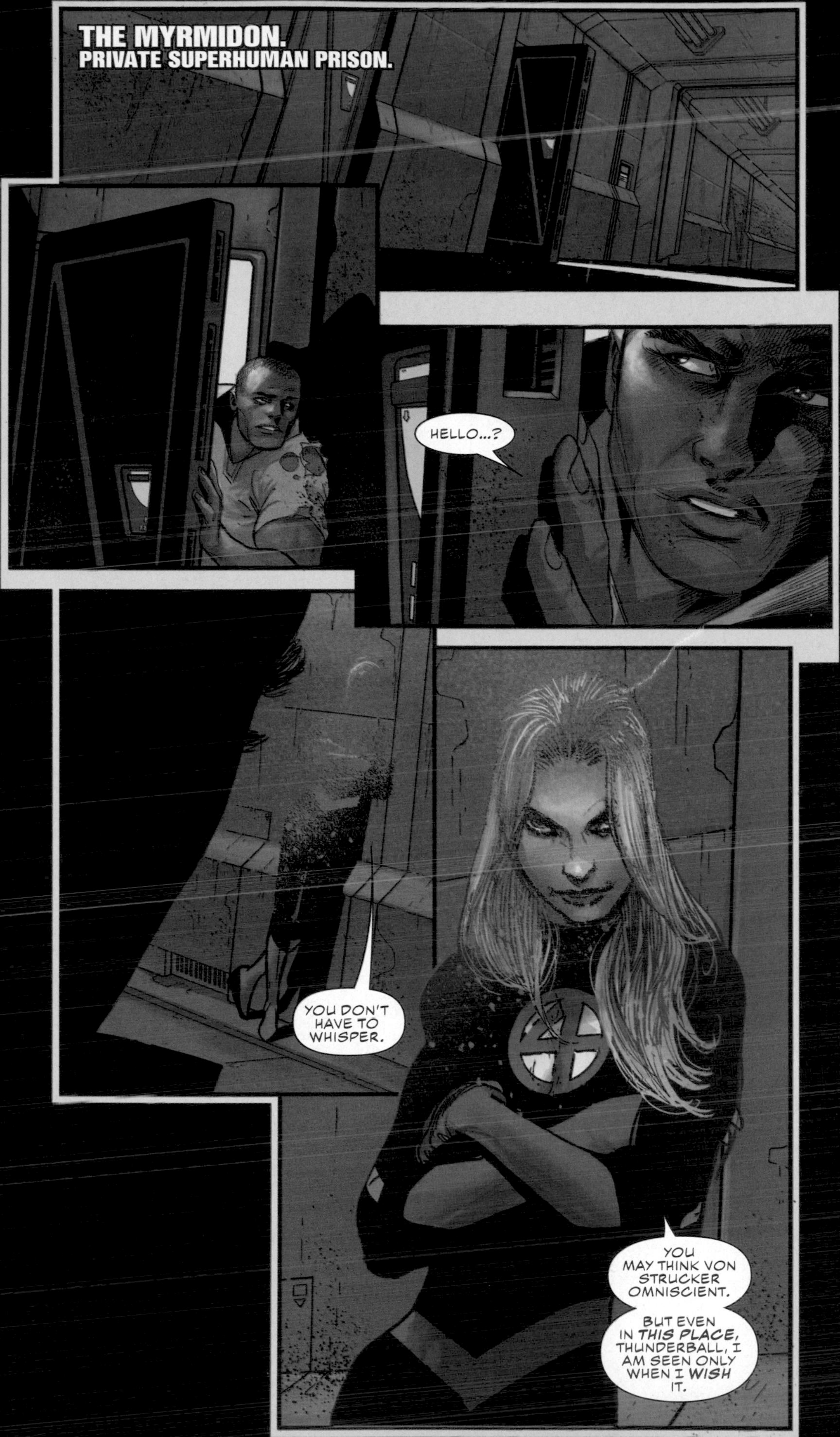
THE MYRMIDON.
PRIVATE SUPERHUMAN PRISON.
HELLO...?
YOU DON'T HAVE TO WHISPER.
YOU MAY THINK VON STRUCKER OMNISCIENT.
BUT EVEN IN *THIS PLACE,* THUNDERBALL, I AM SEEN ONLY WHEN I *WISH* IT.

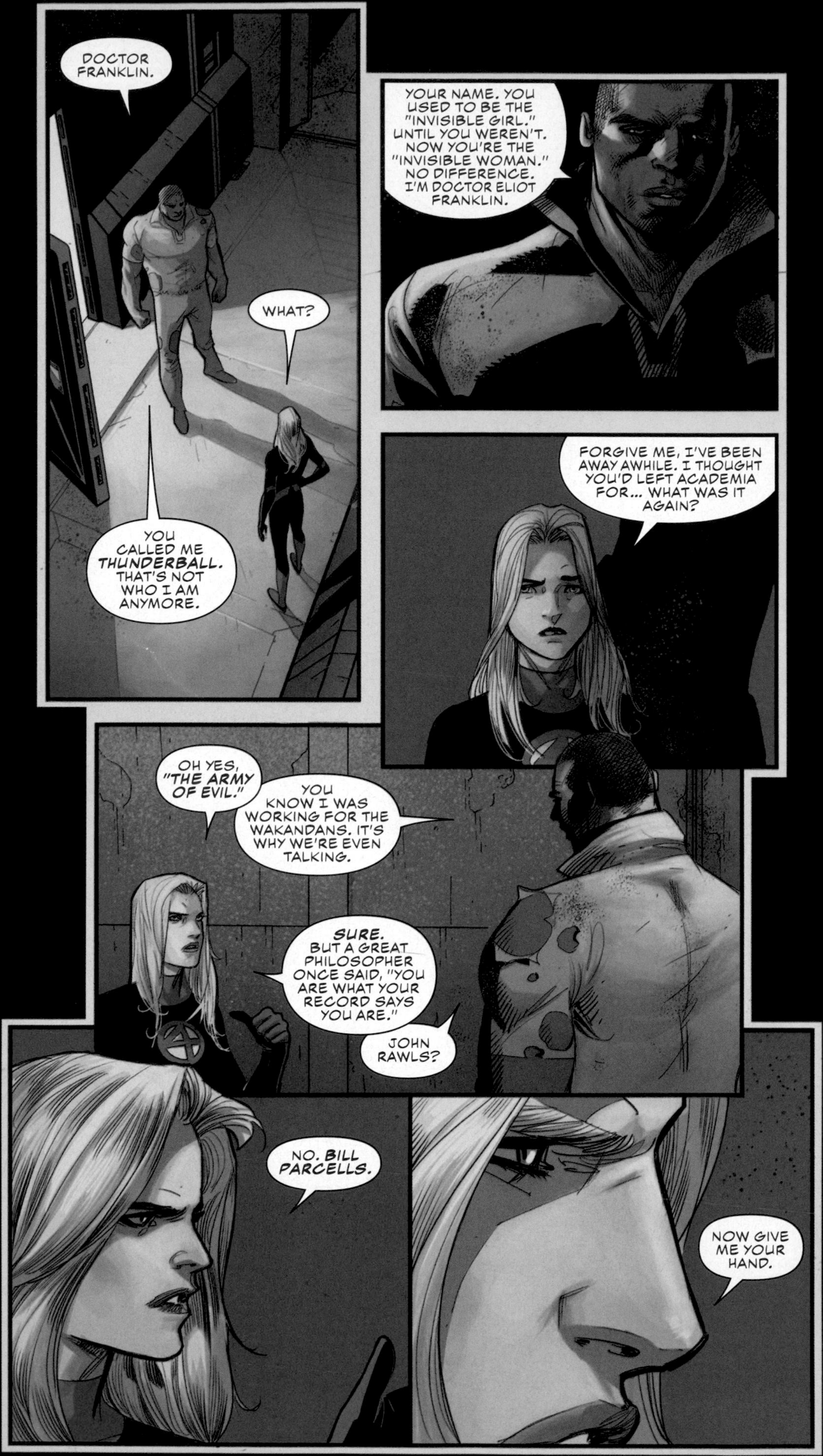

DOCTOR FRANKLIN.
WHAT?
YOU CALLED ME THUNDERBALL. THAT'S NOT WHO I AM ANYMORE.
YOUR NAME. YOU USED TO BE THE "INVISIBLE GIRL." UNTIL YOU WEREN'T. NOW YOU'RE THE "INVISIBLE WOMAN." NO DIFFERENCE. I'M DOCTOR ELIOT FRANKLIN.
FORGIVE ME, I'VE BEEN AWAY AWHILE. I THOUGHT YOU'D LEFT ACADEMIA FOR... WHAT WAS IT AGAIN?
OH YES, "THE ARMY OF EVIL."
YOU KNOW I WAS WORKING FOR THE WAKANDANS. IT'S WHY WE'RE EVEN TALKING.
SURE. BUT A GREAT PHILOSOPHER ONCE SAID, "YOU ARE WHAT YOUR RECORD SAYS YOU ARE."
JOHN RAWLS?
NO. BILL PARCELLS.
NOW GIVE ME YOUR HAND.

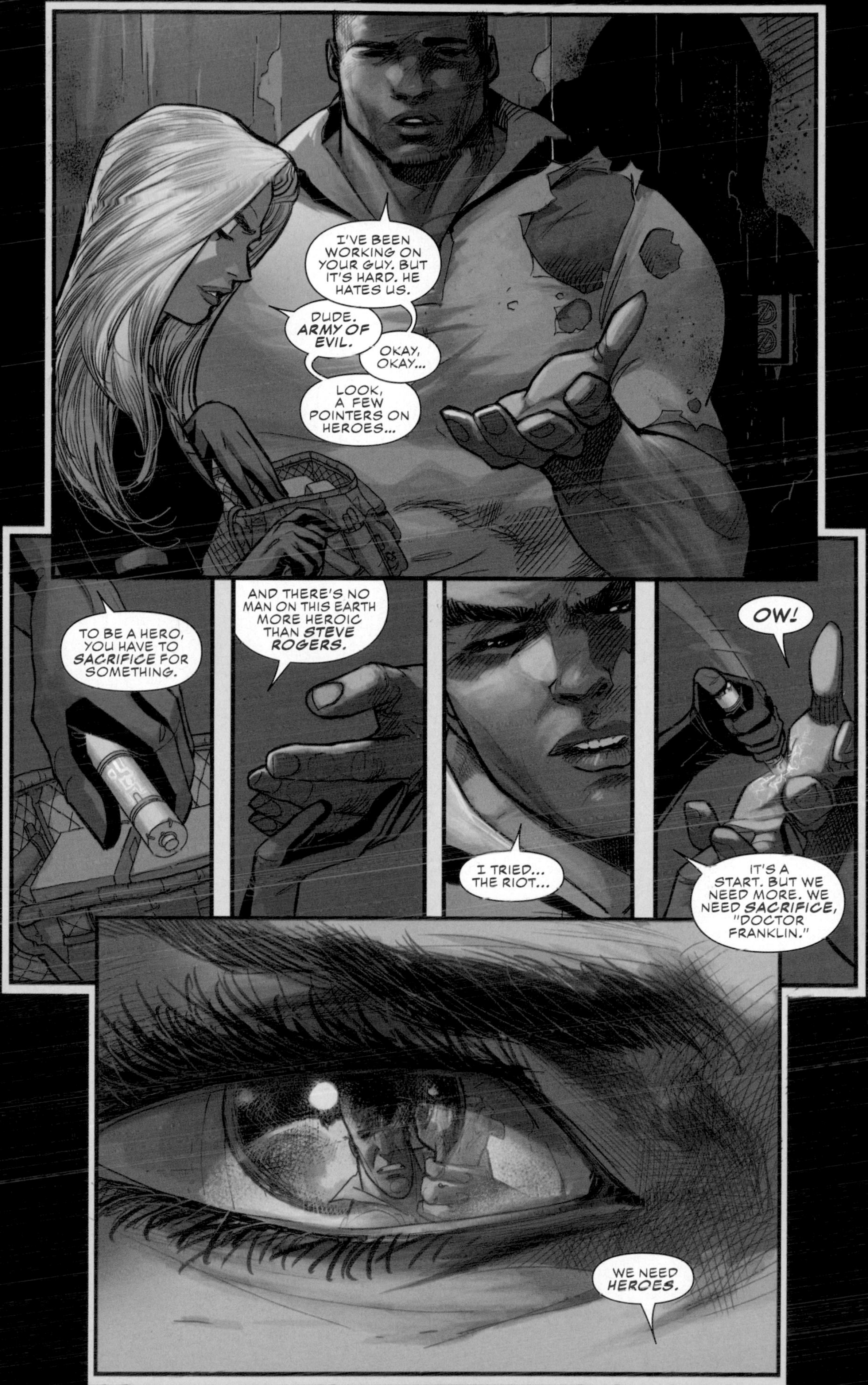
I'VE BEEN WORKING ON YOUR GUY. BUT IT'S HARD. HE HATES US.
DUDE. ARMY OF EVIL.
OKAY, OKAY...
LOOK, A FEW POINTERS ON HEROES...
TO BE A HERO, YOU HAVE TO SACRIFICE FOR SOMETHING.
AND THERE'S NO MAN ON THIS EARTH MORE HEROIC THAN STEVE ROGERS.
I TRIED... THE RIOT...
OW!
IT'S A START. BUT WE NEED MORE. WE NEED SACRIFICE, "DOCTOR FRANKLIN."
WE NEED HEROES.

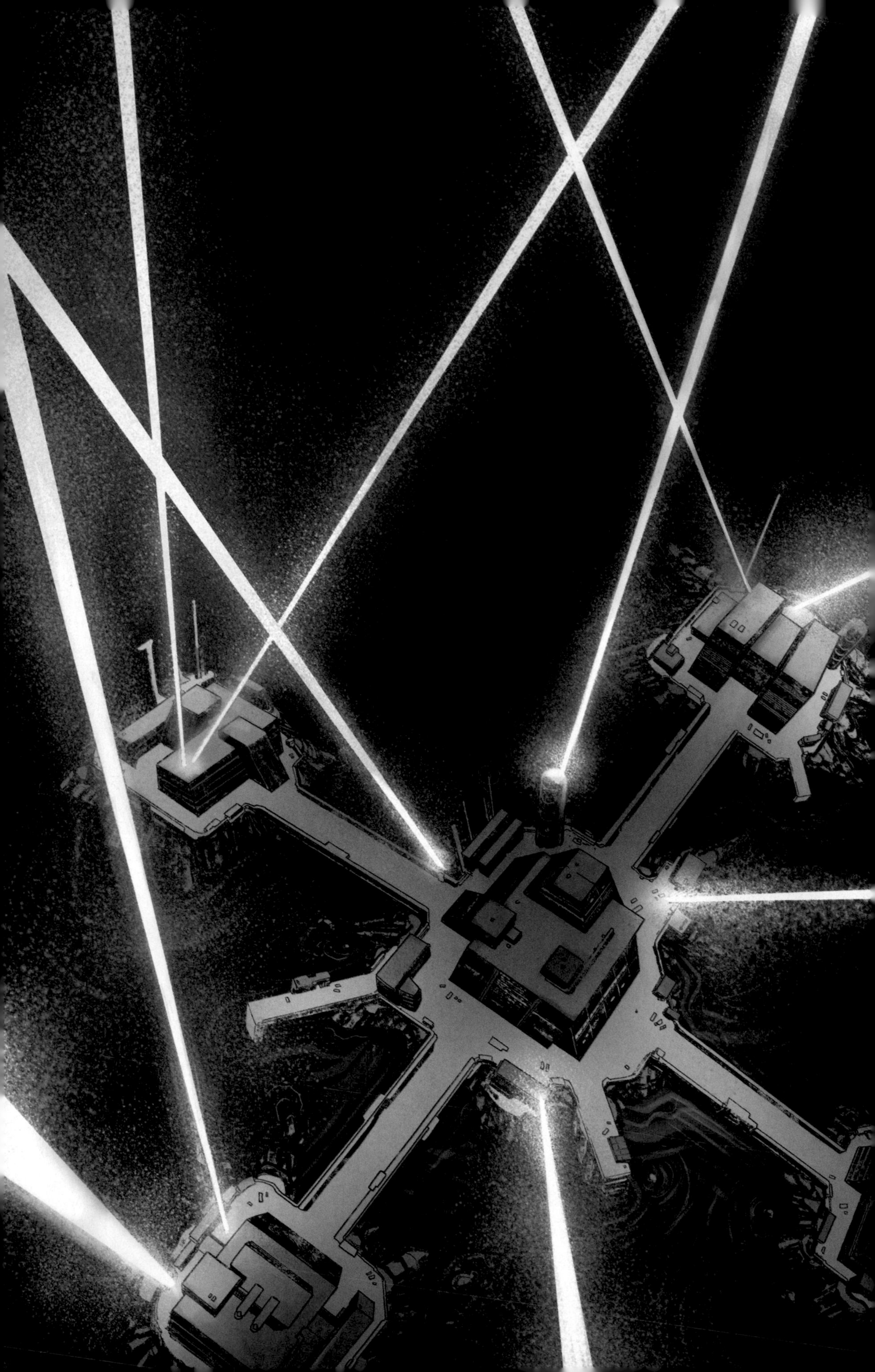

A FEW YEARS BACK, I WORKED AS A POLICE OFFICER.
THE BEAT GAVE ME THE STREET-LEVEL VIEW OF CRIMINALS.
I GOT TO SEE THAT A GUY LIKE THE GRIFFIN HAS A MOTHER CRYING ABOUT HIM SOMEWHERE.
THAT, TO SOMEONE, THIS MAN ISN'T PILEDRIVER. HE'S BRIAN.
AND SOMETIMES, BEHIND THE MASK, THERE'S A JADED VETERAN...
...WHO ALSO JUST HAPPENS TO BE A SHARK AT UNO.
HAHA! THIRD STRAIGHT GAME, YOU BUMS!

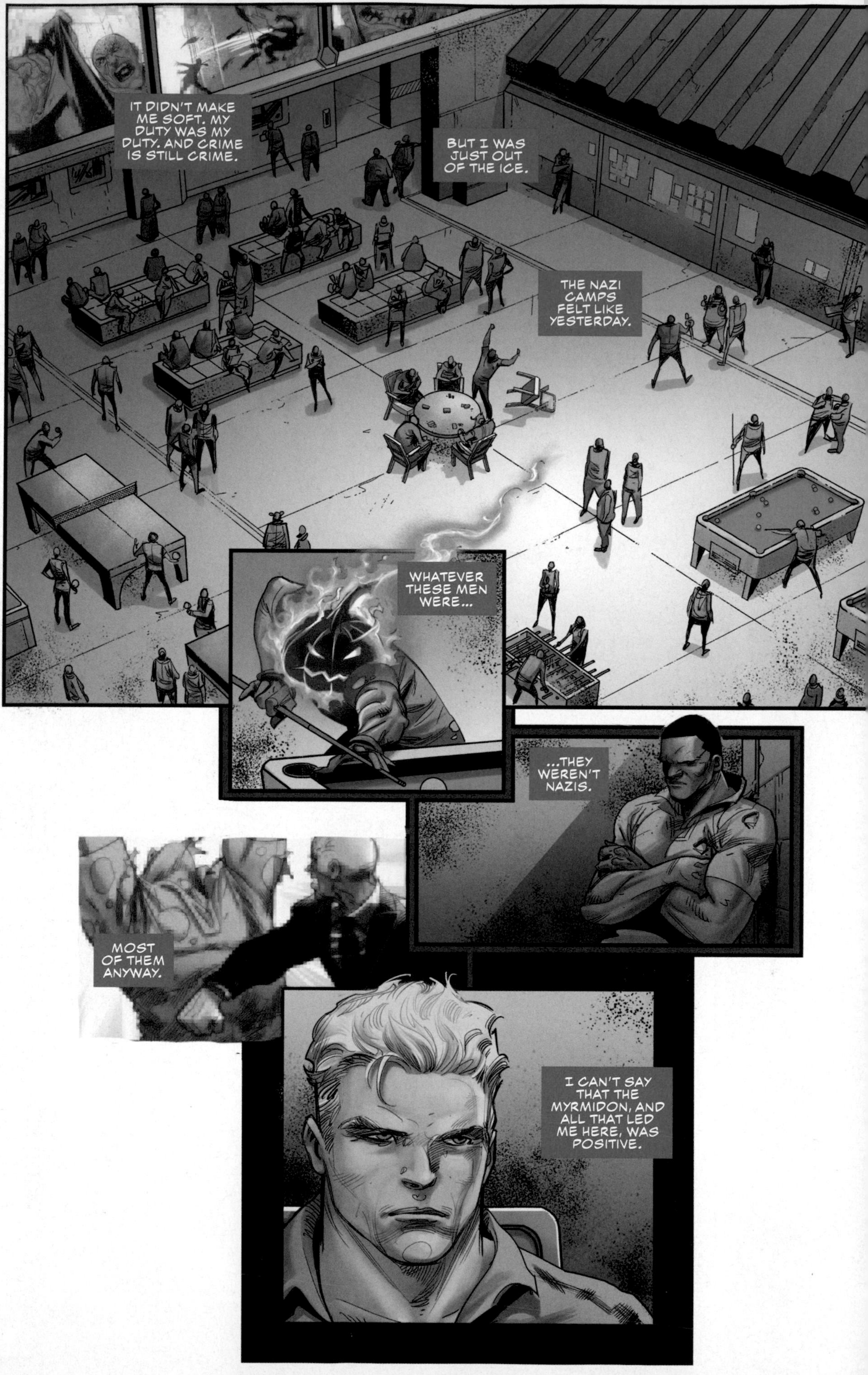
IT DIDN'T MAKE ME SOFT. MY DUTY WAS MY DUTY. AND CRIME IS STILL CRIME.
BUT I WAS JUST OUT OF THE ICE.
THE NAZI CAMPS FELT LIKE YESTERDAY.
WHATEVER THESE MEN WERE...
...THEY WEREN'T NAZIS.
MOST OF THEM ANYWAY.
I CAN'T SAY THAT THE MYRMIDON, AND ALL THAT LED ME HERE, WAS POSITIVE.

PEOPLE SUFFERED AND DIED-- THADDEUS ROSS AMONG THEM.

AMERICA'S ENEMIES WERE WELCOMED INTO ITS LIVING ROOM.

ALEXA, SO NICE TO SEE YOU AGAIN.

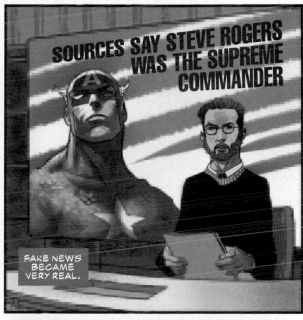

SOURCES SAY STEVE ROGERS WAS THE SUPREME COMMANDER

FAKE NEWS BECAME VERY REAL.

KRONOS

AND INTO THE CHAOS, INTO THE VACUUM...

...OLD FOES RETURNED TO REAP THE PROFITS.

THE BOARD IS READY, ALEKSANDER.

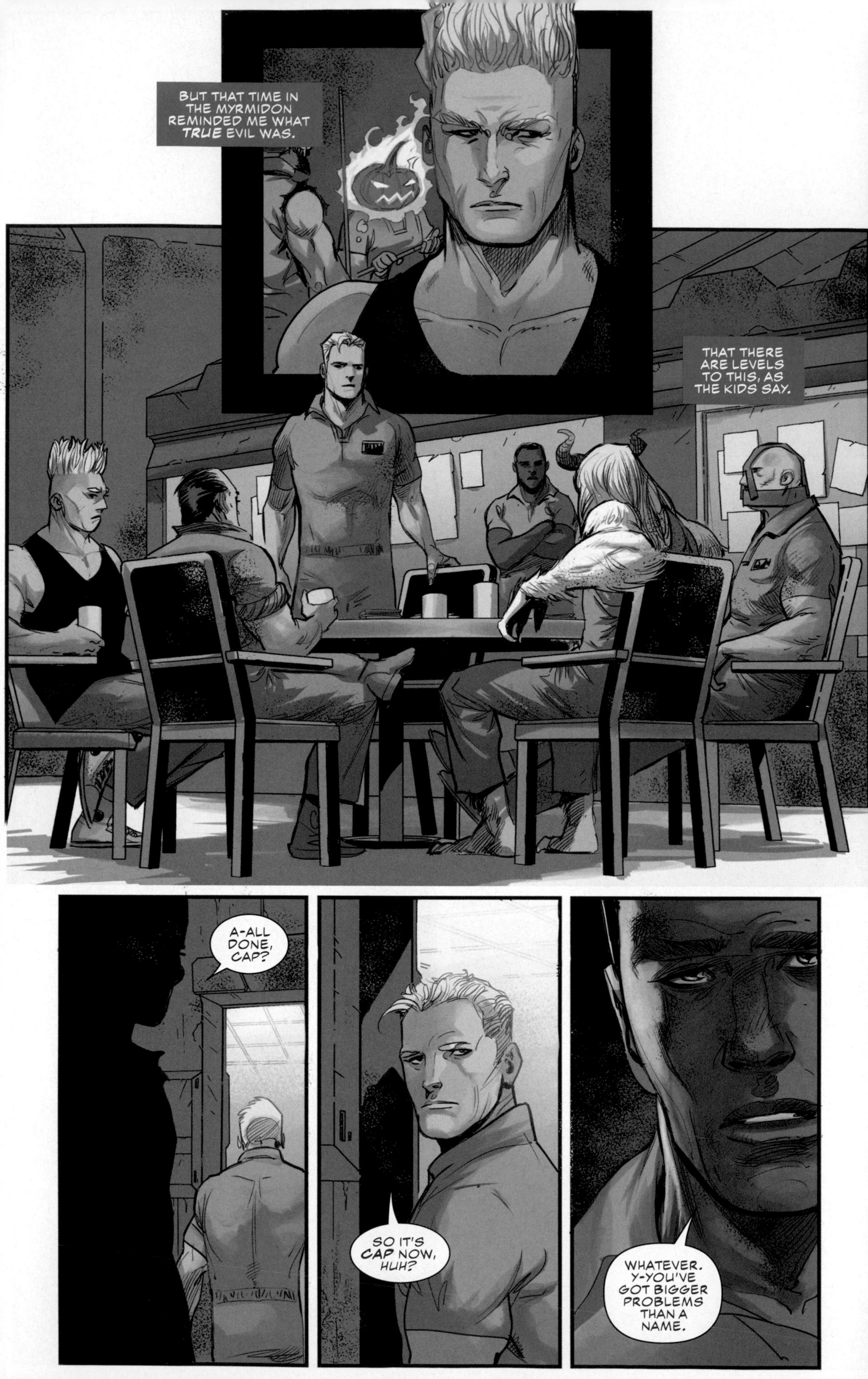
BUT THAT TIME IN THE MYRMIDON REMINDED ME WHAT TRUE EVIL WAS.
THAT THERE ARE LEVELS TO THIS, AS THE KIDS SAY.
A-ALL DONE, CAP?
SO IT'S CAP NOW, HUH?
WHATEVER. Y-YOU'VE GOT BIGGER PROBLEMS THAN A NAME.

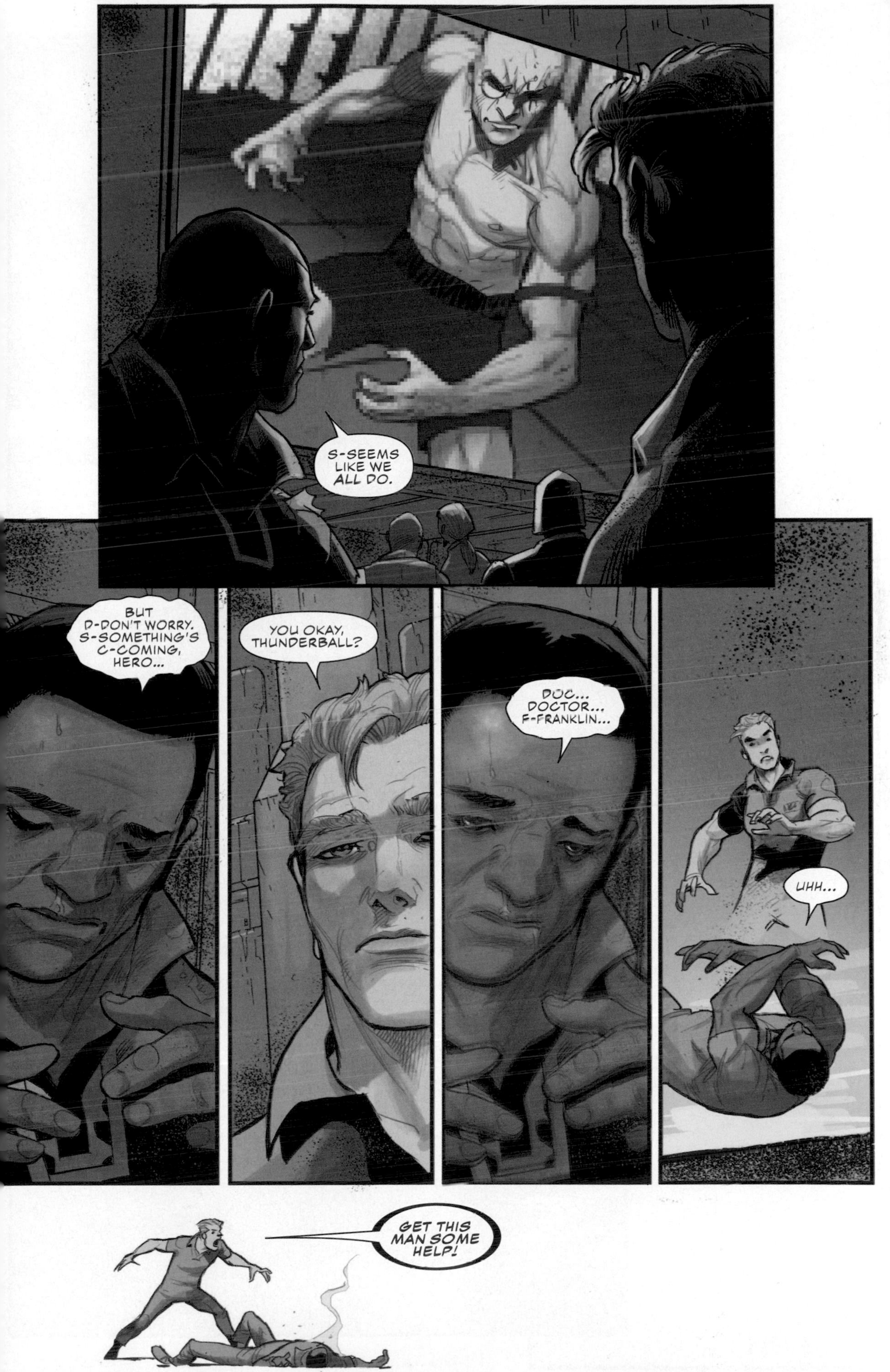
S-SEEMS LIKE WE ALL DO.
BUT D-DON'T WORRY. S-SOMETHING'S C-COMING, HERO...
YOU OKAY, THUNDERBALL?
DOC... DOCTOR... F-FRANKLIN...
UHH...
GET THIS MAN SOME HELP!

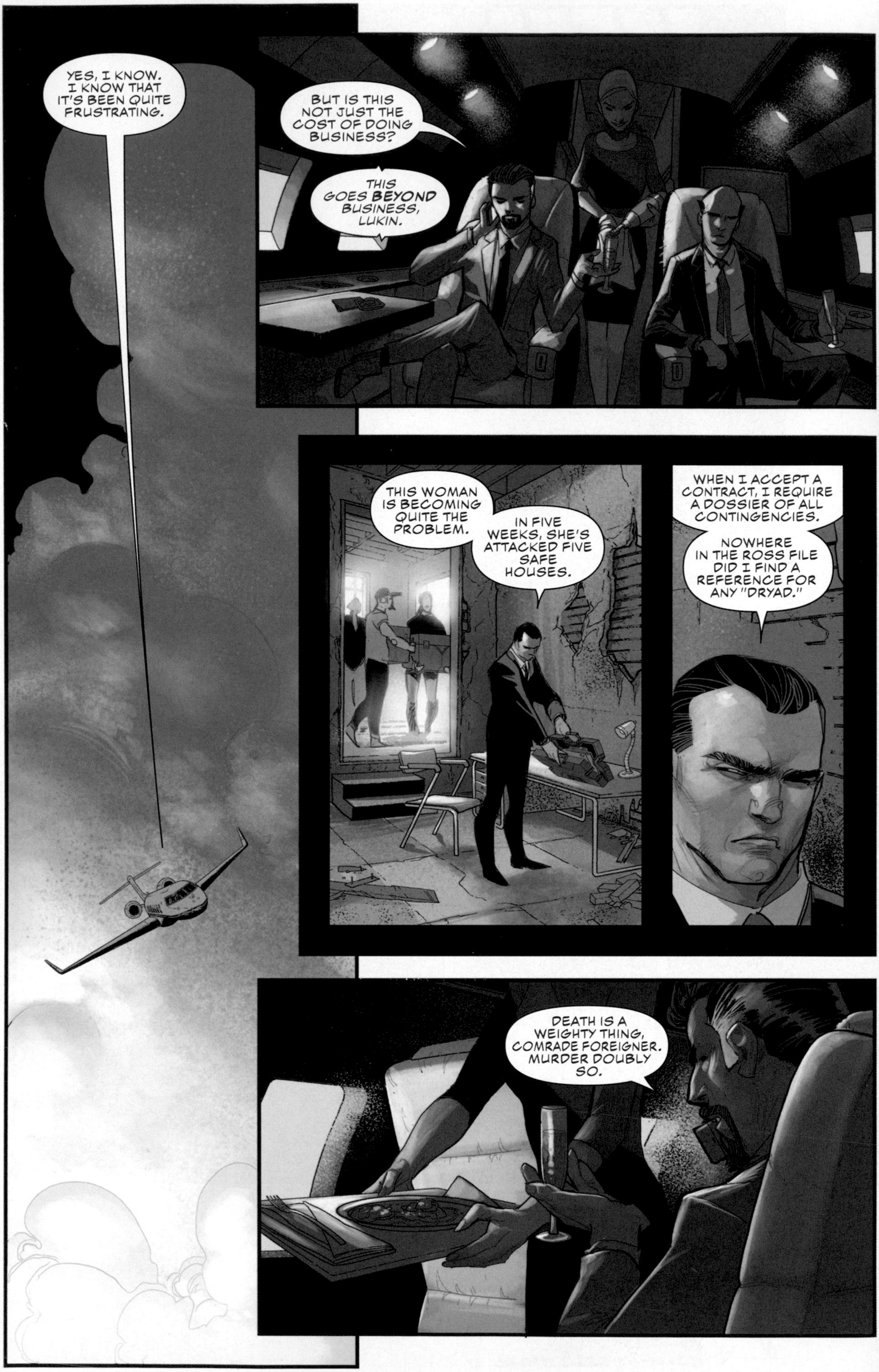
YES, I KNOW. I KNOW THAT IT'S BEEN QUITE FRUSTRATING.
BUT IS THIS NOT JUST THE COST OF DOING BUSINESS?
THIS GOES **BEYOND** BUSINESS, LUKIN.
THIS WOMAN IS BECOMING QUITE THE PROBLEM.
IN FIVE WEEKS, SHE'S ATTACKED FIVE SAFE HOUSES.
WHEN I ACCEPT A CONTRACT, I REQUIRE A DOSSIER OF ALL CONTINGENCIES.
NOWHERE IN THE ROSS FILE DID I FIND A REFERENCE FOR ANY "DRYAD."
DEATH IS A WEIGHTY THING, COMRADE FOREIGNER. MURDER DOUBLY SO.

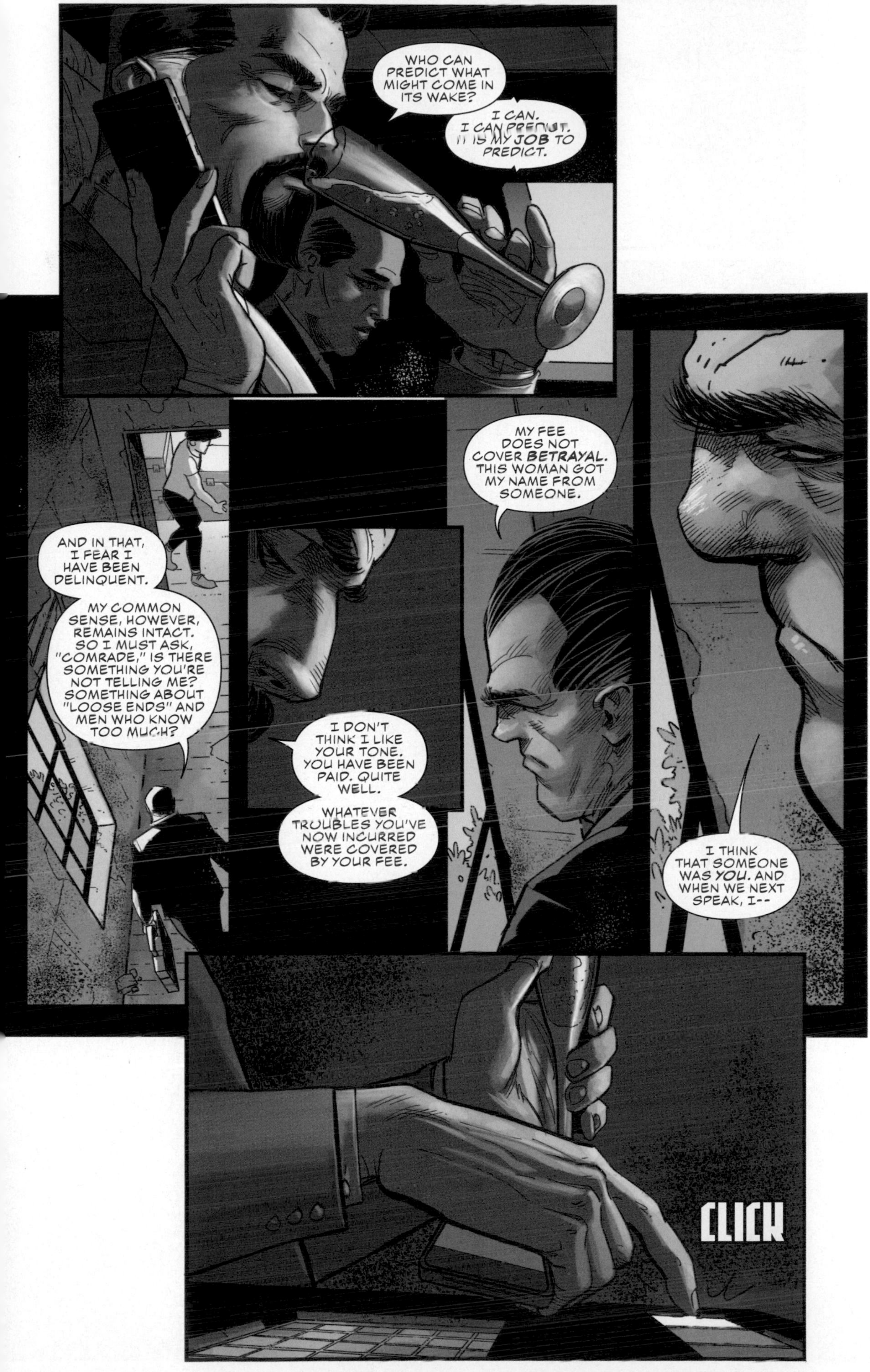
WHO CAN PREDICT WHAT MIGHT COME IN ITS WAKE?
I CAN. I CAN PREDICT. IT IS MY JOB TO PREDICT.
AND IN THAT, I FEAR I HAVE BEEN DELINQUENT.
MY COMMON SENSE, HOWEVER, REMAINS INTACT. SO I MUST ASK, "COMRADE," IS THERE SOMETHING YOU'RE NOT TELLING ME? SOMETHING ABOUT "LOOSE ENDS" AND MEN WHO KNOW TOO MUCH?
I DON'T THINK I LIKE YOUR TONE. YOU HAVE BEEN PAID. QUITE WELL.
WHATEVER TROUBLES YOU'VE NOW INCURRED WERE COVERED BY YOUR FEE.
MY FEE DOES NOT COVER BETRAYAL. THIS WOMAN GOT MY NAME FROM SOMEONE.
I THINK THAT SOMEONE WAS YOU. AND WHEN WE NEXT SPEAK, I--
CLICK

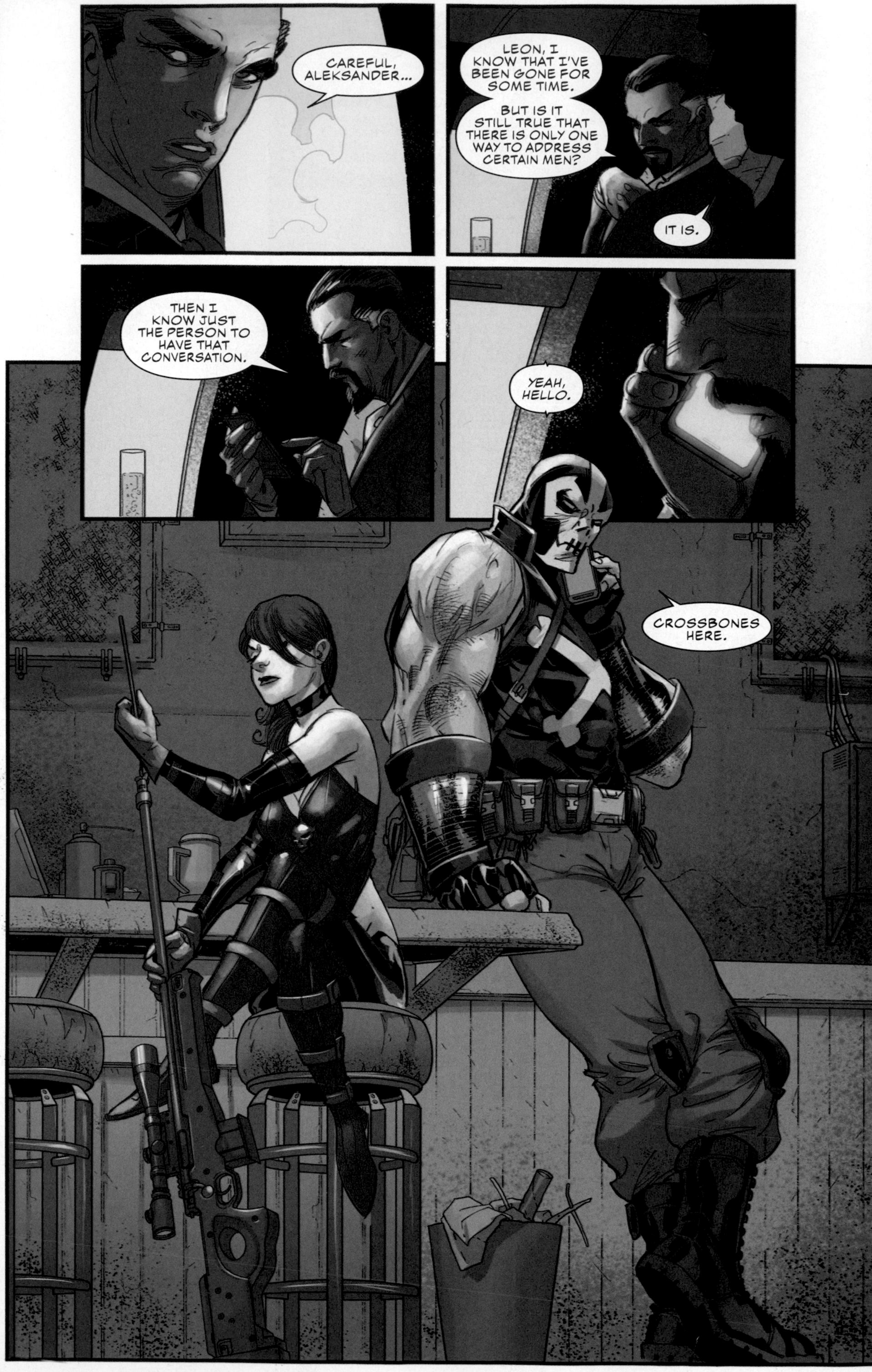
CAREFUL, ALEKSANDER...
LEON, I KNOW THAT I'VE BEEN GONE FOR SOME TIME.
BUT IS IT STILL TRUE THAT THERE IS ONLY ONE WAY TO ADDRESS CERTAIN MEN?
IT IS.
THEN I KNOW JUST THE PERSON TO HAVE THAT CONVERSATION.
YEAH, HELLO.
CROSSBONES HERE.

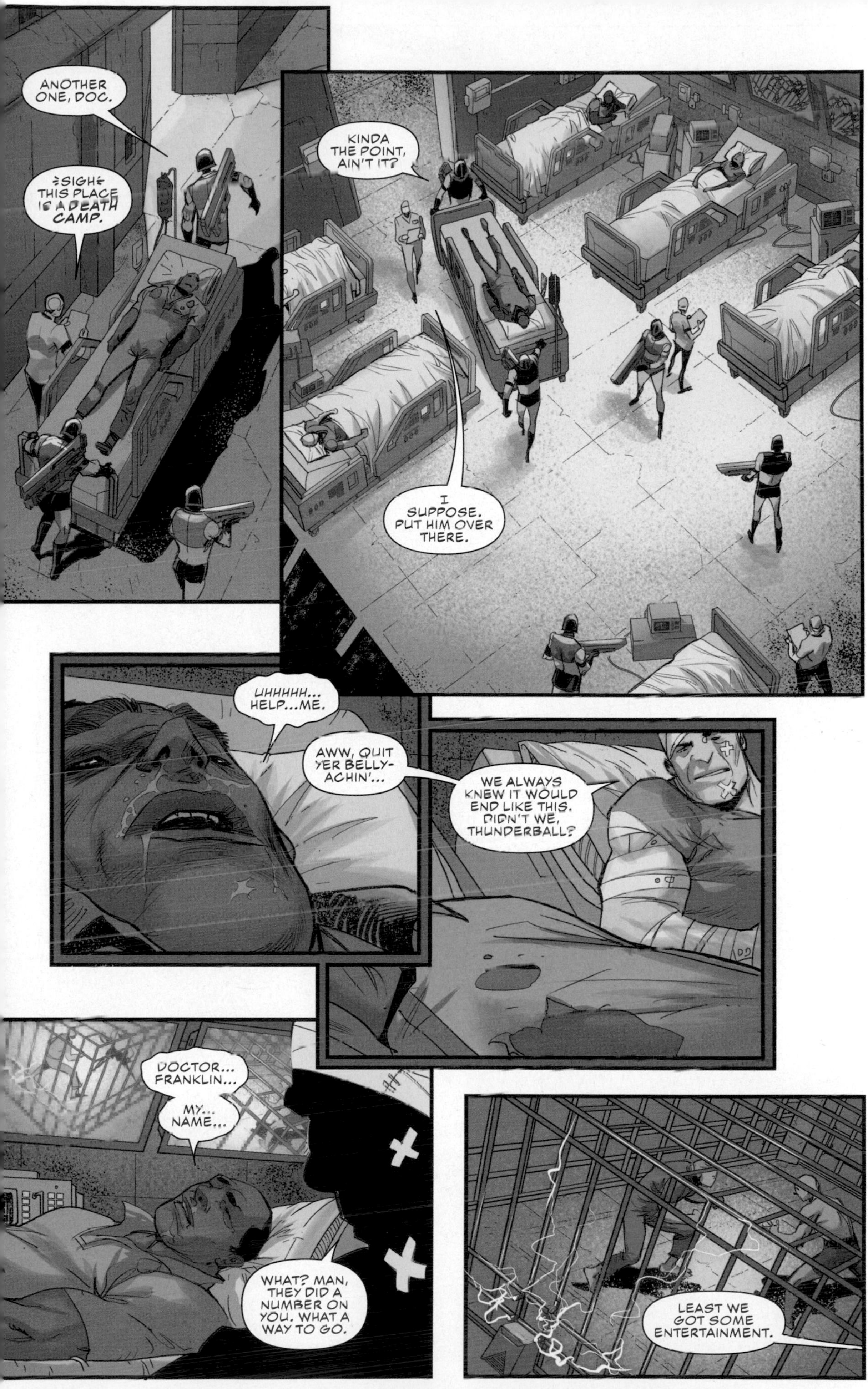
ANOTHER ONE, DOC.
SIGH THIS PLACE IS A DEATH CAMP.
KINDA THE POINT, AIN'T IT?
I SUPPOSE. PUT HIM OVER THERE.
UHHHHH... HELP...ME.
AWW, QUIT YER BELLY-ACHIN'...
WE ALWAYS KNEW IT WOULD END LIKE THIS. DIDN'T WE, THUNDERBALL?
DOCTOR... FRANKLIN...
MY... NAME...
WHAT? MAN, THEY DID A NUMBER ON YOU. WHAT A WAY TO GO.
LEAST WE GOT SOME ENTERTAINMENT.

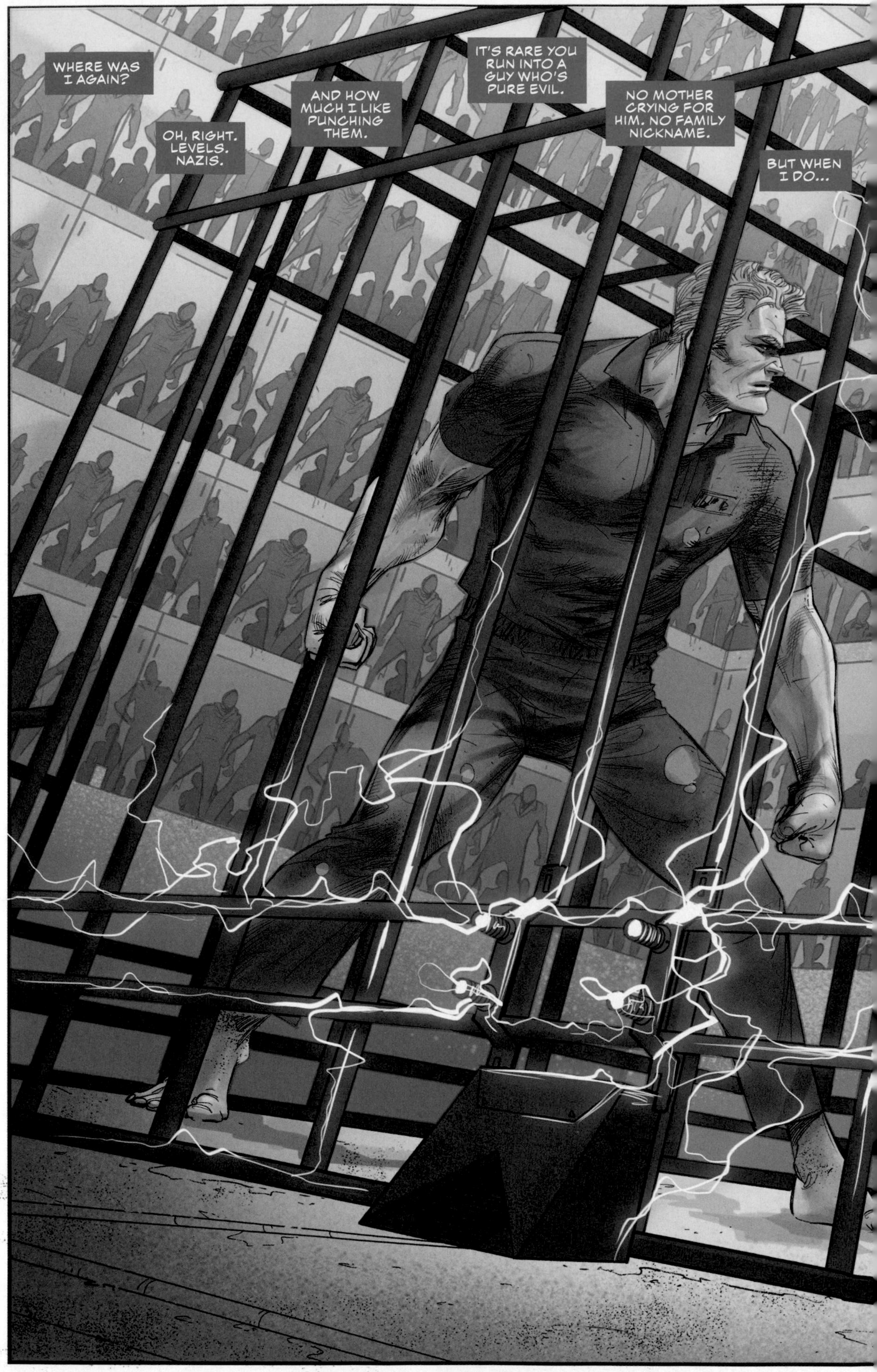
WHERE WAS I AGAIN?
OH, RIGHT. LEVELS. NAZIS.
AND HOW MUCH I LIKE PUNCHING THEM.
IT'S RARE YOU RUN INTO A GUY WHO'S PURE EVIL.
NO MOTHER CRYING FOR HIM. NO FAMILY NICKNAME.
BUT WHEN I DO...

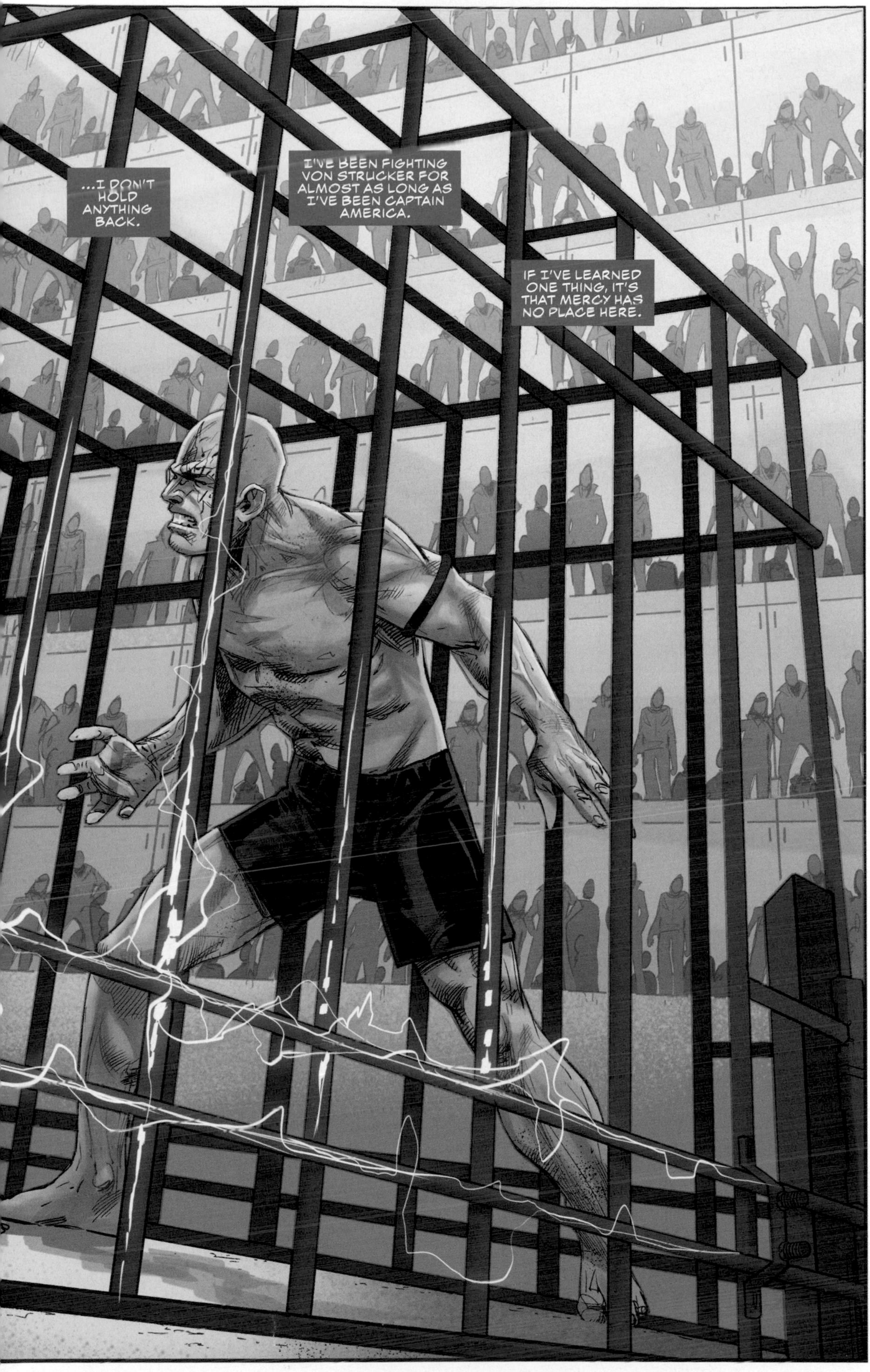
...I DON'T HOLD ANYTHING BACK.
I'VE BEEN FIGHTING VON STRUCKER FOR ALMOST AS LONG AS I'VE BEEN CAPTAIN AMERICA.
IF I'VE LEARNED ONE THING, IT'S THAT MERCY HAS NO PLACE HERE.

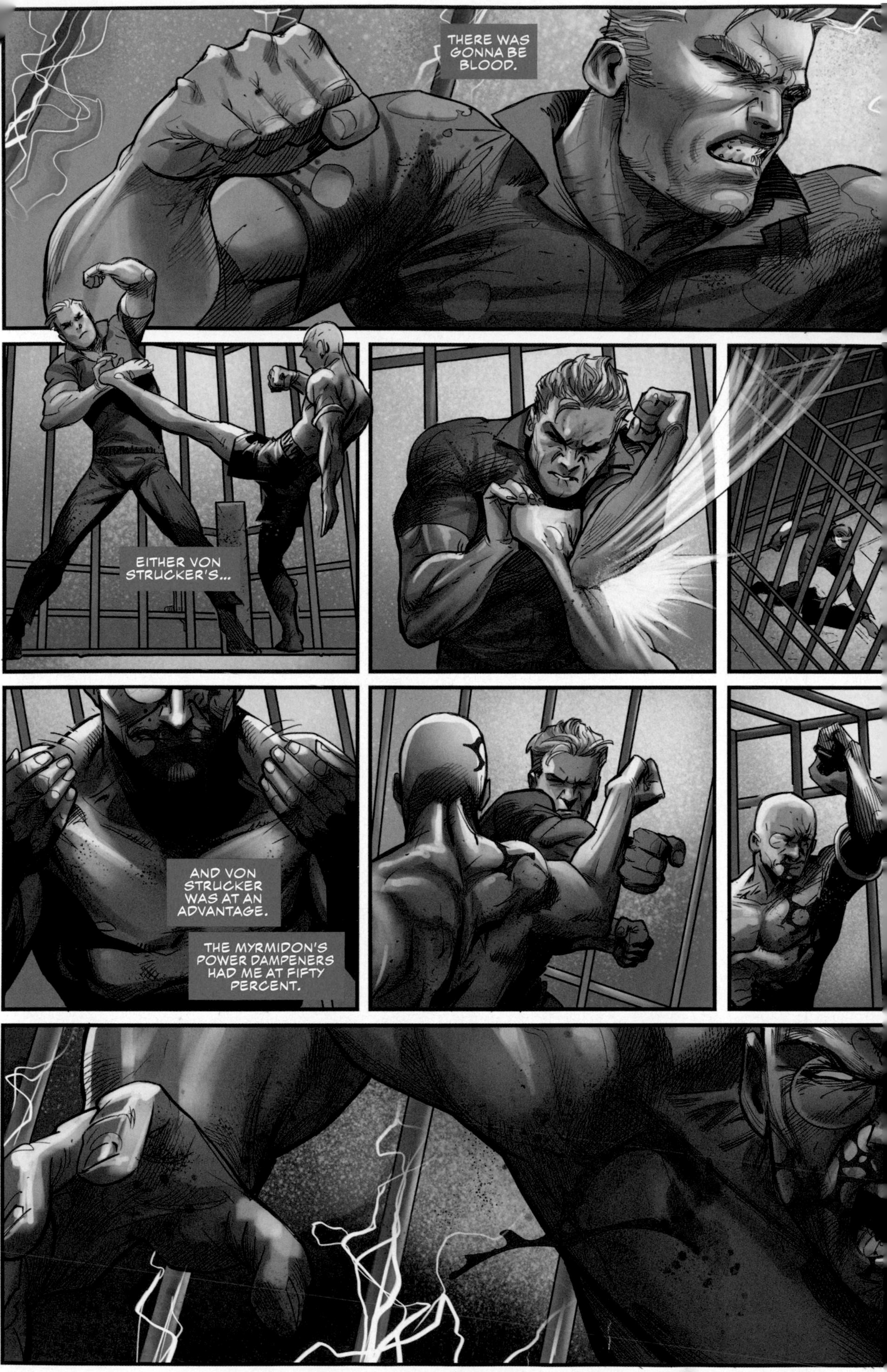
THERE WAS GONNA BE BLOOD.
EITHER VON STRUCKER'S...
AND VON STRUCKER WAS AT AN ADVANTAGE.
THE MYRMIDON'S POWER DAMPENERS HAD ME AT FIFTY PERCENT.

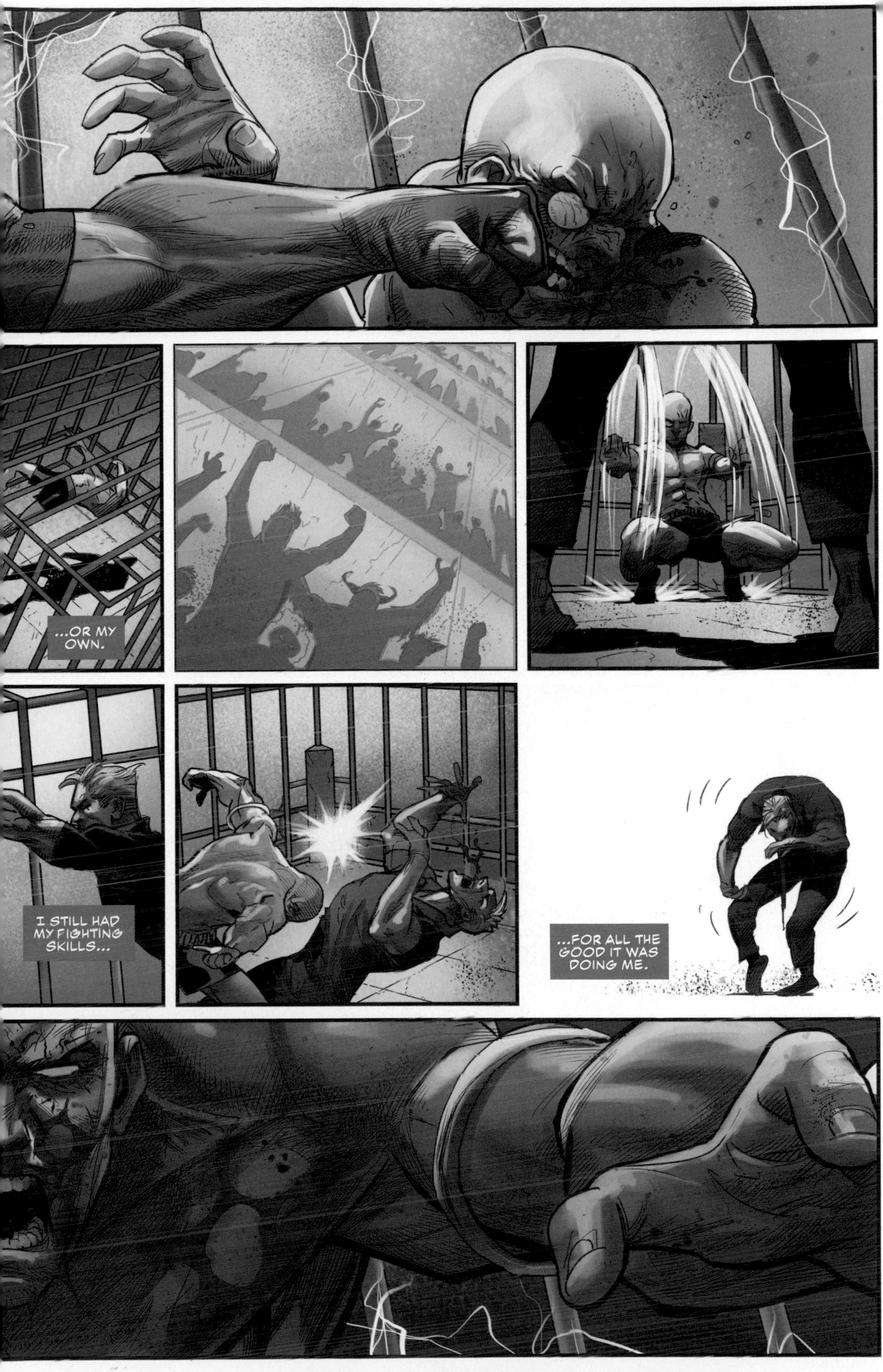
...OR MY OWN.
I STILL HAD MY FIGHTING SKILLS...
...FOR ALL THE GOOD IT WAS DOING ME.

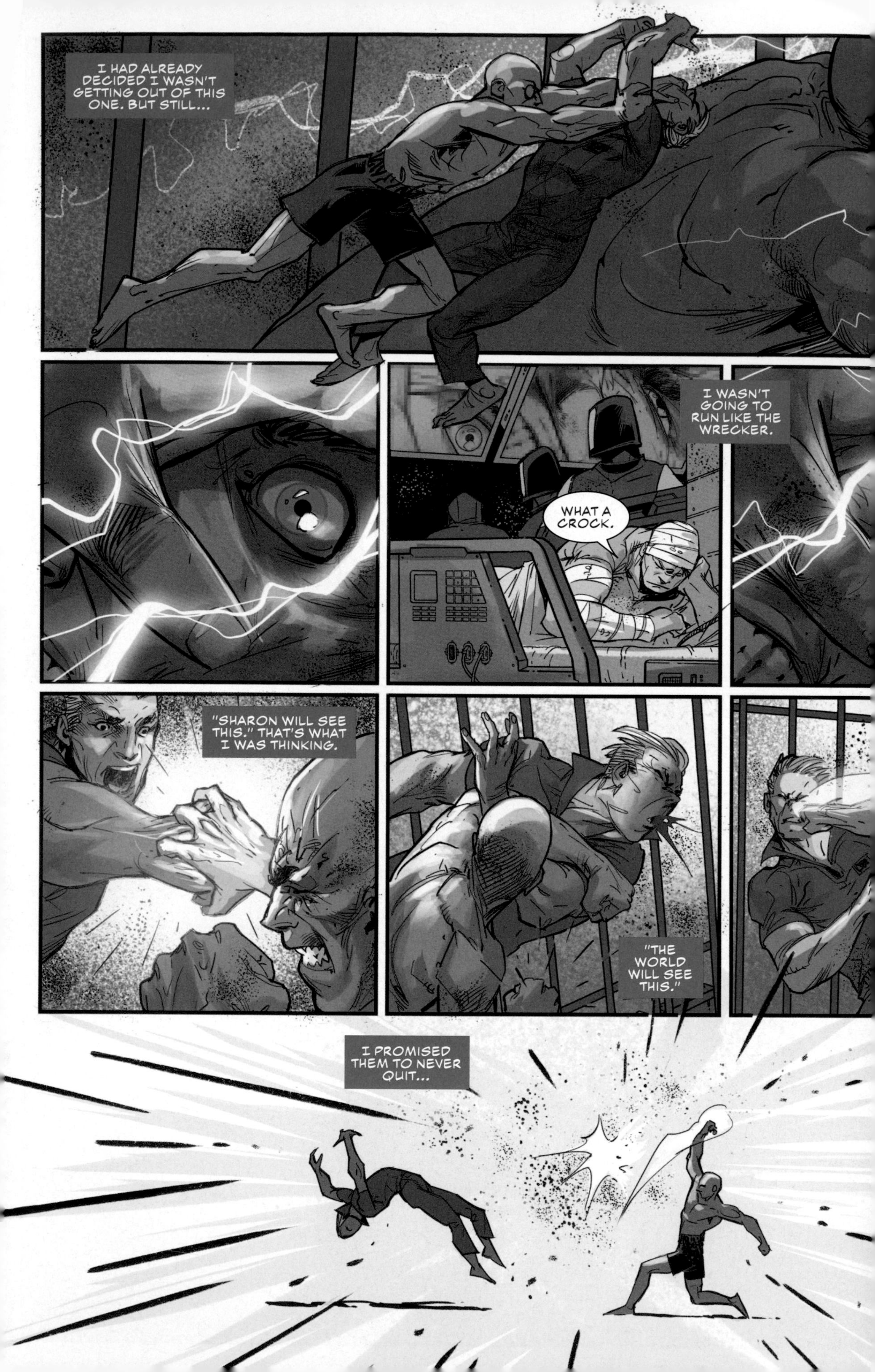
I HAD ALREADY DECIDED I WASN'T GETTING OUT OF THIS ONE. BUT STILL...
I WASN'T GOING TO RUN LIKE THE WRECKER.
WHAT A CROCK.
"SHARON WILL SEE THIS." THAT'S WHAT I WAS THINKING.
"THE WORLD WILL SEE THIS."
I PROMISED THEM TO NEVER QUIT...

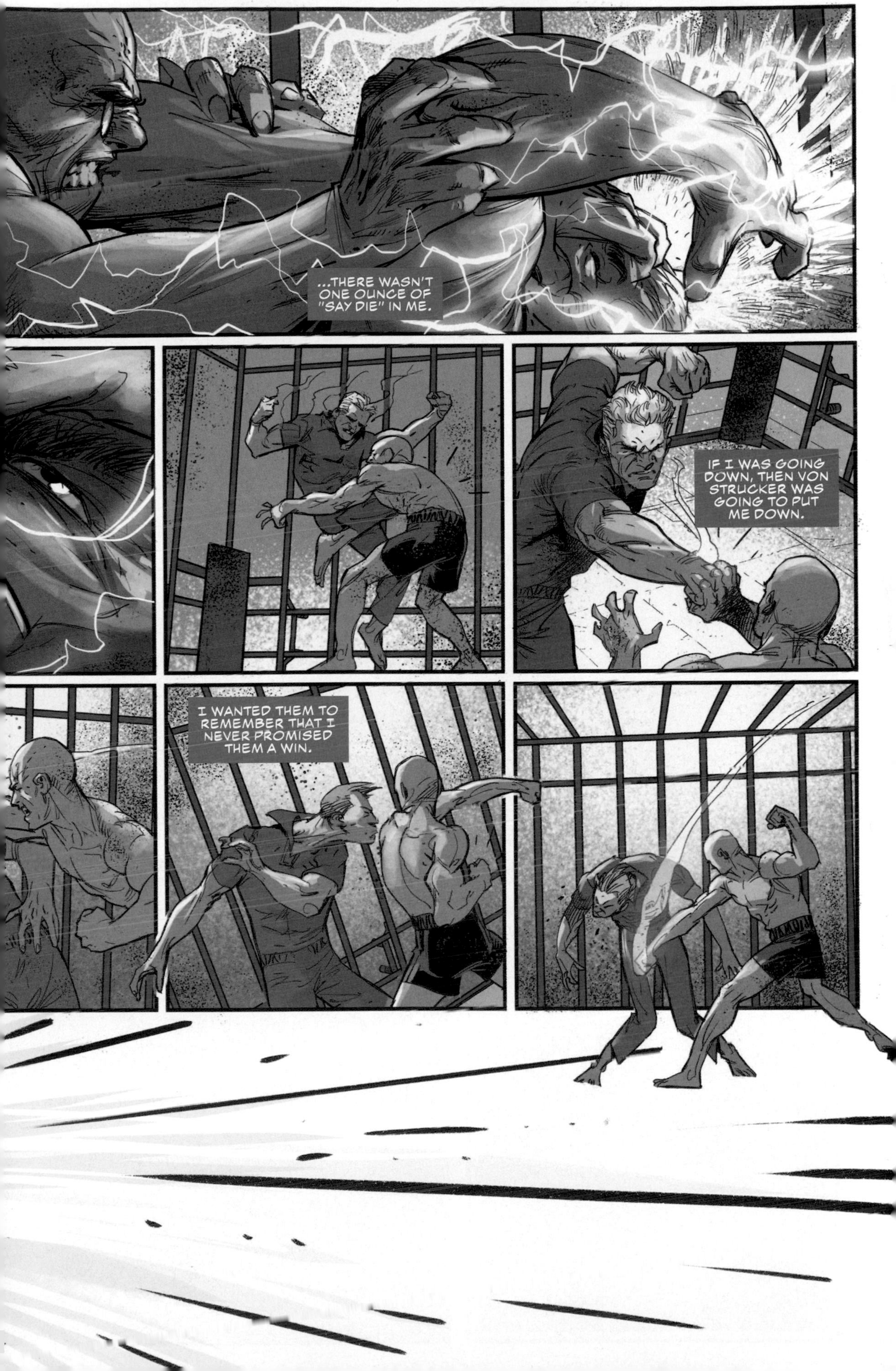
...THERE WASN'T ONE OUNCE OF "SAY DIE" IN ME.
IF I WAS GOING DOWN, THEN VON STRUCKER WAS GOING TO PUT ME DOWN.
I WANTED THEM TO REMEMBER THAT I NEVER PROMISED THEM A WIN.

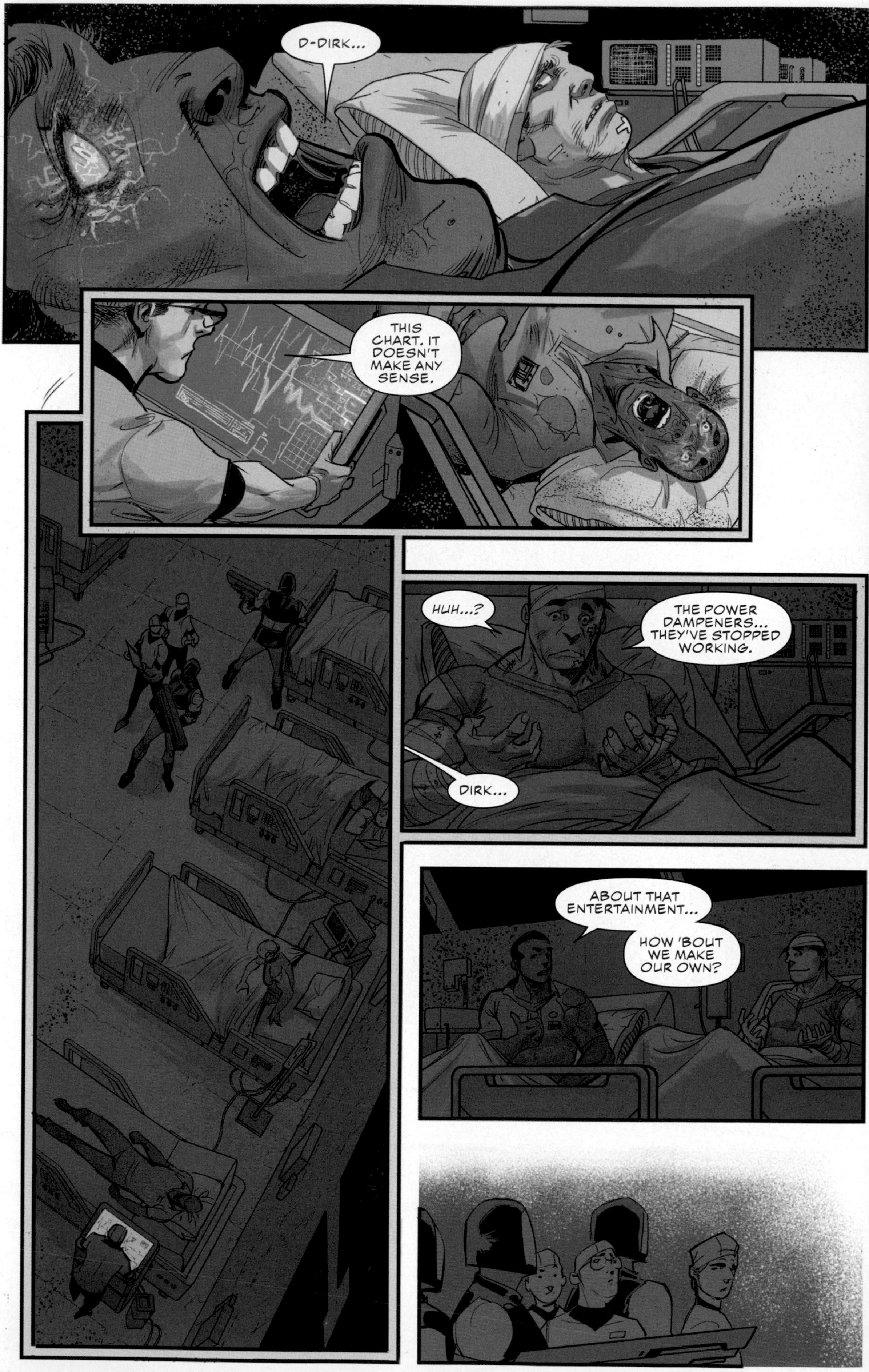
D-DIRK...
THIS CHART. IT DOESN'T MAKE ANY SENSE.
HUH...?
THE POWER DAMPENERS... THEY'VE STOPPED WORKING.
DIRK...
ABOUT THAT ENTERTAINMENT...
HOW 'BOUT WE MAKE OUR OWN?

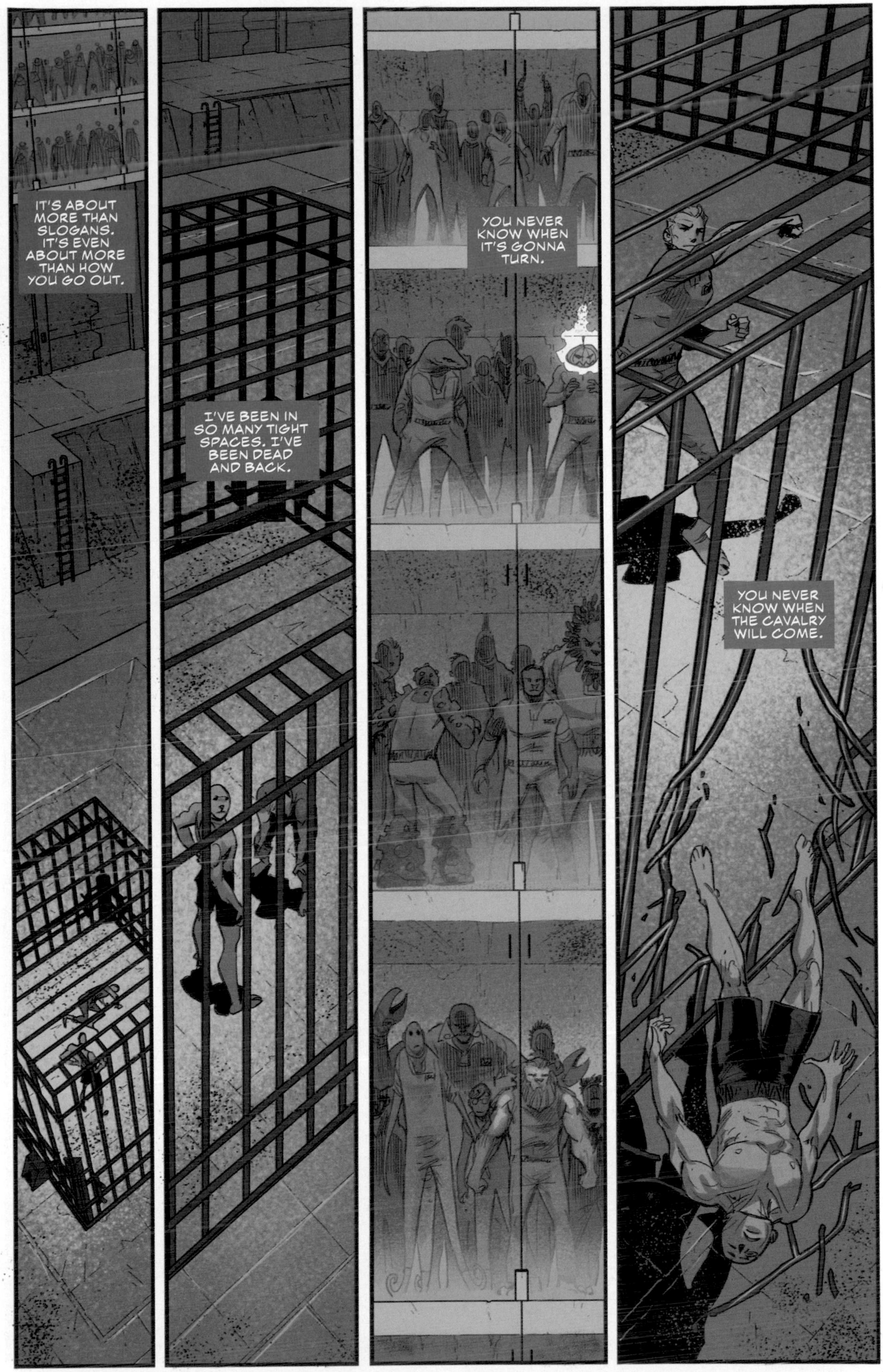
IT'S ABOUT MORE THAN SLOGANS. IT'S EVEN ABOUT MORE THAN HOW YOU GO OUT.
I'VE BEEN IN SO MANY TIGHT SPACES. I'VE BEEN DEAD AND BACK.
YOU NEVER KNOW WHEN IT'S GONNA TURN.
YOU NEVER KNOW WHEN THE CAVALRY WILL COME.

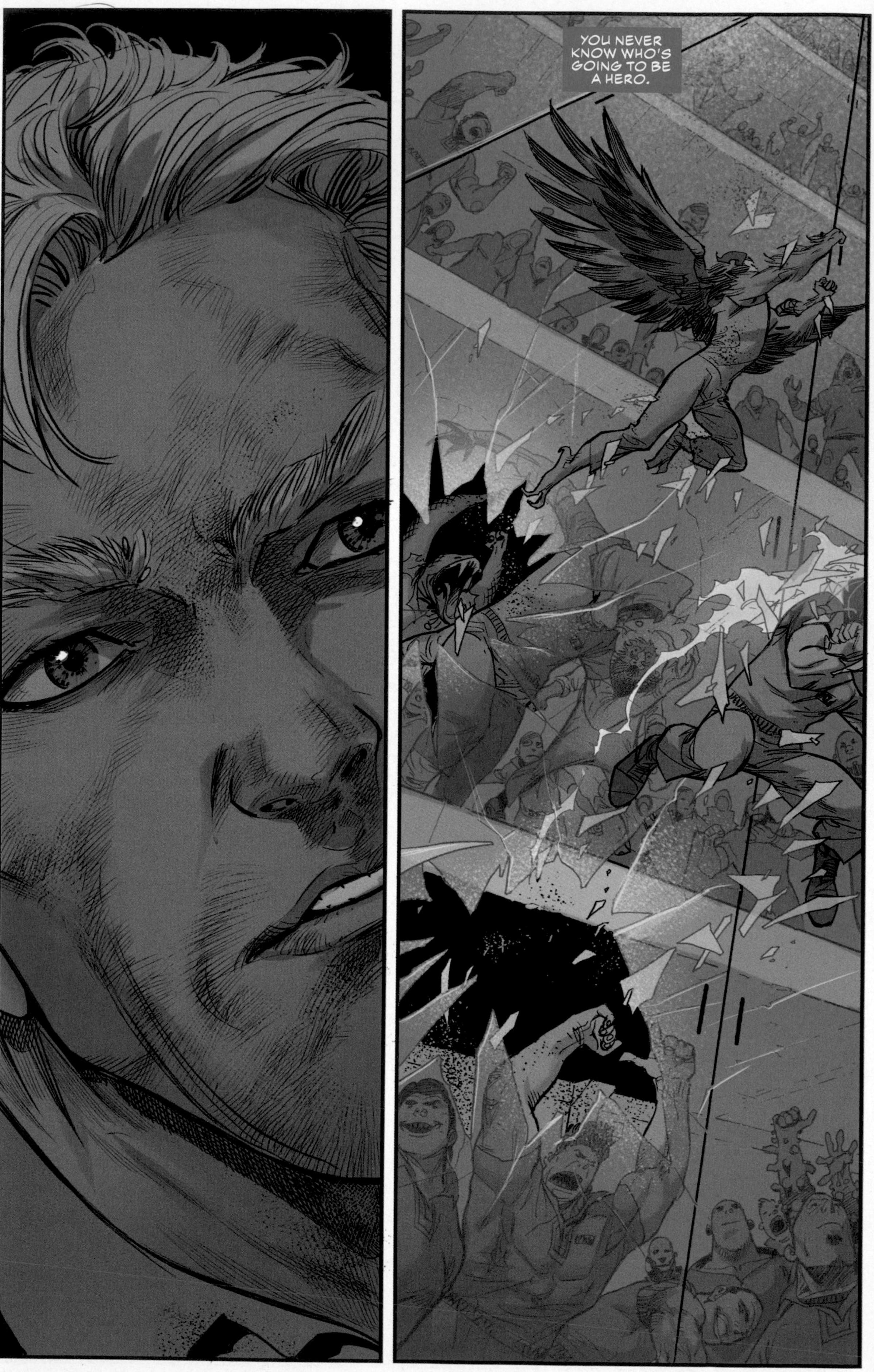
YOU NEVER KNOW WHO'S GOING TO BE A HERO.

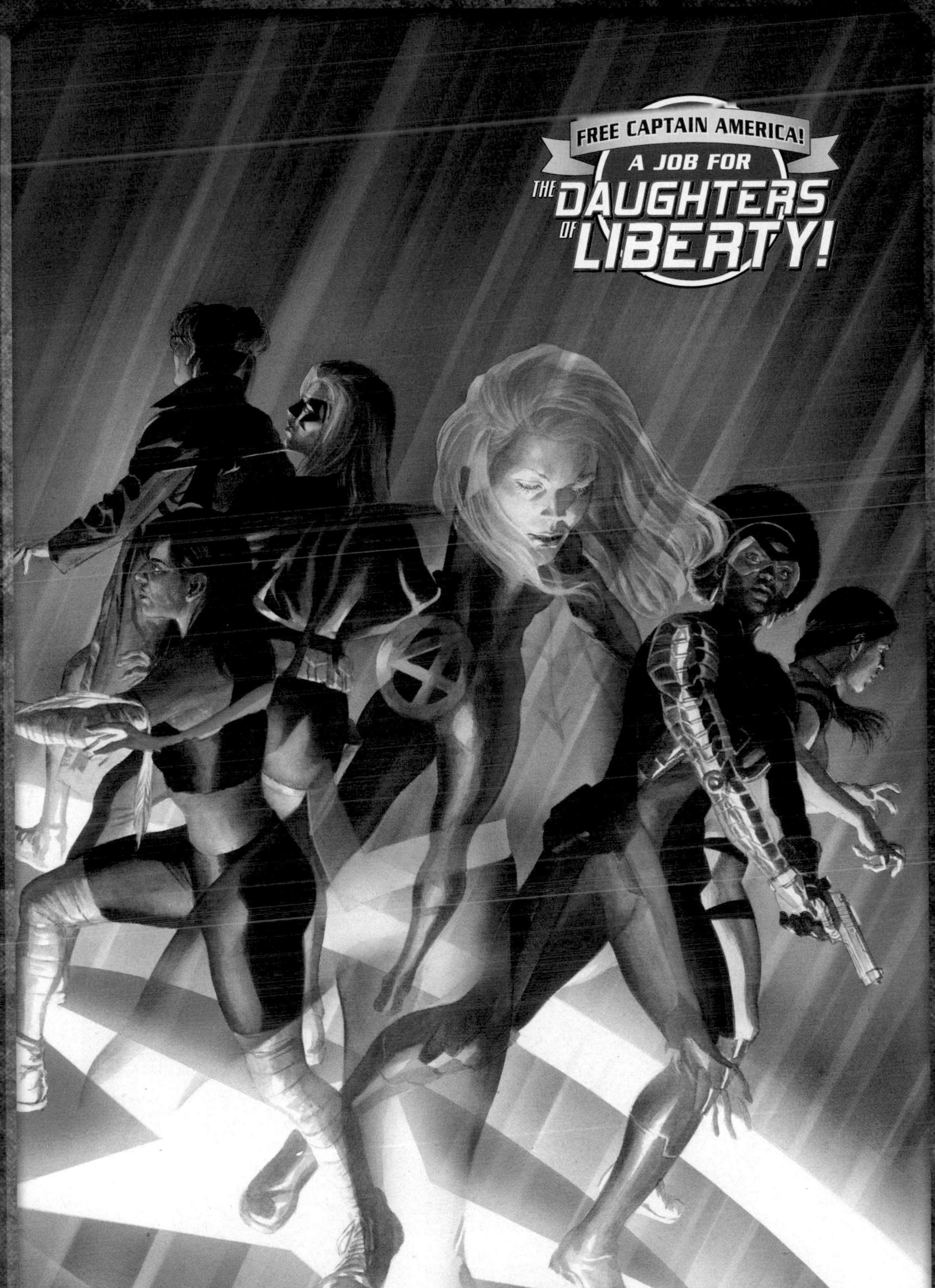
FREE CAPTAIN AMERICA!
A JOB FOR
THE DAUGHTERS OF LIBERTY!

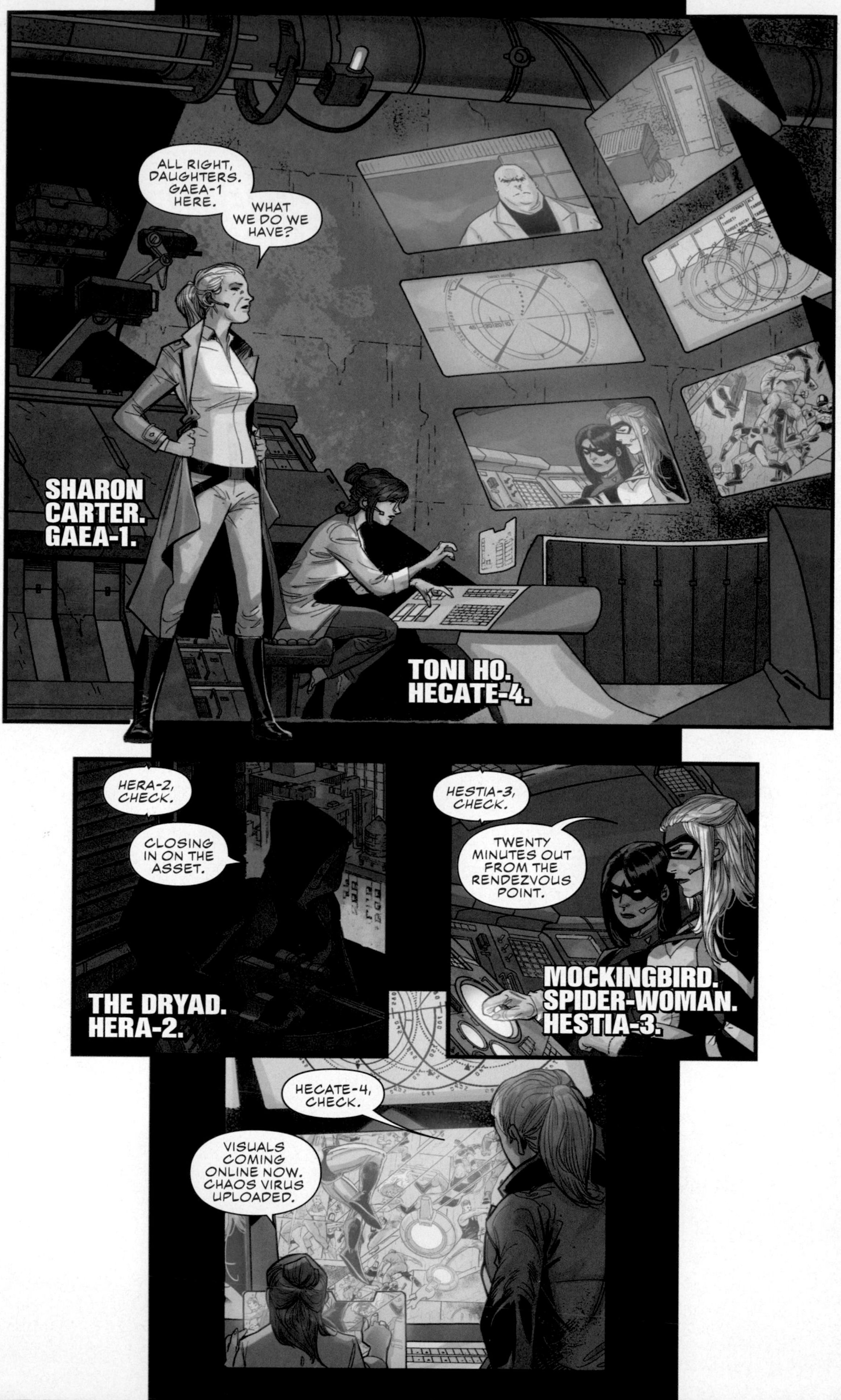
ALL RIGHT, DAUGHTERS. GAEA-1 HERE.
WHAT WE DO WE HAVE?
SHARON CARTER. GAEA-1.
TONI HO. HECATE-4.
HERA-2, CHECK.
CLOSING IN ON THE ASSET.
THE DRYAD. HERA-2.
HESTIA-3, CHECK.
TWENTY MINUTES OUT FROM THE RENDEZVOUS POINT.
MOCKINGBIRD. SPIDER-WOMAN. HESTIA-3.
HECATE-4, CHECK.
VISUALS COMING ONLINE NOW. CHAOS VIRUS UPLOADED.

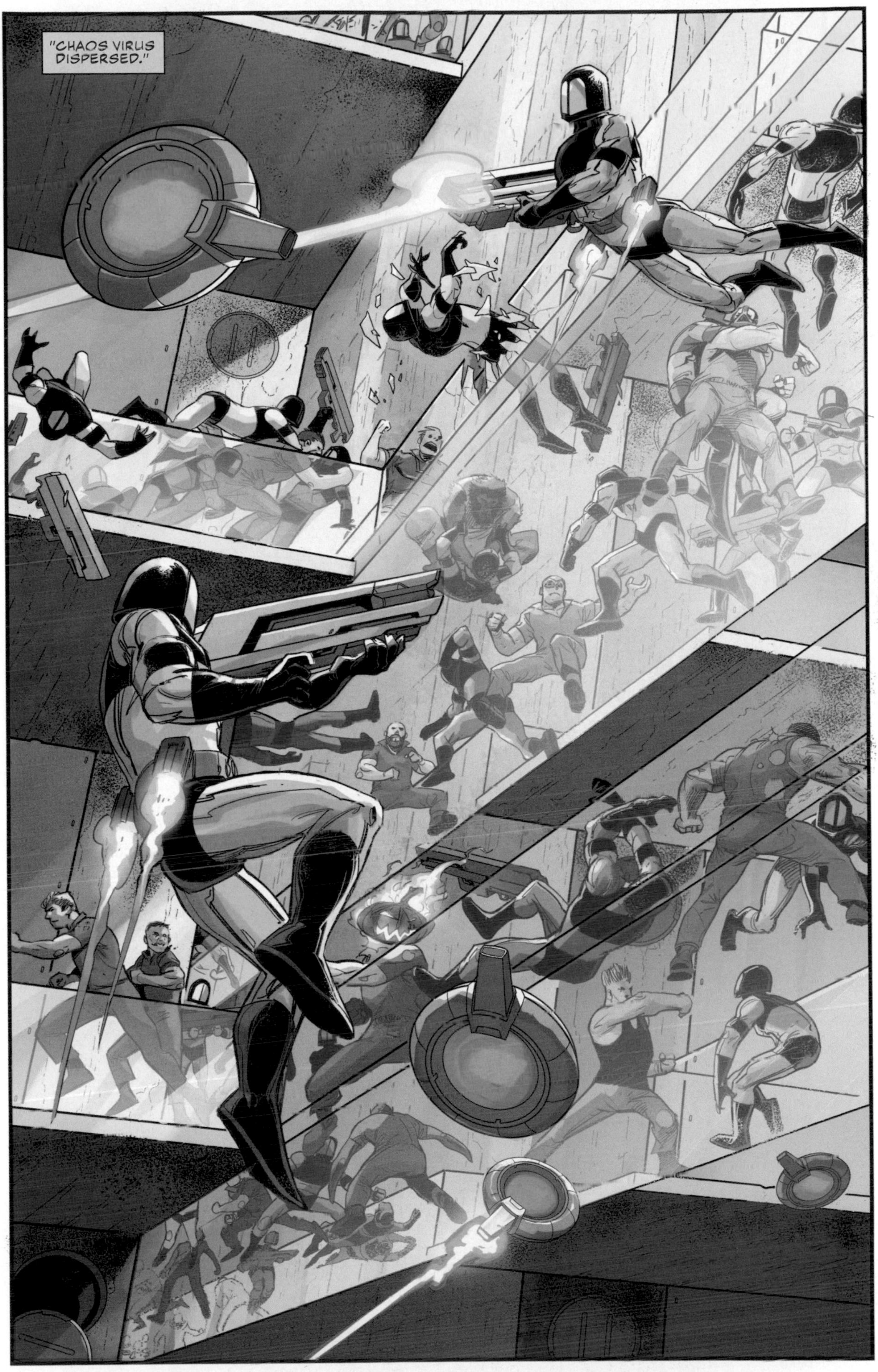
"CHAOS VIRUS DISPERSED."

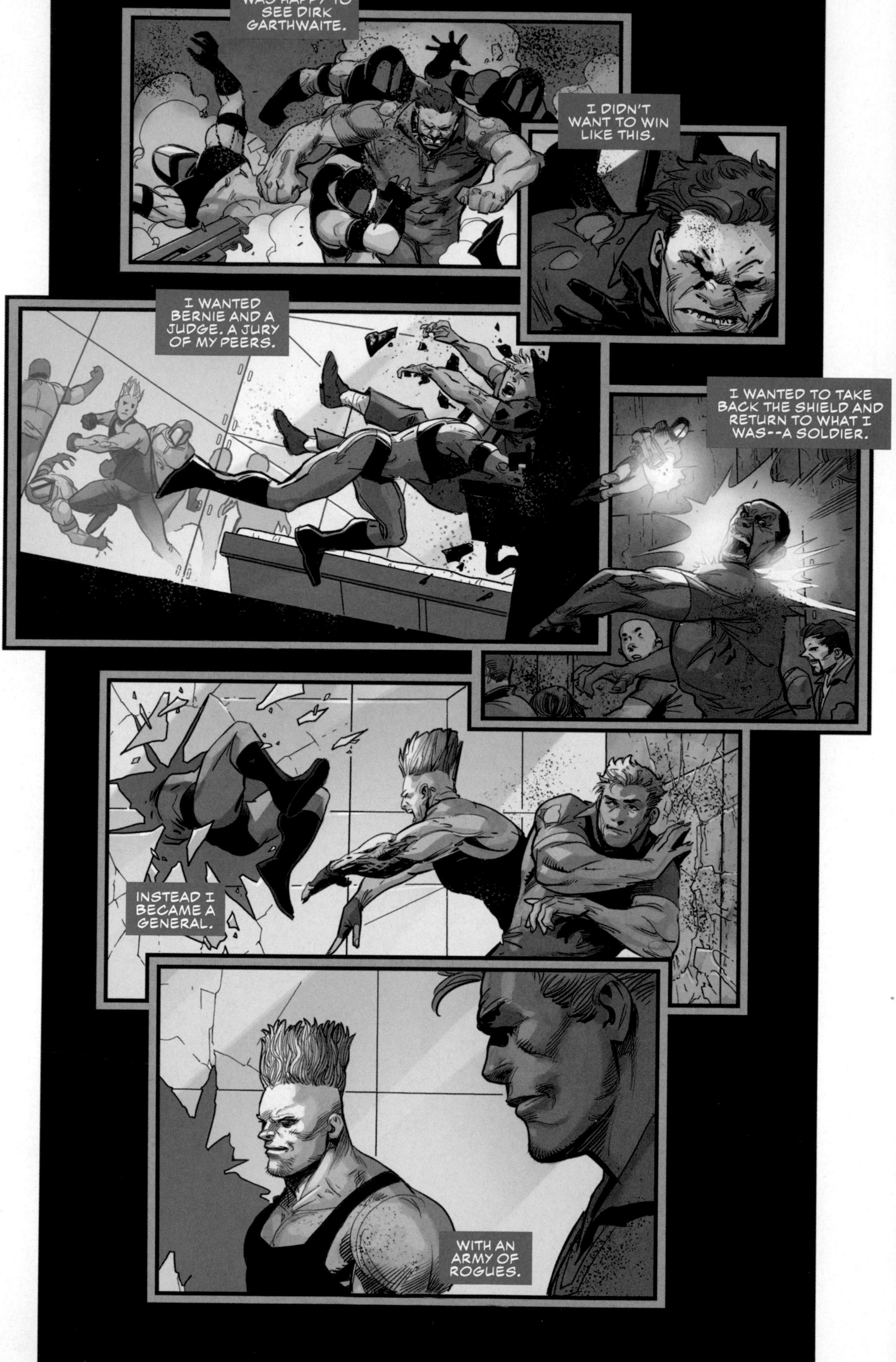
I CAN'T SAY I WAS HAPPY TO SEE DIRK GARTHWAITE.
I DIDN'T WANT TO WIN LIKE THIS.
I WANTED BERNIE AND A JUDGE. A JURY OF MY PEERS.
I WANTED TO TAKE BACK THE SHIELD AND RETURN TO WHAT I WAS--A SOLDIER.
INSTEAD I BECAME A GENERAL.
WITH AN ARMY OF ROGUES.

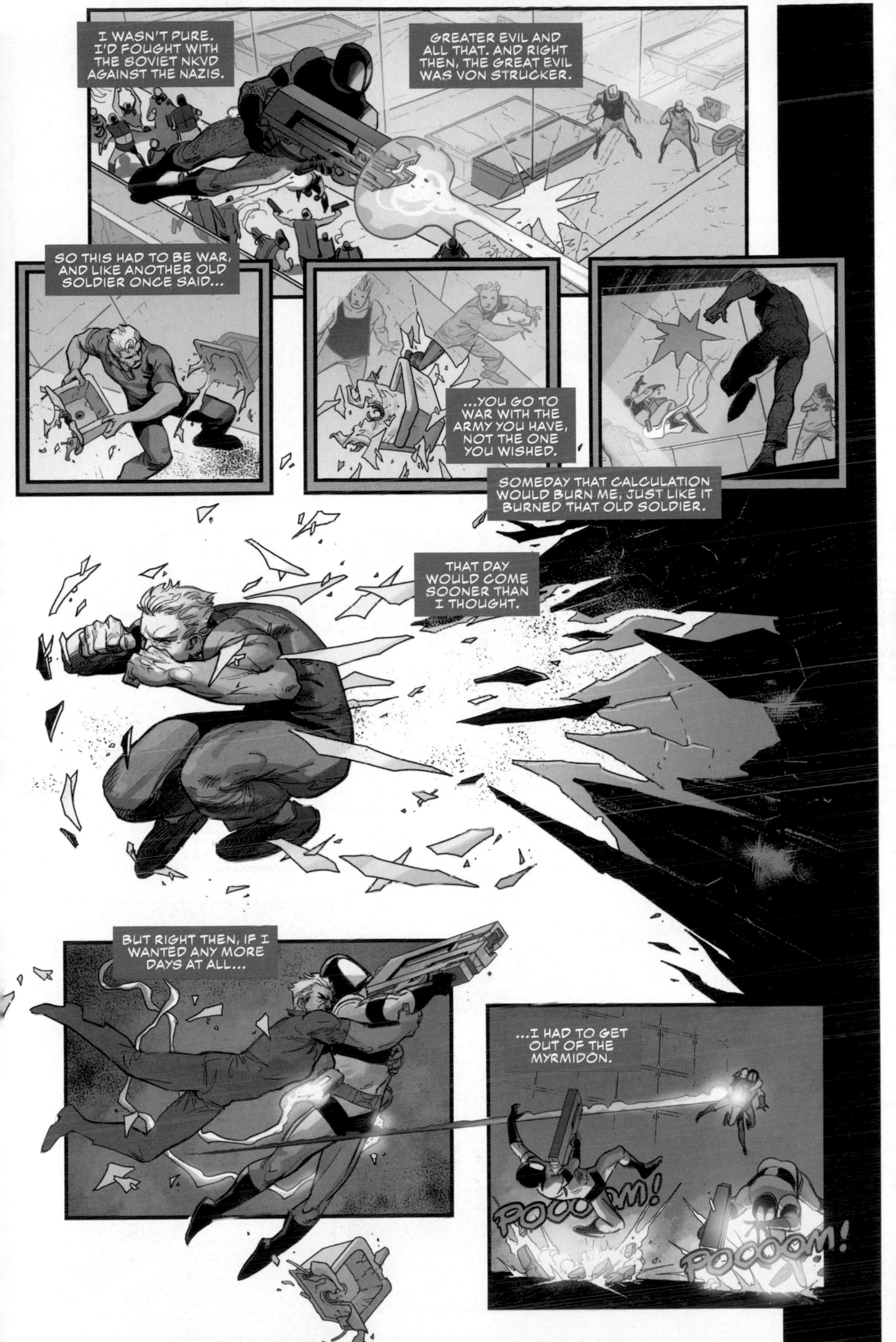
I WASN'T PURE. I'D FOUGHT WITH THE SOVIET NKVD AGAINST THE NAZIS.
GREATER EVIL AND ALL THAT. AND RIGHT THEN, THE GREAT EVIL WAS VON STRUCKER.
SO THIS HAD TO BE WAR, AND LIKE ANOTHER OLD SOLDIER ONCE SAID...
...YOU GO TO WAR WITH THE ARMY YOU HAVE, NOT THE ONE YOU WISHED.
SOMEDAY THAT CALCULATION WOULD BURN ME, JUST LIKE IT BURNED THAT OLD SOLDIER.
THAT DAY WOULD COME SOONER THAN I THOUGHT.
BUT RIGHT THEN, IF I WANTED ANY MORE DAYS AT ALL...
...I HAD TO GET OUT OF THE MYRMIDON.
POOOOM!
POOOOM!

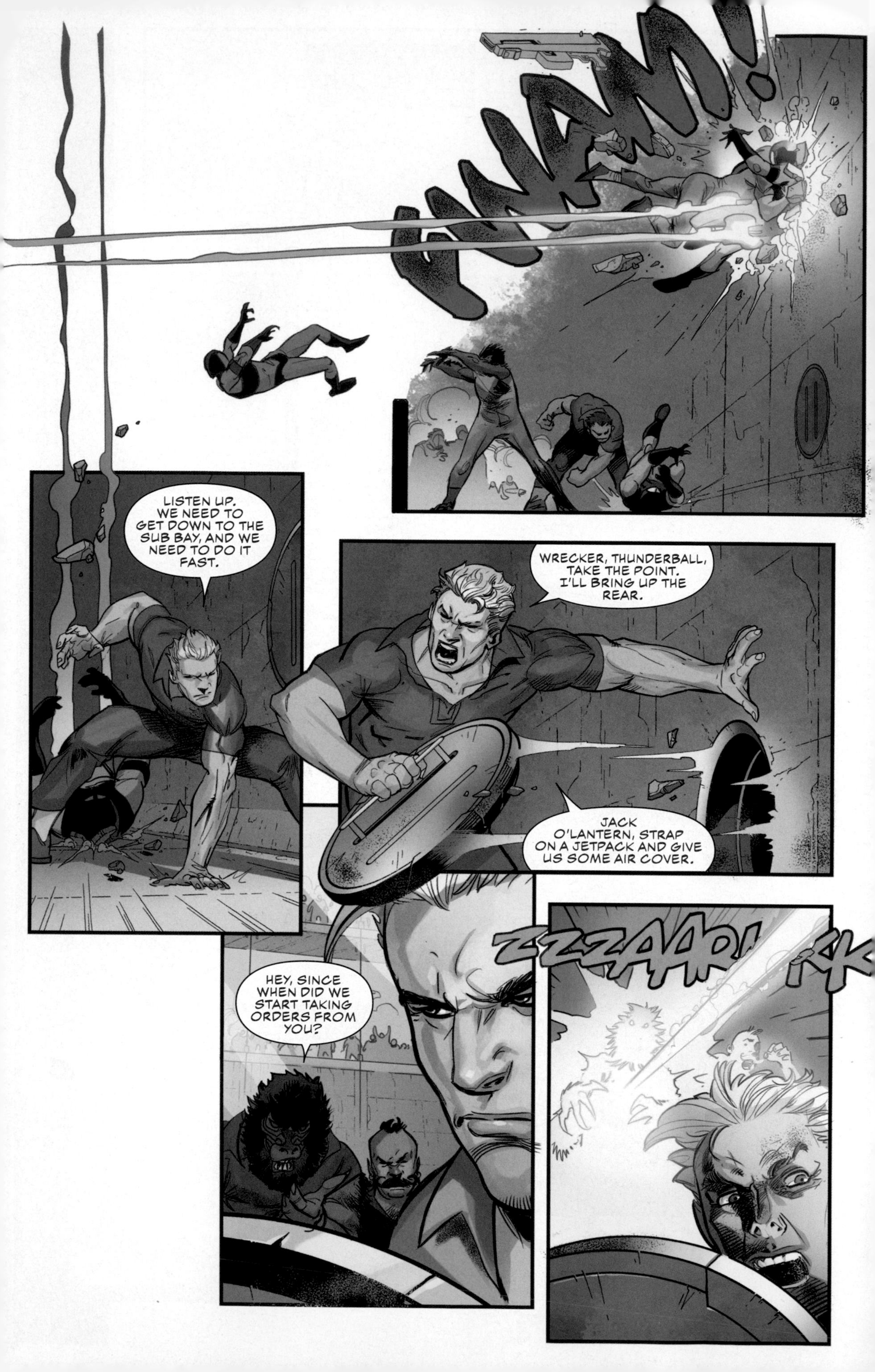
WHAM!
LISTEN UP. WE NEED TO GET DOWN TO THE SUB BAY, AND WE NEED TO DO IT FAST.
WRECKER, THUNDERBALL, TAKE THE POINT. I'LL BRING UP THE REAR.
JACK O'LANTERN, STRAP ON A JETPACK AND GIVE US SOME AIR COVER.
HEY, SINCE WHEN DID WE START TAKING ORDERS FROM YOU?
ZZZAARKK

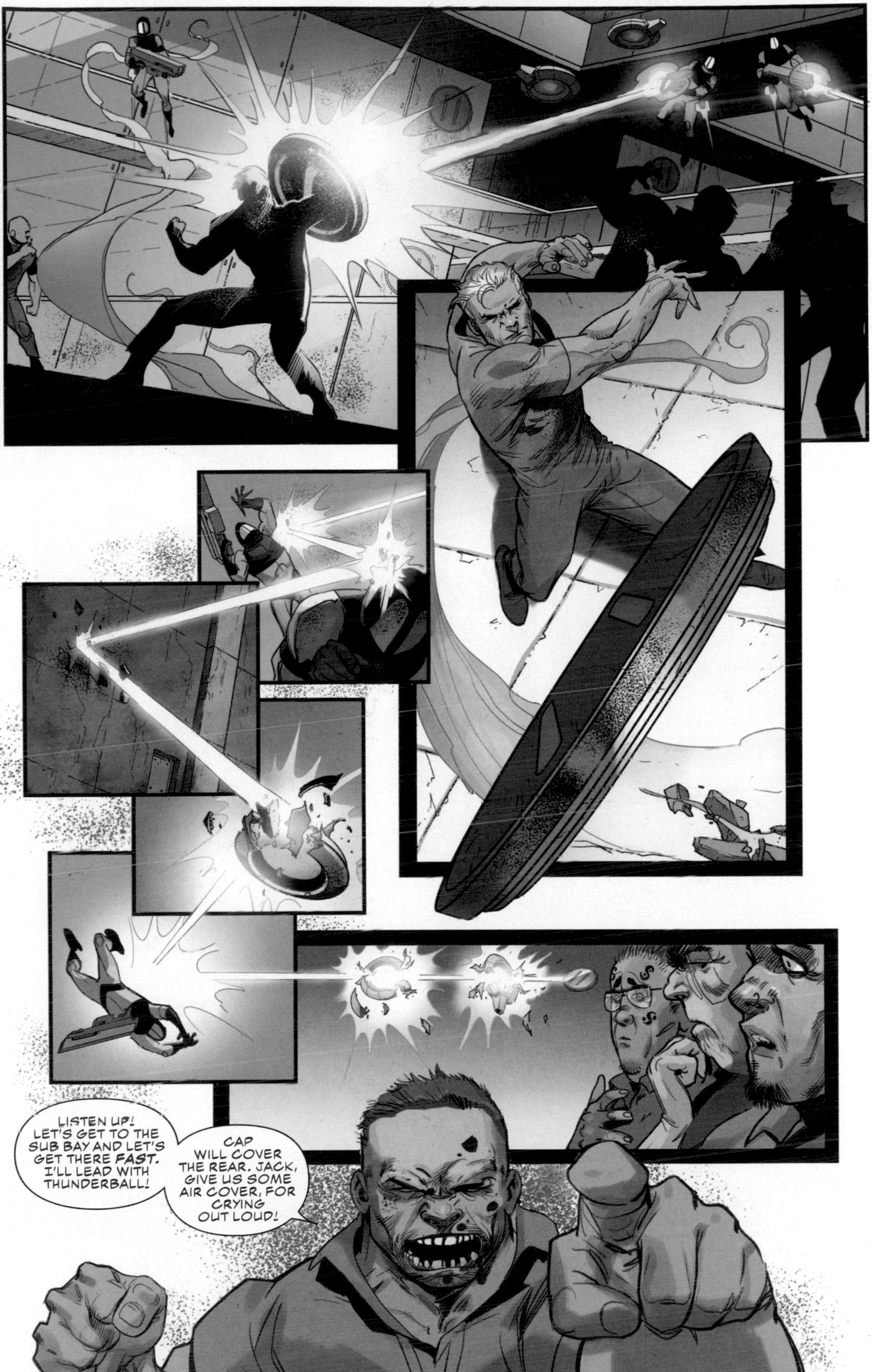
LISTEN UP! LET'S GET TO THE SUB BAY AND LET'S GET THERE **FAST.** I'LL LEAD WITH THUNDERBALL!
CAP WILL COVER THE REAR. JACK, GIVE US SOME AIR COVER, FOR CRYING OUT LOUD!

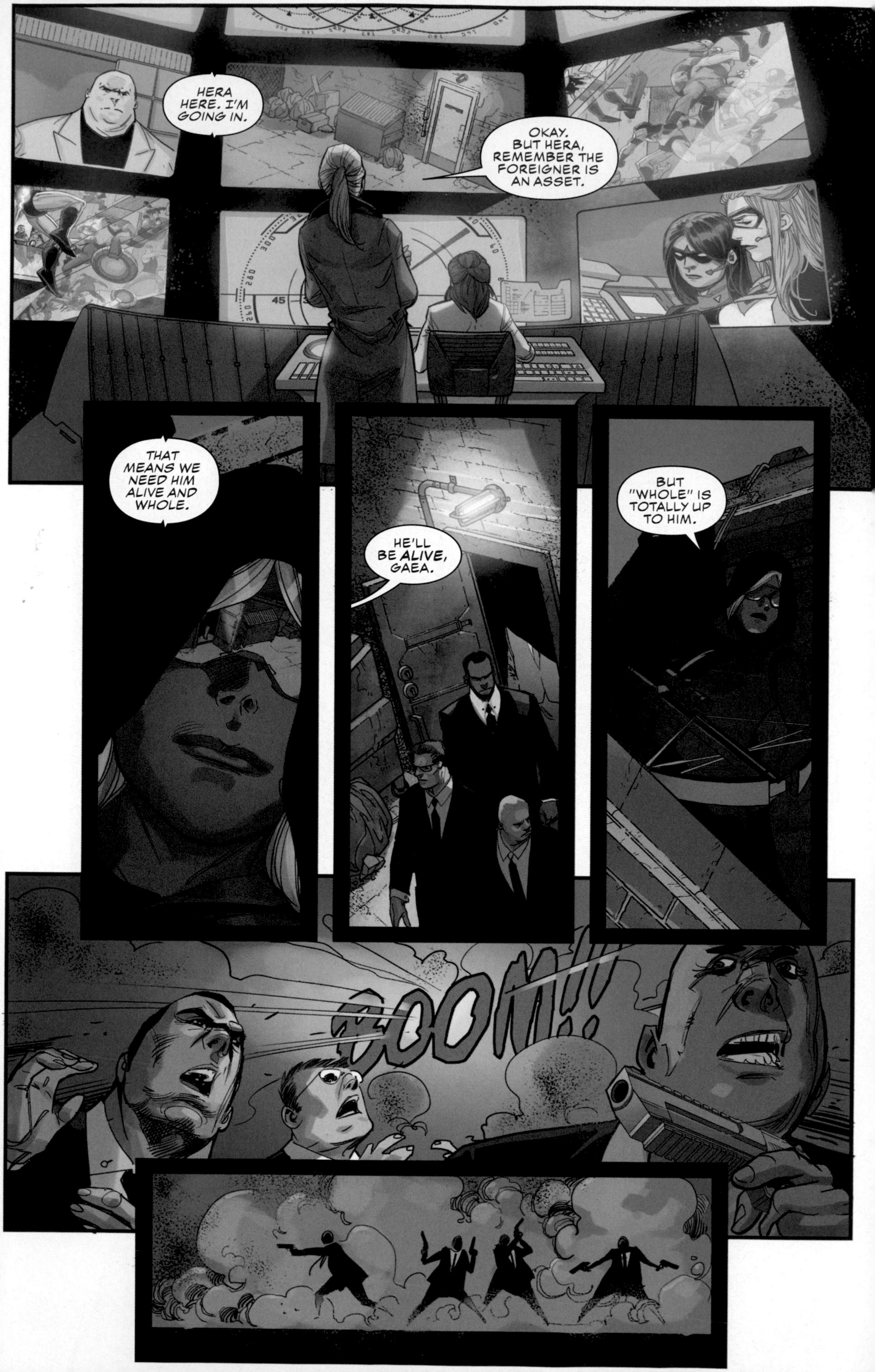

HERA HERE. I'M GOING IN.
OKAY. BUT HERA, REMEMBER THE FOREIGNER IS AN ASSET.
THAT MEANS WE NEED HIM ALIVE AND WHOLE.
HE'LL BE ALIVE, GAEA.
BUT "WHOLE" IS TOTALLY UP TO HIM.
BOOM!!

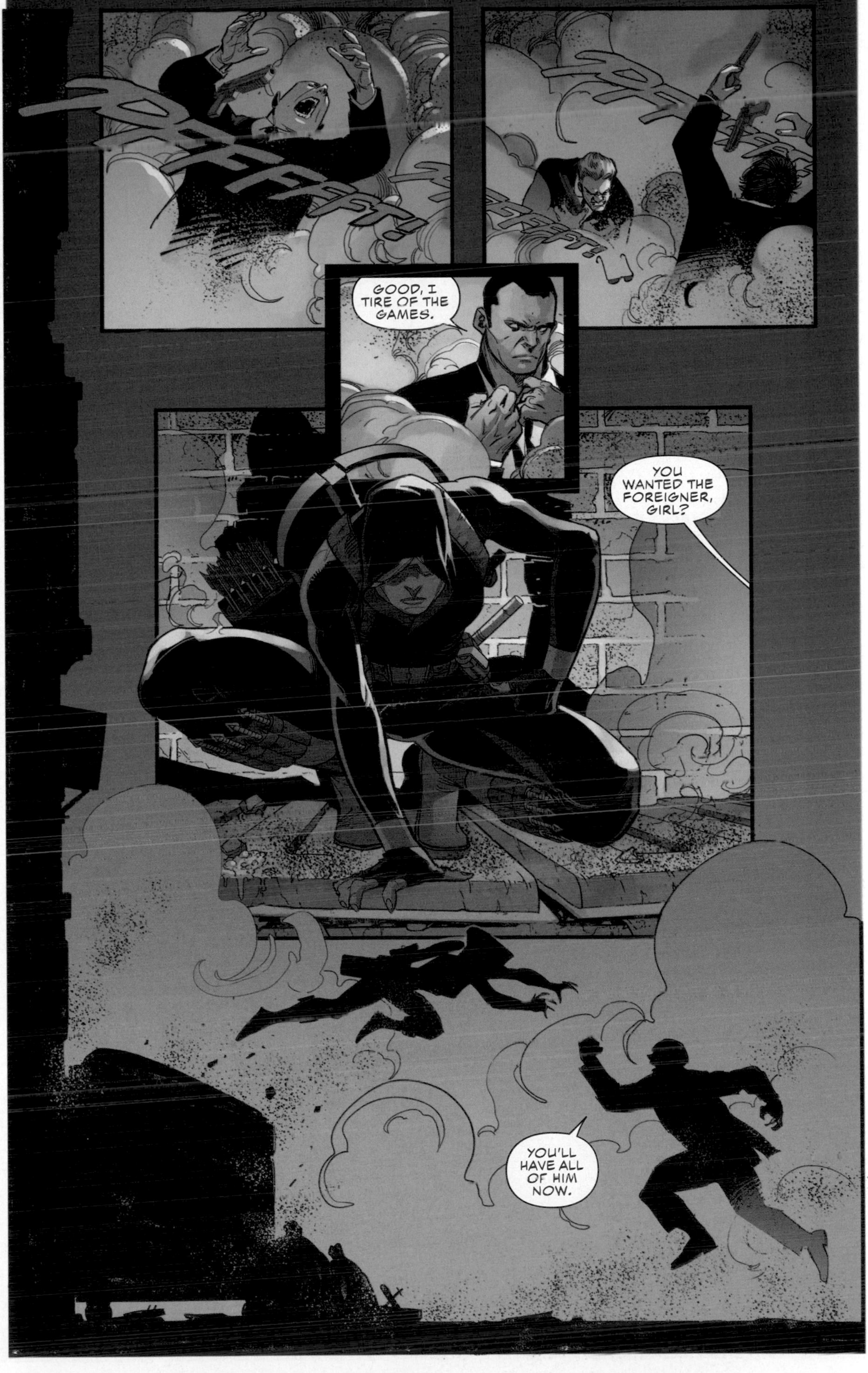
GOOD, I TIRE OF THE GAMES.
YOU WANTED THE FOREIGNER, GIRL?
YOU'LL HAVE ALL OF HIM NOW.

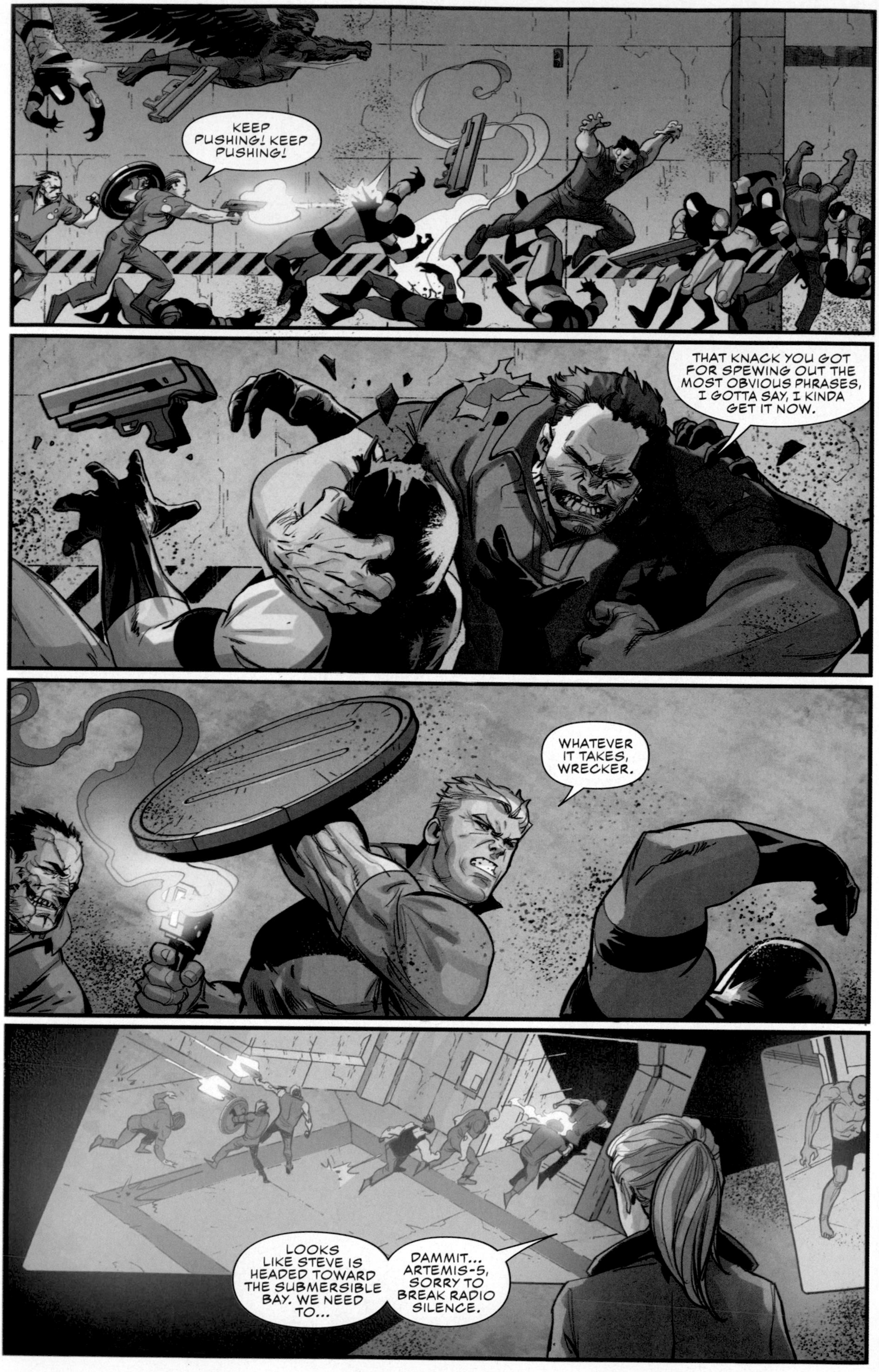
KEEP PUSHING! KEEP PUSHING!
THAT KNACK YOU GOT FOR SPEWING OUT THE MOST OBVIOUS PHRASES, I GOTTA SAY, I KINDA GET IT NOW.
WHATEVER IT TAKES, WRECKER.
DAMMIT... ARTEMIS-5, SORRY TO BREAK RADIO SILENCE.
LOOKS LIKE STEVE IS HEADED TOWARD THE SUBMERSIBLE BAY. WE NEED TO...

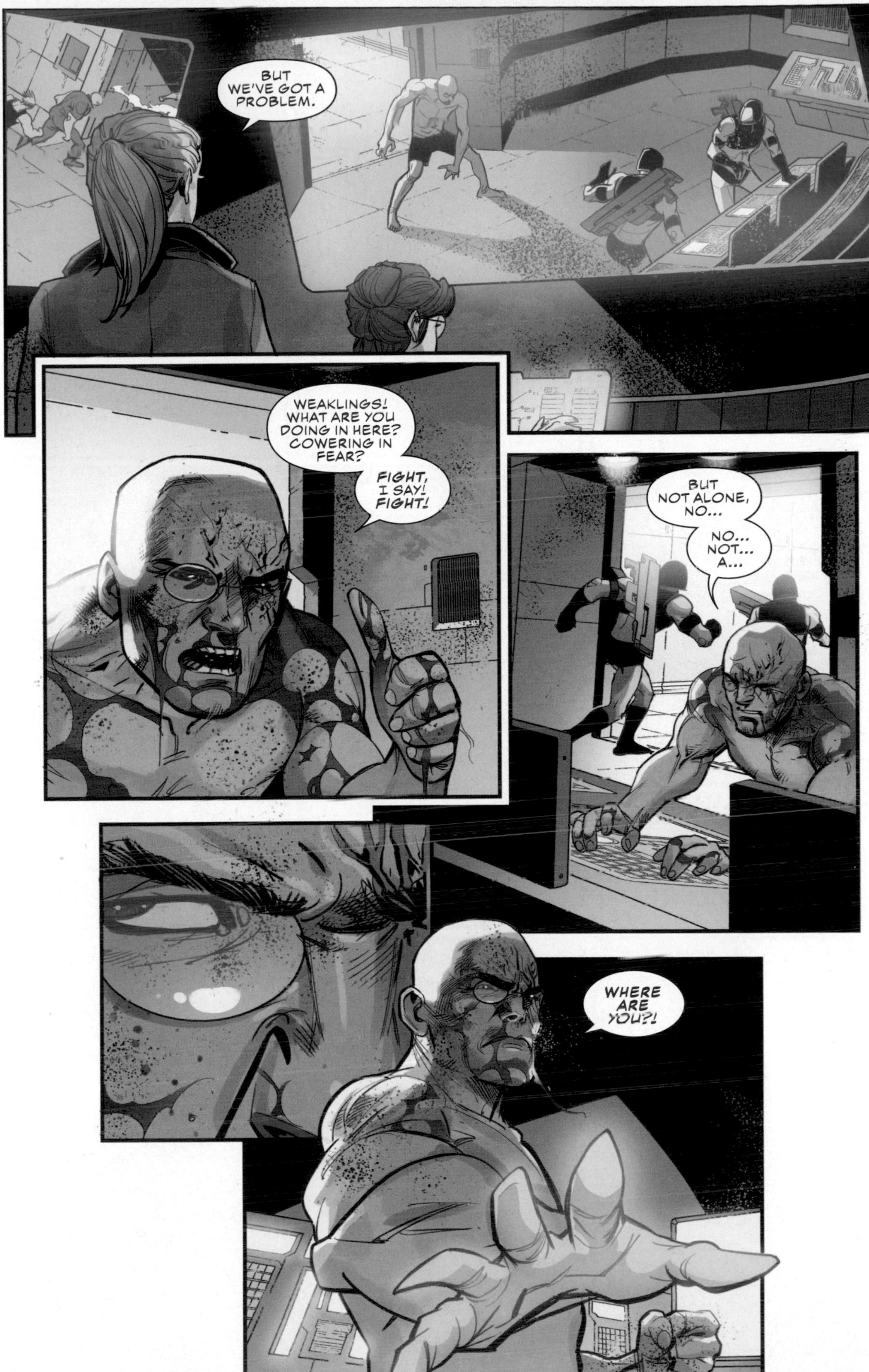
BUT WE'VE GOT A PROBLEM.
WEAKLINGS! WHAT ARE YOU DOING IN HERE? COWERING IN FEAR?
FIGHT, I SAY! FIGHT!
BUT NOT ALONE, NO...
NO... NOT... A...
WHERE ARE YOU?!

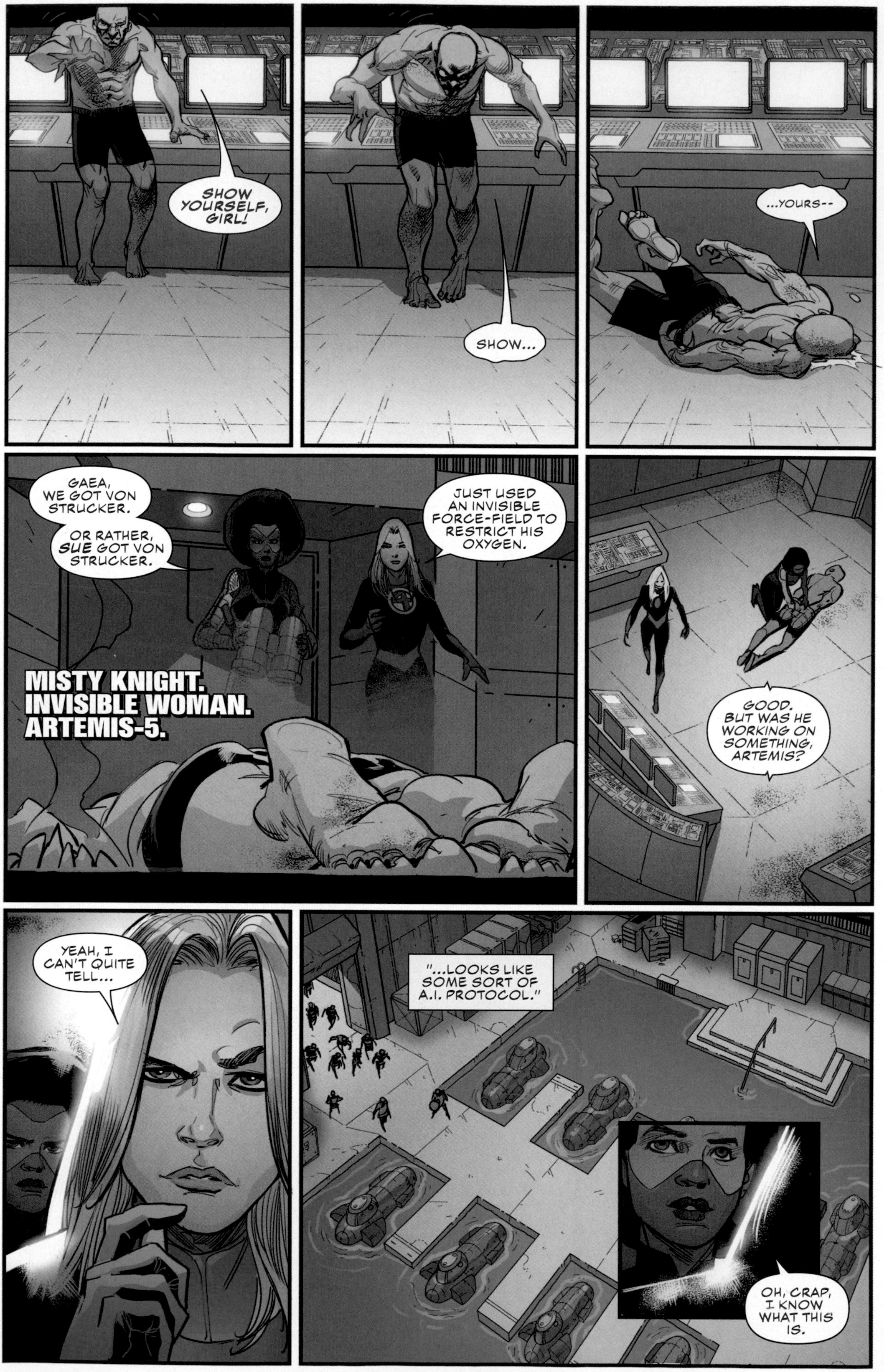
SHOW YOURSELF, GIRL!
SHOW...
...YOURS--
GAEA, WE GOT VON STRUCKER.
OR RATHER, SUE GOT VON STRUCKER.
JUST USED AN INVISIBLE FORCE-FIELD TO RESTRICT HIS OXYGEN.
MISTY KNIGHT. INVISIBLE WOMAN. ARTEMIS-5.
GOOD. BUT WAS HE WORKING ON SOMETHING, ARTEMIS?
YEAH, I CAN'T QUITE TELL...
"...LOOKS LIKE SOME SORT OF A.I. PROTOCOL."
OH, CRAP, I KNOW WHAT THIS IS.

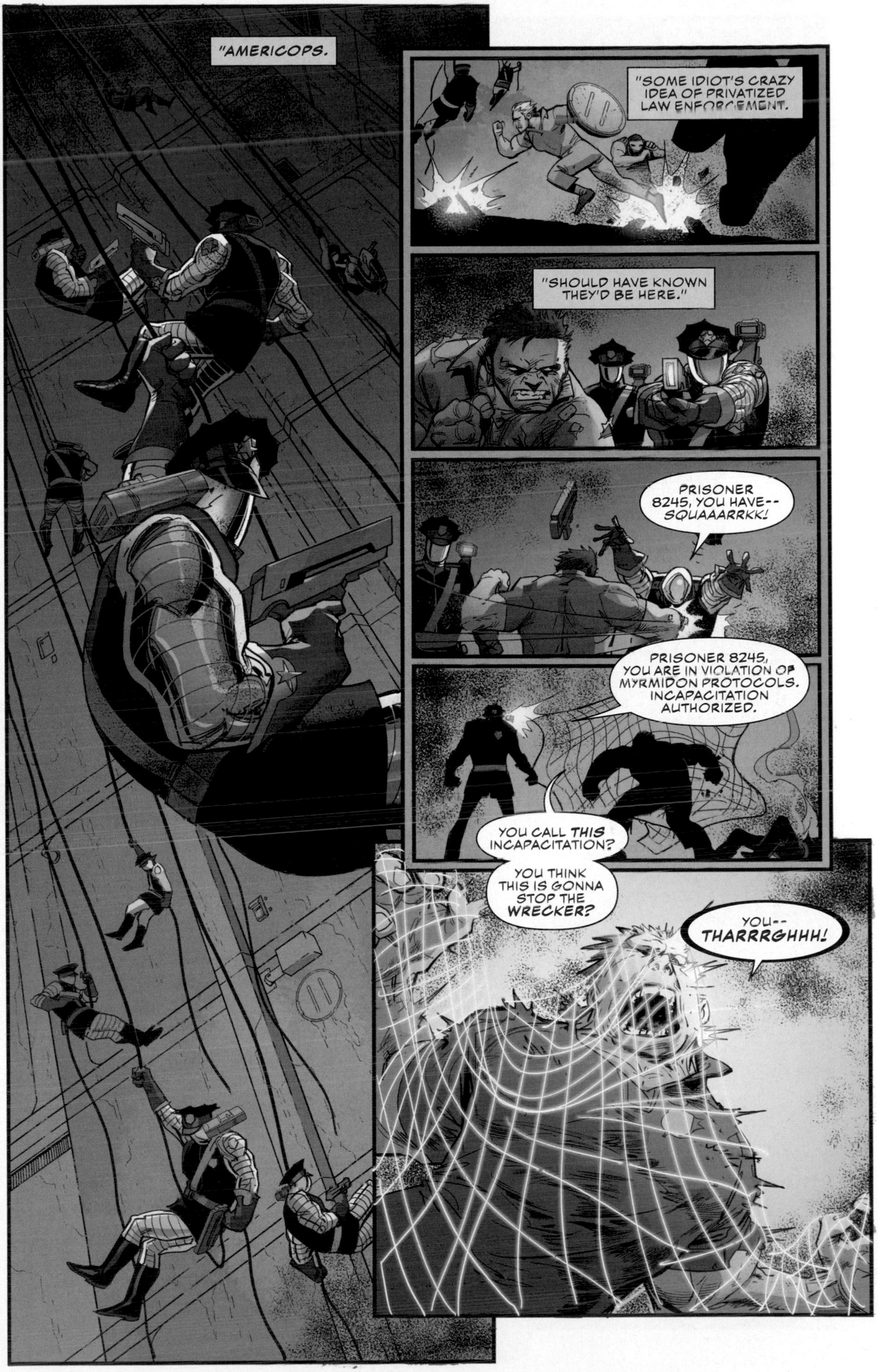

"AMERICOPS.
"SOME IDIOT'S CRAZY IDEA OF PRIVATIZED LAW ENFORCEMENT.
"SHOULD HAVE KNOWN THEY'D BE HERE."
PRISONER 8245, YOU HAVE-- SQUAAARRKK!
PRISONER 8245, YOU ARE IN VIOLATION OF MYRMIDON PROTOCOLS. INCAPACITATION AUTHORIZED.
YOU CALL THIS INCAPACITATION?
YOU THINK THIS IS GONNA STOP THE WRECKER?
YOU-- THARRRGHHH!

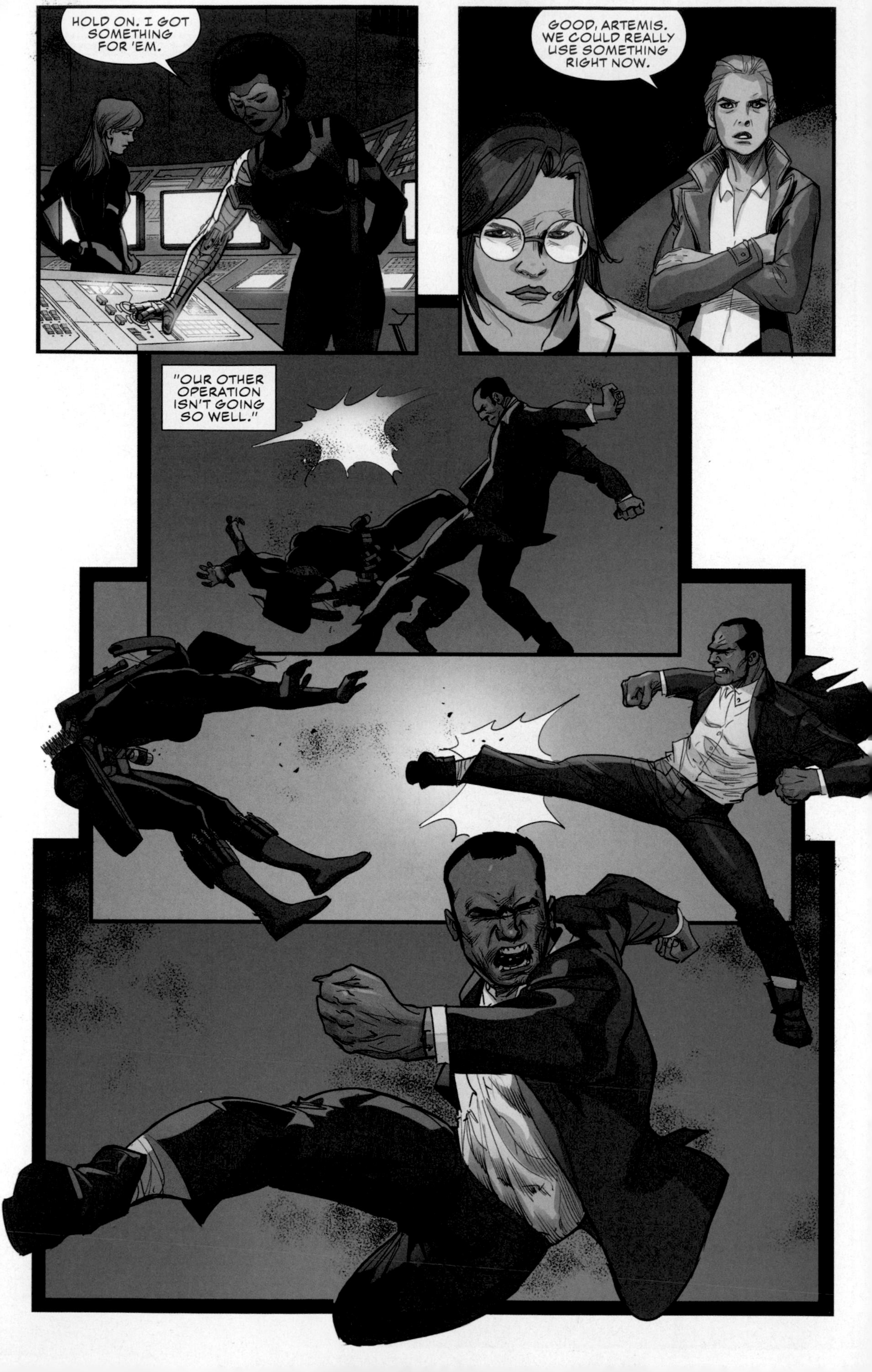
HOLD ON. I GOT SOMETHING FOR 'EM.
GOOD, ARTEMIS. WE COULD REALLY USE SOMETHING RIGHT NOW.
"OUR OTHER OPERATION ISN'T GOING SO WELL."

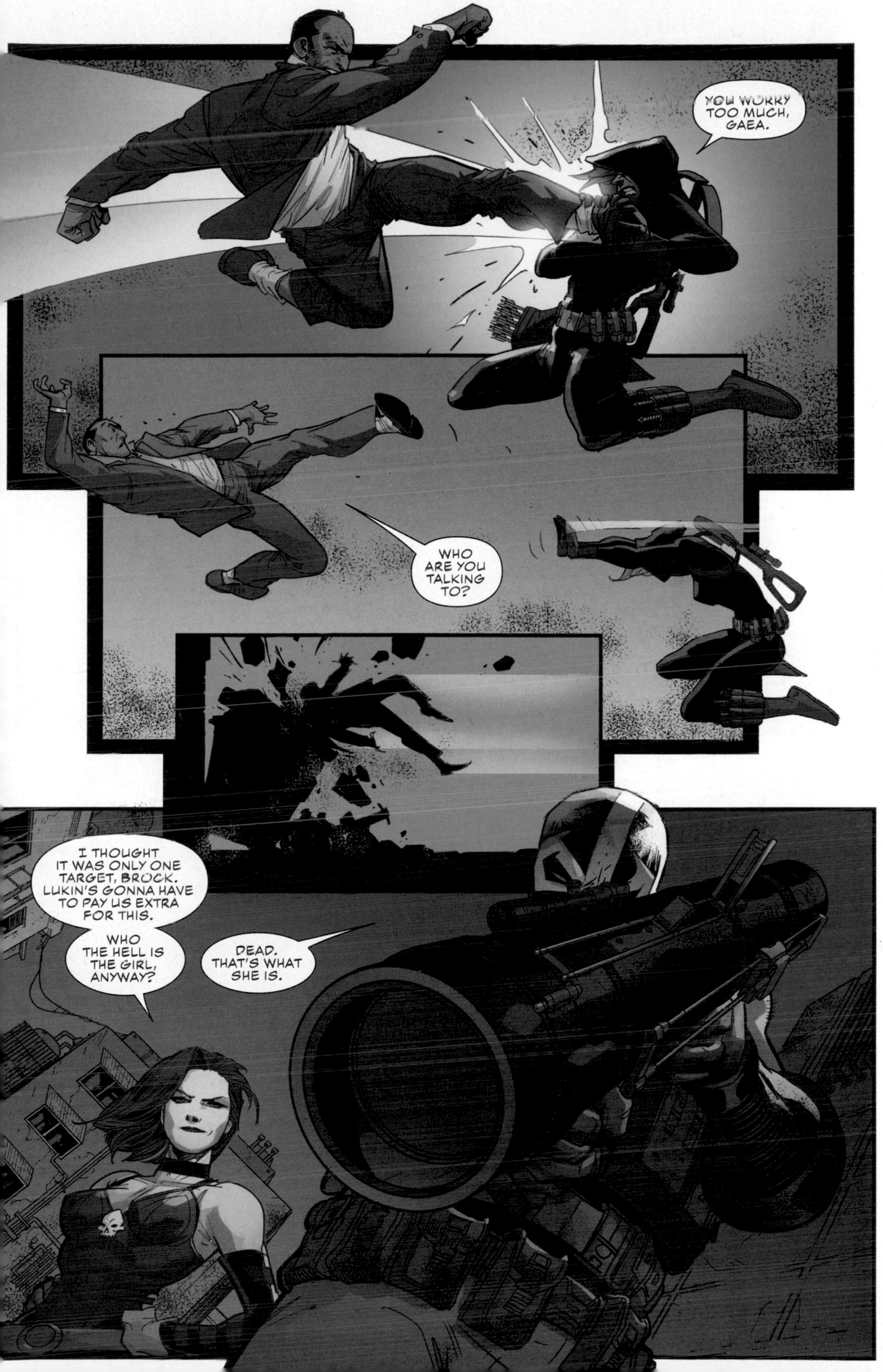
YOU WORRY TOO MUCH, GAEA.
WHO ARE YOU TALKING TO?
I THOUGHT IT WAS ONLY ONE TARGET, BROCK. LUKIN'S GONNA HAVE TO PAY US EXTRA FOR THIS.
WHO THE HELL IS THE GIRL, ANYWAY?
DEAD. THAT'S WHAT SHE IS.

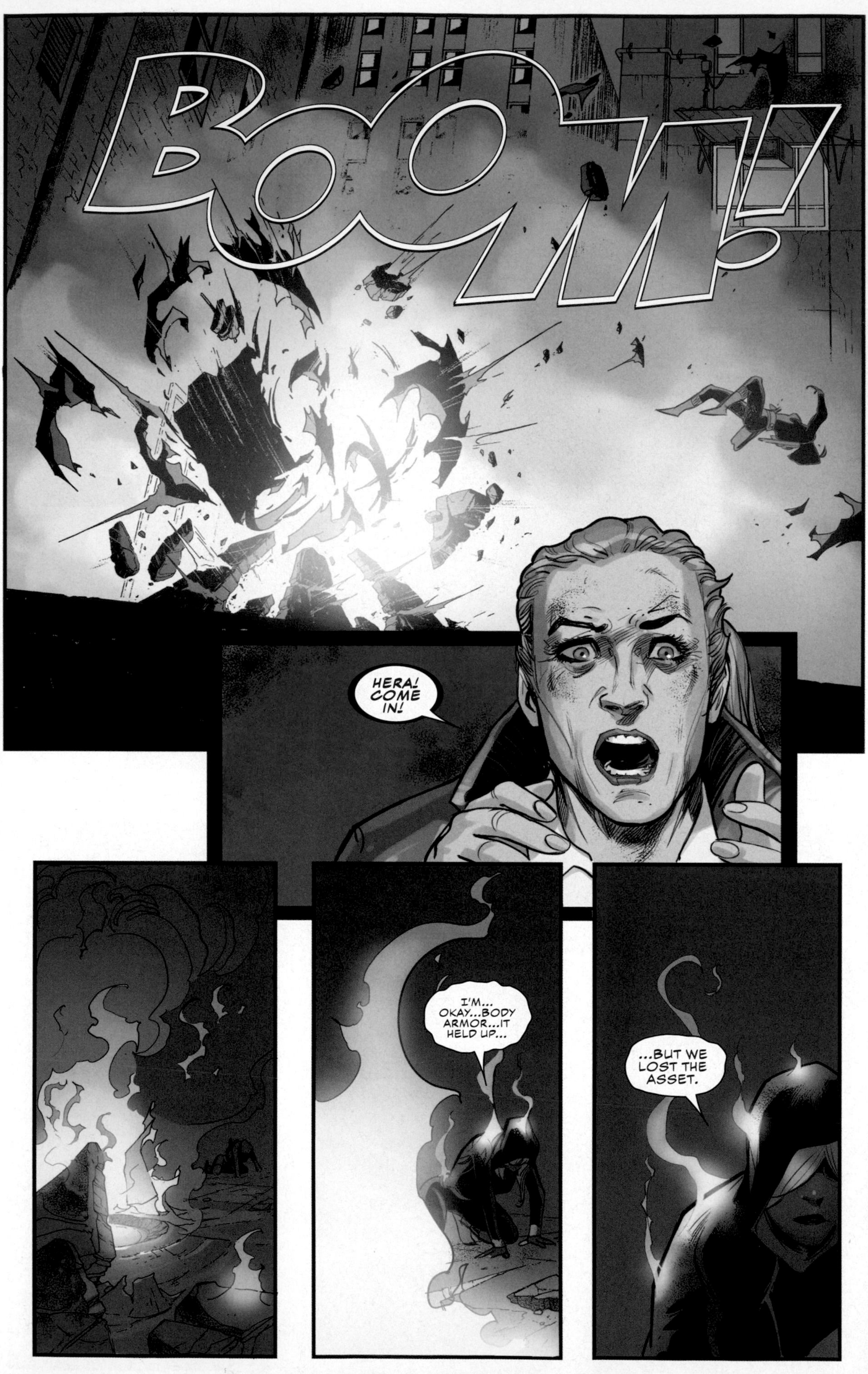
BOOM!
HERA! COME IN!
I'M... OKAY...BODY ARMOR...IT HELD UP...
...BUT WE LOST THE ASSET.

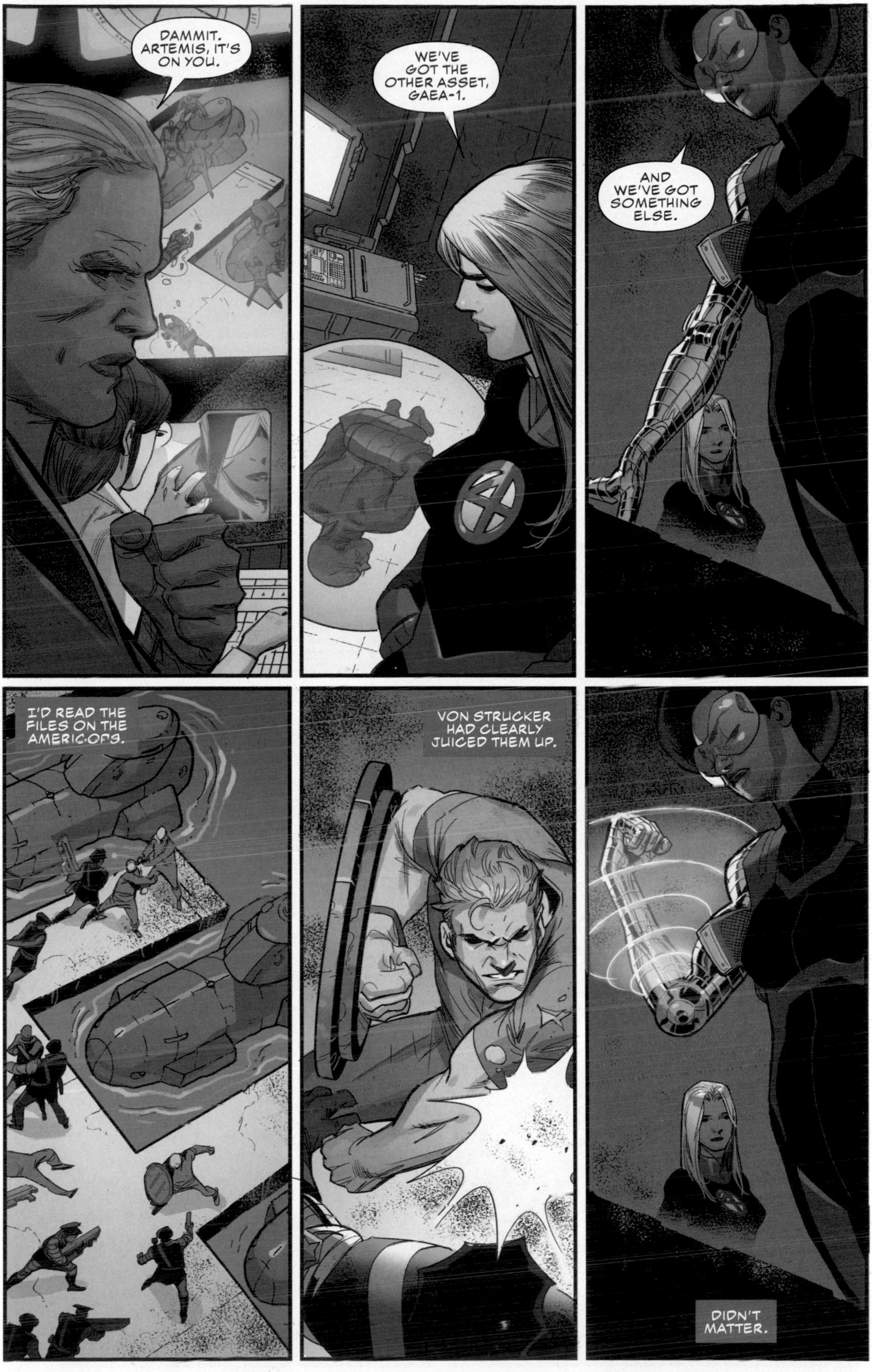
DAMMIT. ARTEMIS, IT'S ON YOU.
WE'VE GOT THE OTHER ASSET, GAEA-1.
AND WE'VE GOT SOMETHING ELSE.
I'D READ THE FILES ON THE AMERICOPS.
VON STRUCKER HAD CLEARLY JUICED THEM UP.
DIDN'T MATTER.

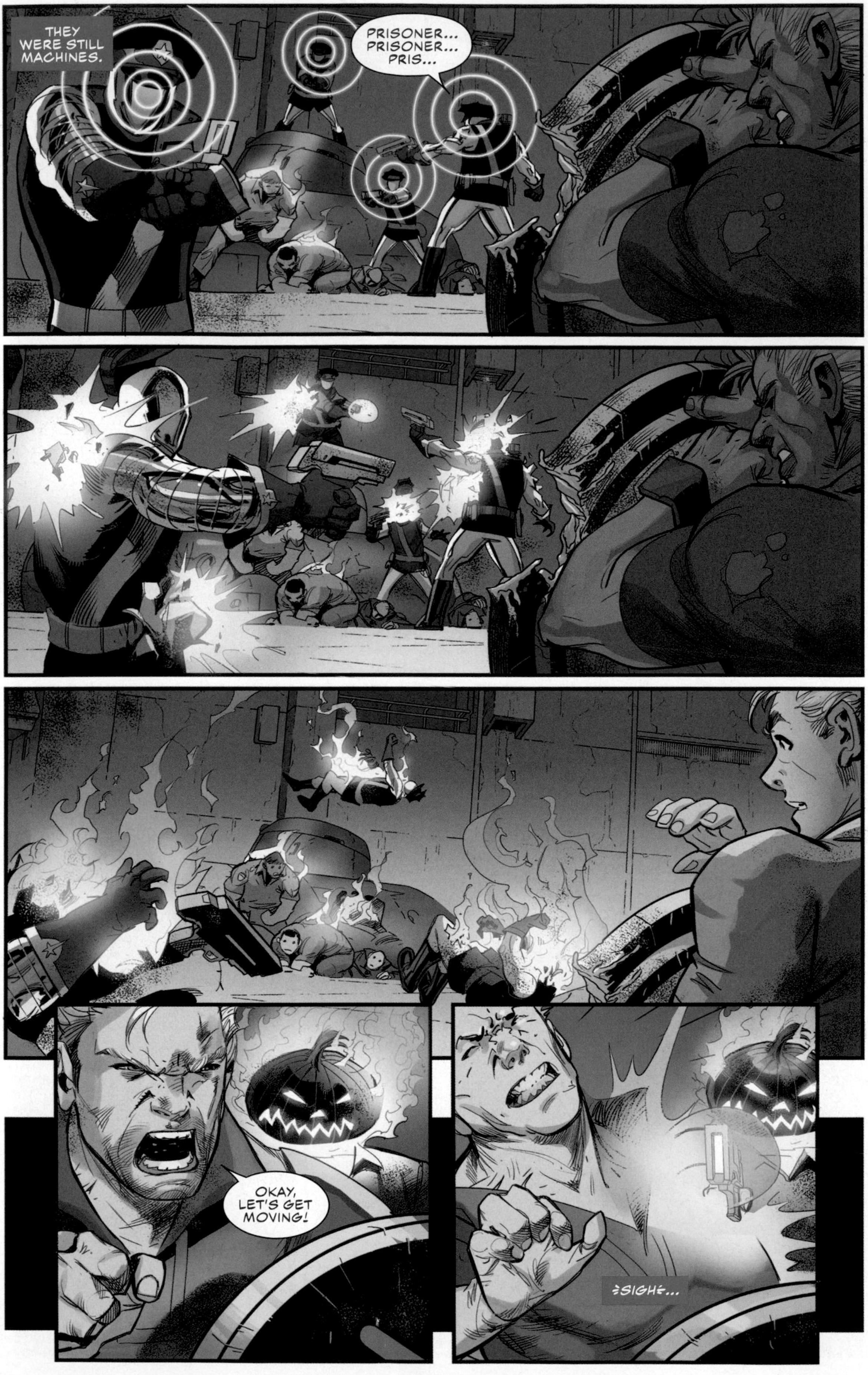
THEY WERE STILL MACHINES.
PRISONER... PRISONER... PRIS...
OKAY, LET'S GET MOVING!
≈SIGH≈...

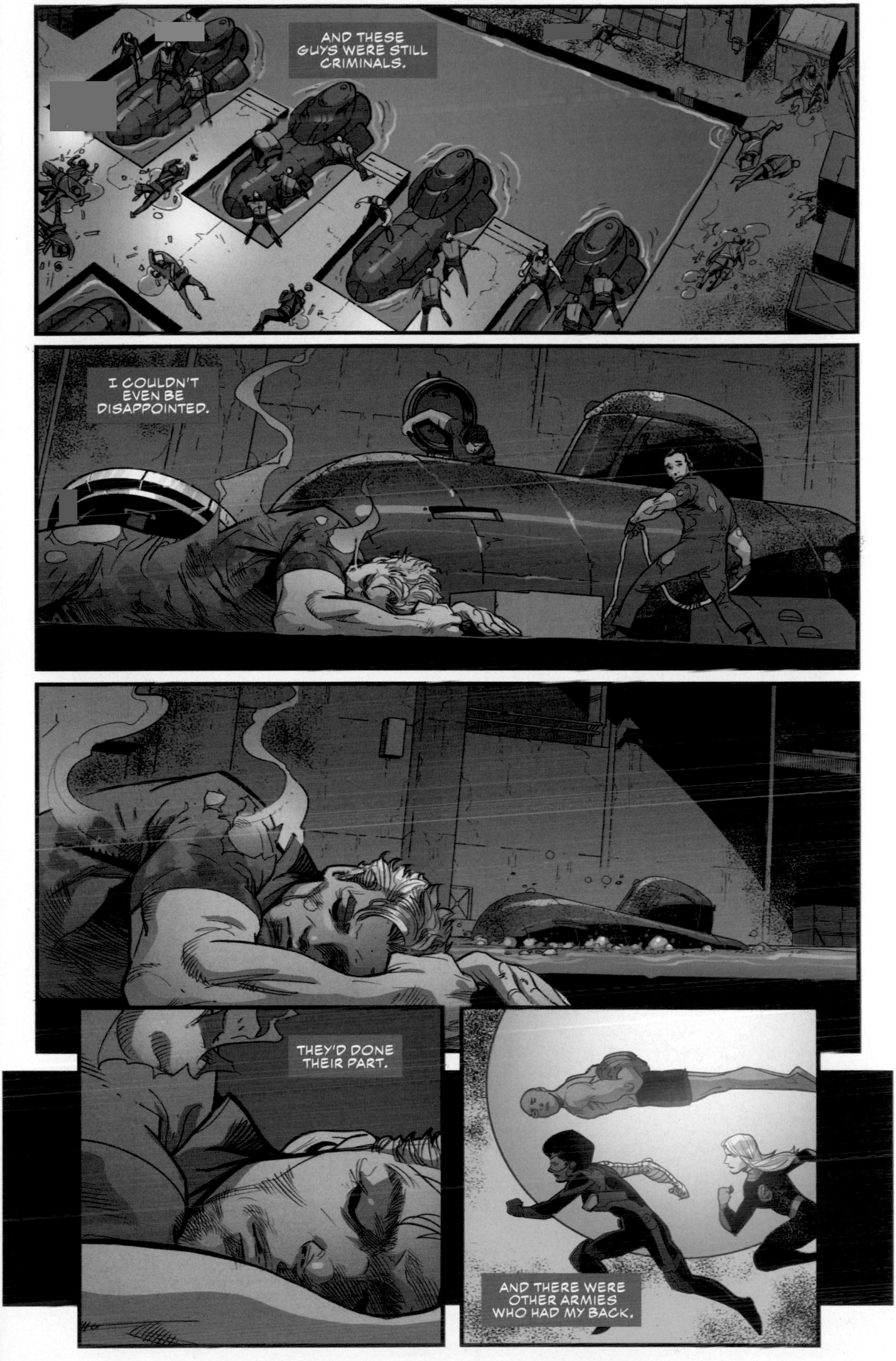
AND THESE GUYS WERE STILL CRIMINALS.
I COULDN'T EVEN BE DISAPPOINTED.
THEY'D DONE THEIR PART.
AND THERE WERE OTHER ARMIES WHO HAD MY BACK.

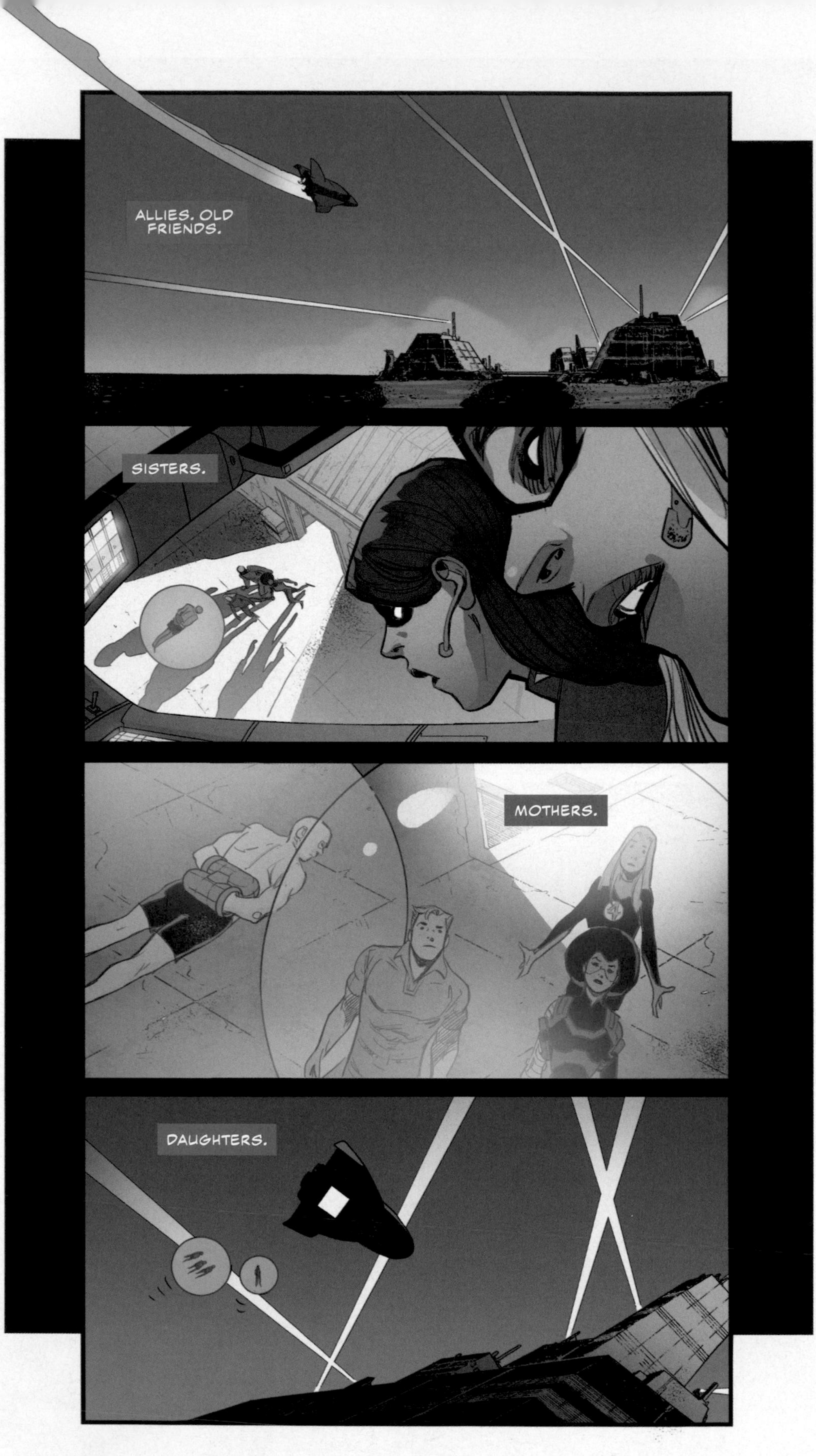
ALLIES. OLD FRIENDS.
SISTERS.
MOTHERS.
DAUGHTERS.

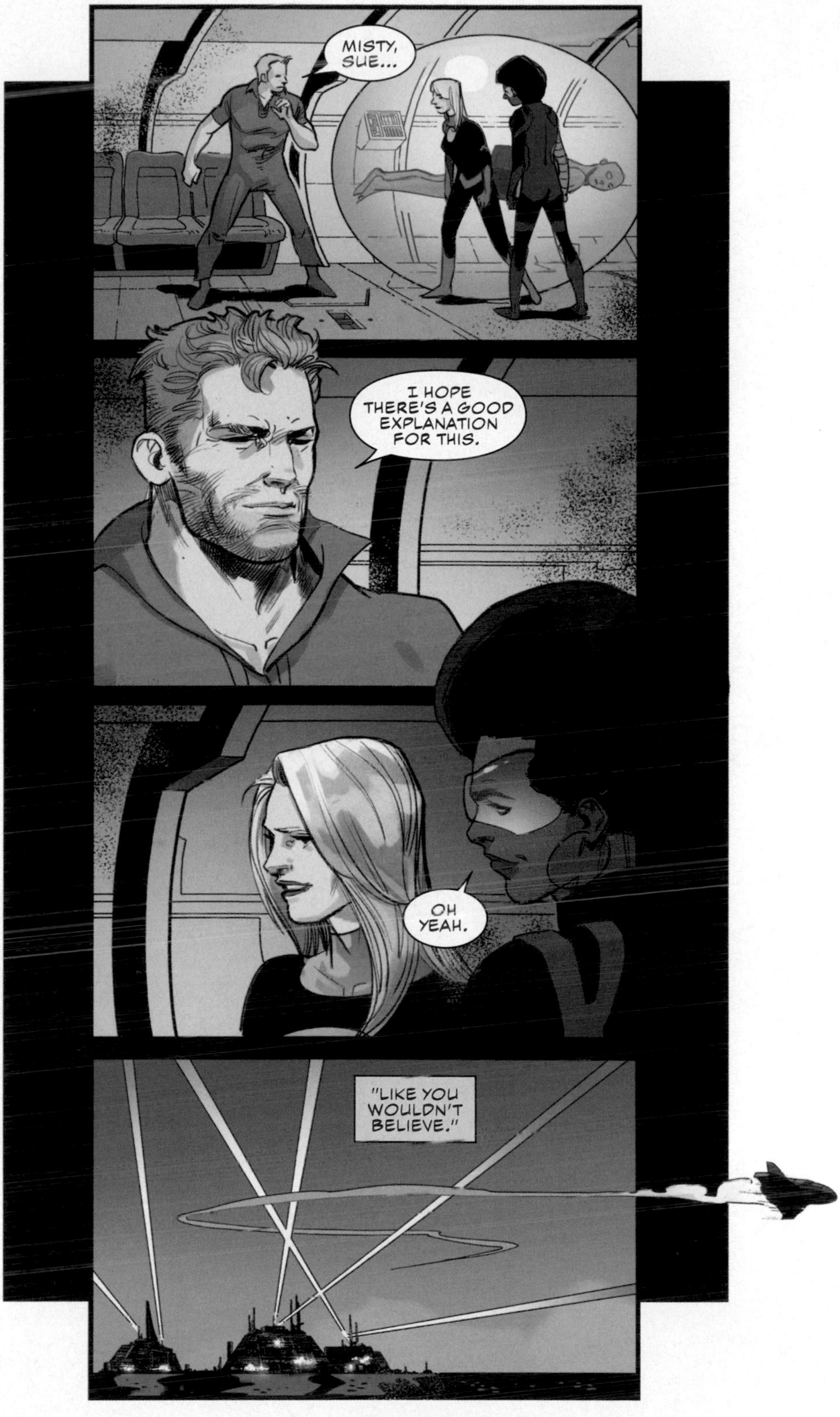
MISTY, SUE...
I HOPE THERE'S A GOOD EXPLANATION FOR THIS.
OH YEAH.
"LIKE YOU WOULDN'T BELIEVE."

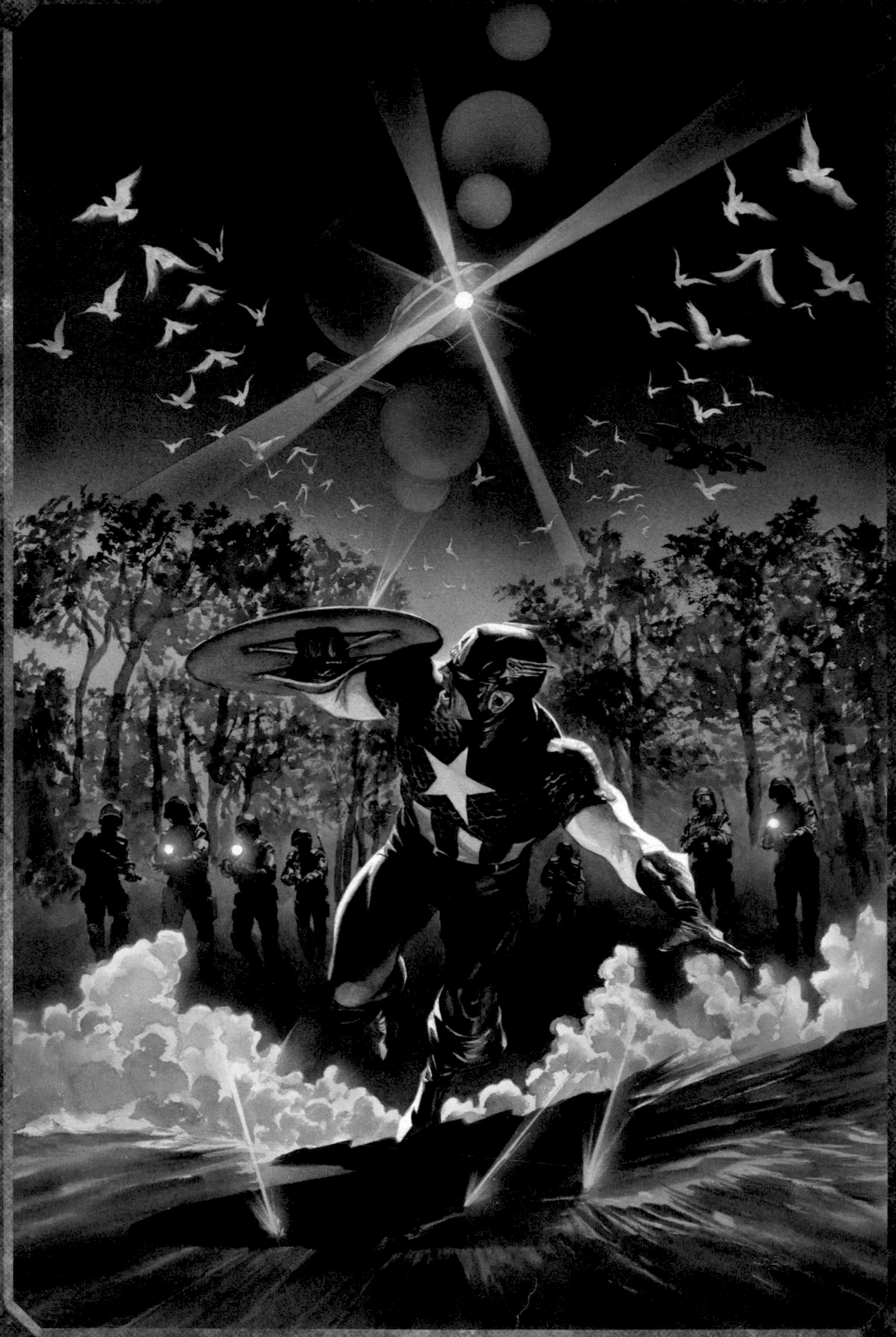

12

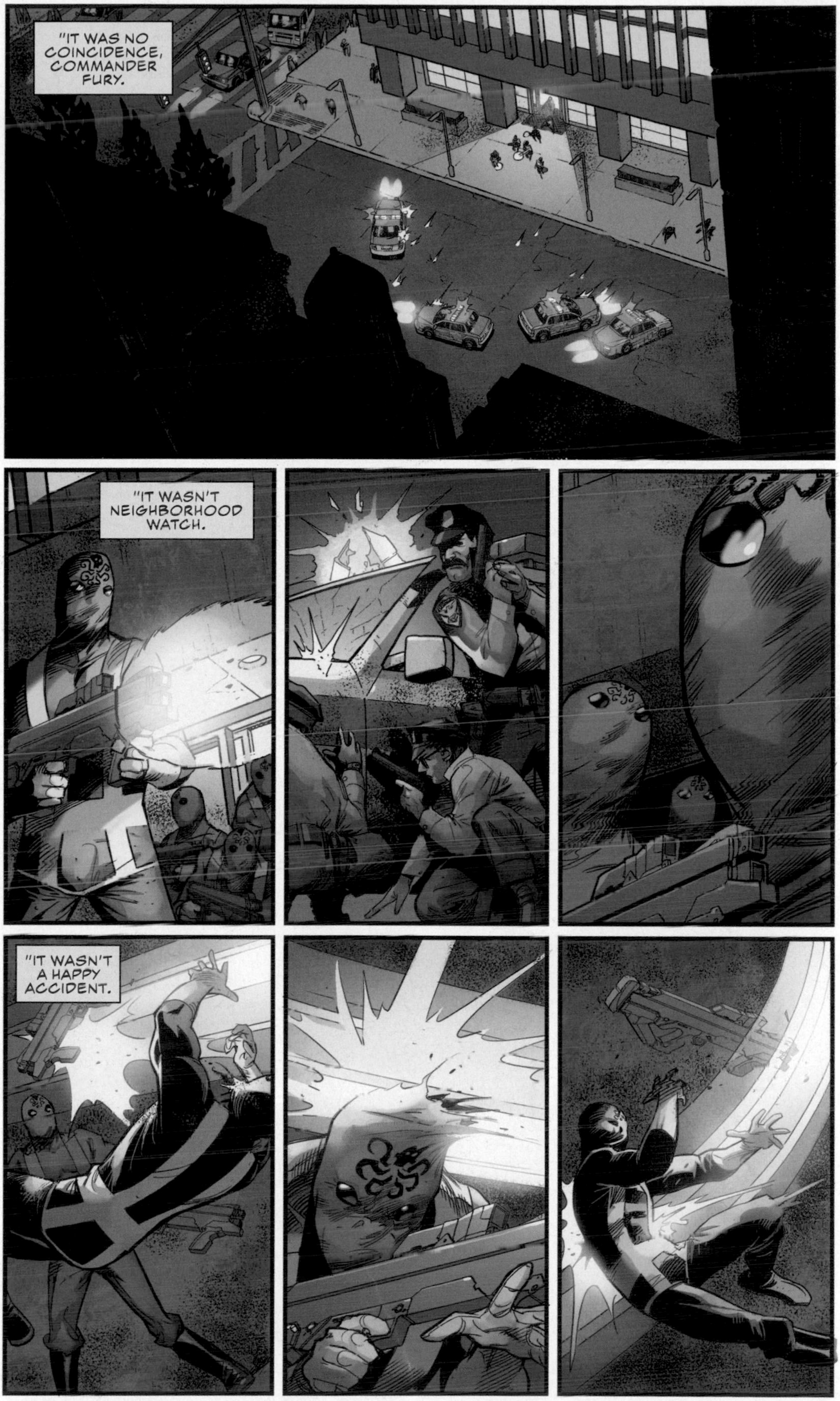
"IT WAS NO COINCIDENCE, COMMANDER FURY.
"IT WASN'T NEIGHBORHOOD WATCH.
"IT WASN'T A HAPPY ACCIDENT.

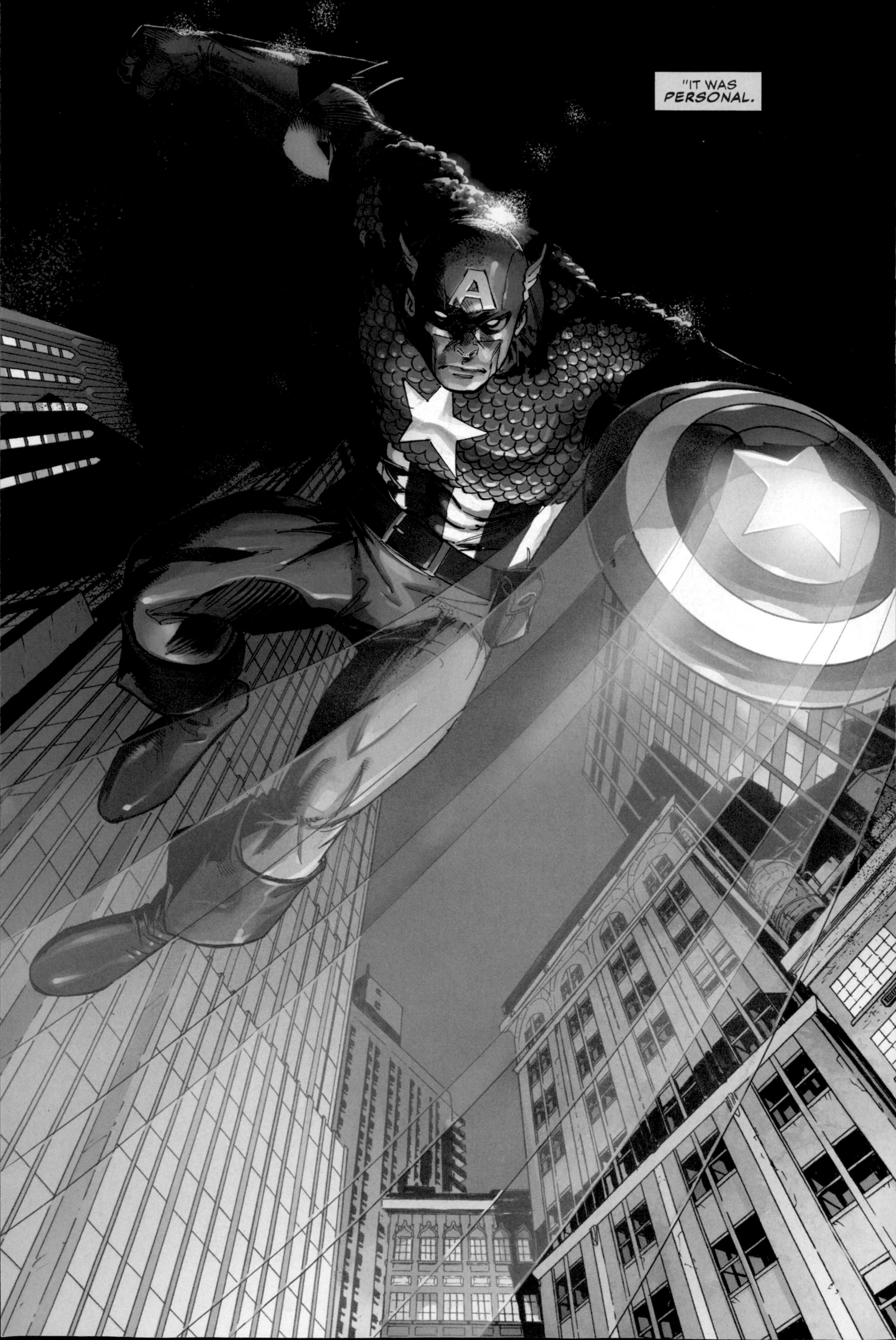
"IT WAS PERSONAL.

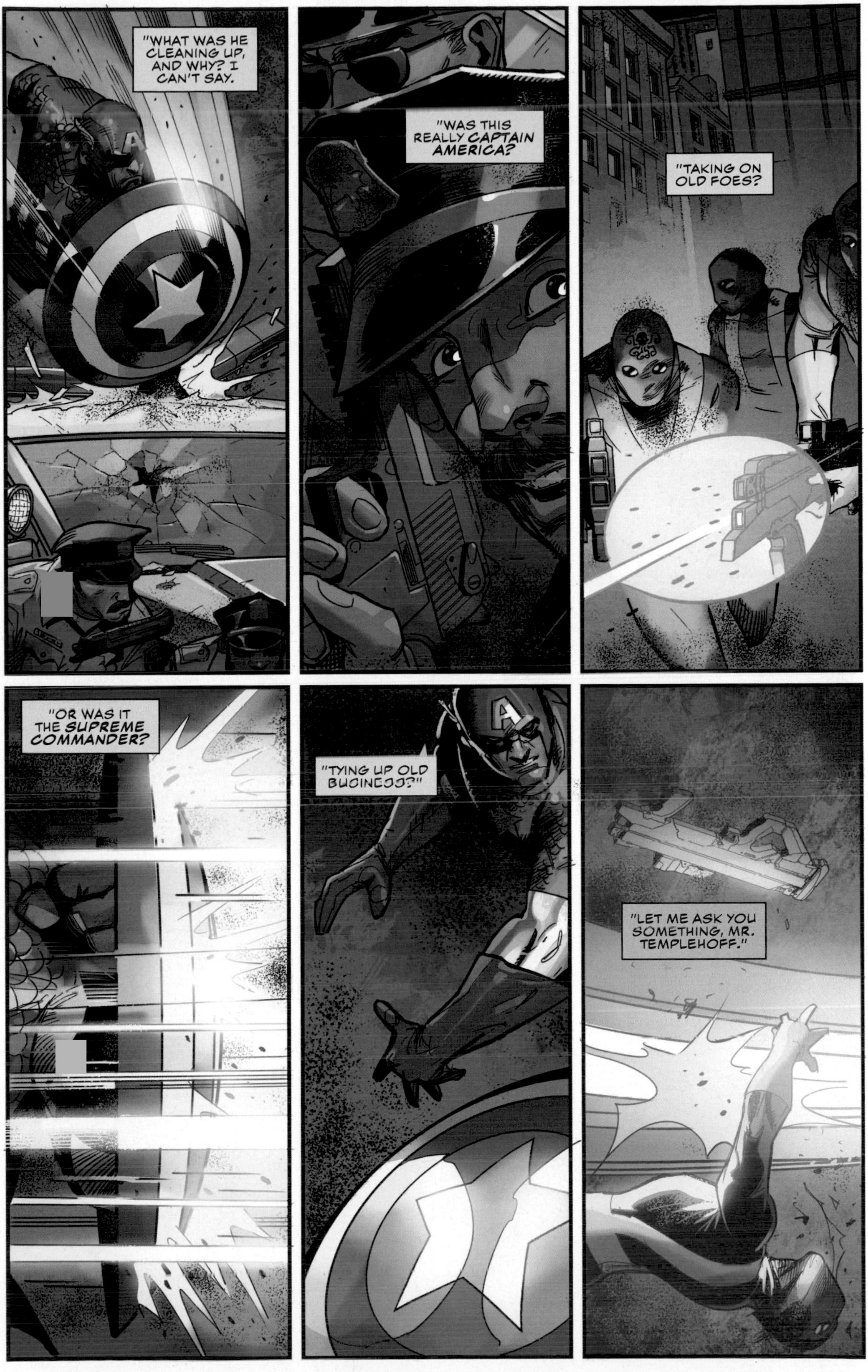
"WHAT WAS HE CLEANING UP, AND WHY? I CAN'T SAY.
"WAS THIS REALLY *CAPTAIN AMERICA?*
"TAKING ON OLD FOES?
"OR WAS IT THE *SUPREME COMMANDER?*
"TYING UP OLD BUSINESS?"
"LET ME ASK YOU SOMETHING, MR. TEMPLEHOFF."

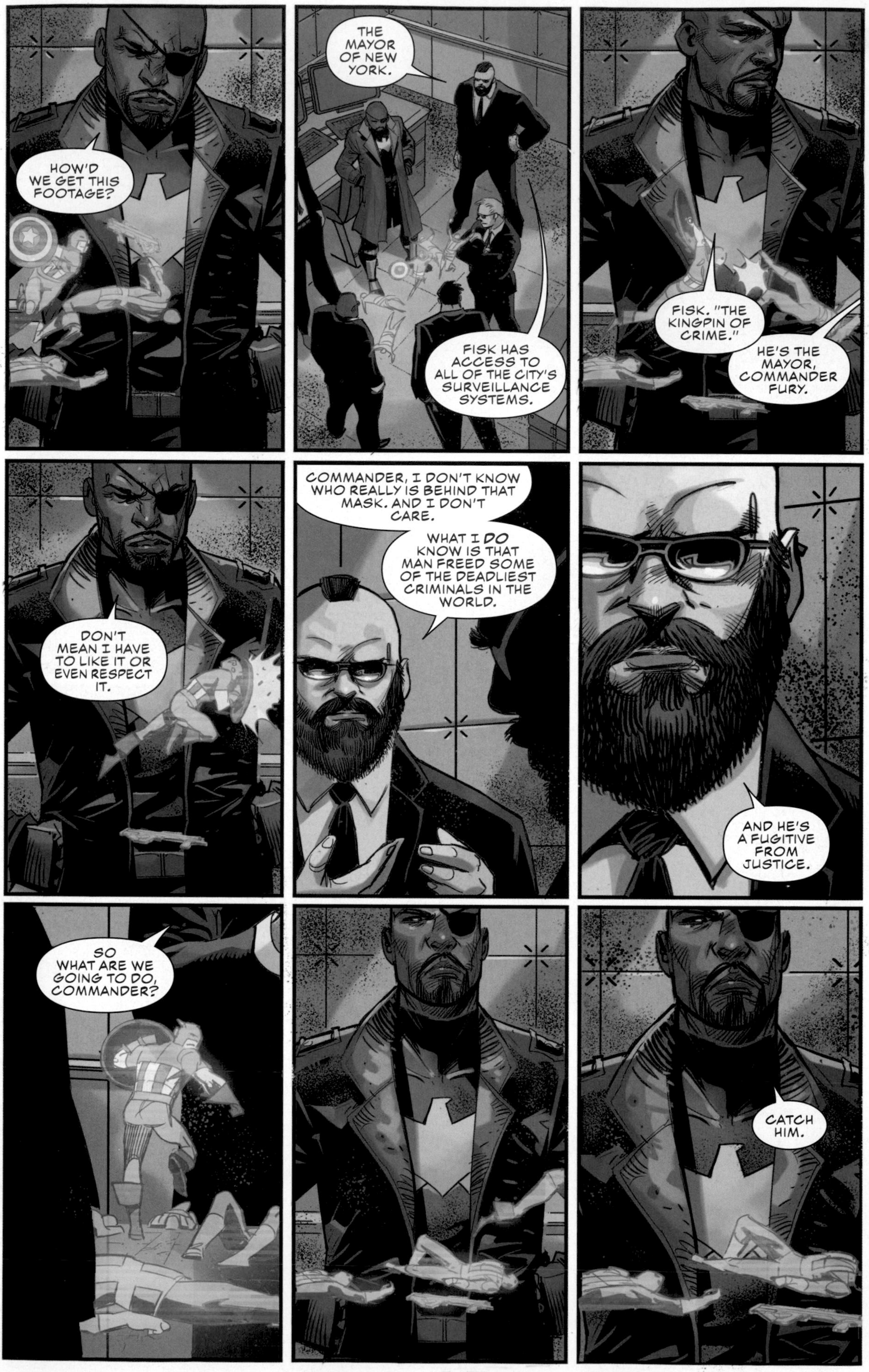
HOW'D WE GET THIS FOOTAGE?
THE MAYOR OF NEW YORK.
FISK HAS ACCESS TO ALL OF THE CITY'S SURVEILLANCE SYSTEMS.
FISK. "THE KINGPIN OF CRIME."
HE'S THE MAYOR, COMMANDER FURY.
DON'T MEAN I HAVE TO LIKE IT OR EVEN RESPECT IT.
COMMANDER, I DON'T KNOW WHO REALLY IS BEHIND THAT MASK. AND I DON'T CARE.
WHAT I DO KNOW IS THAT MAN FREED SOME OF THE DEADLIEST CRIMINALS IN THE WORLD.
AND HE'S A FUGITIVE FROM JUSTICE.
SO WHAT ARE WE GOING TO DO, COMMANDER?
CATCH HIM.

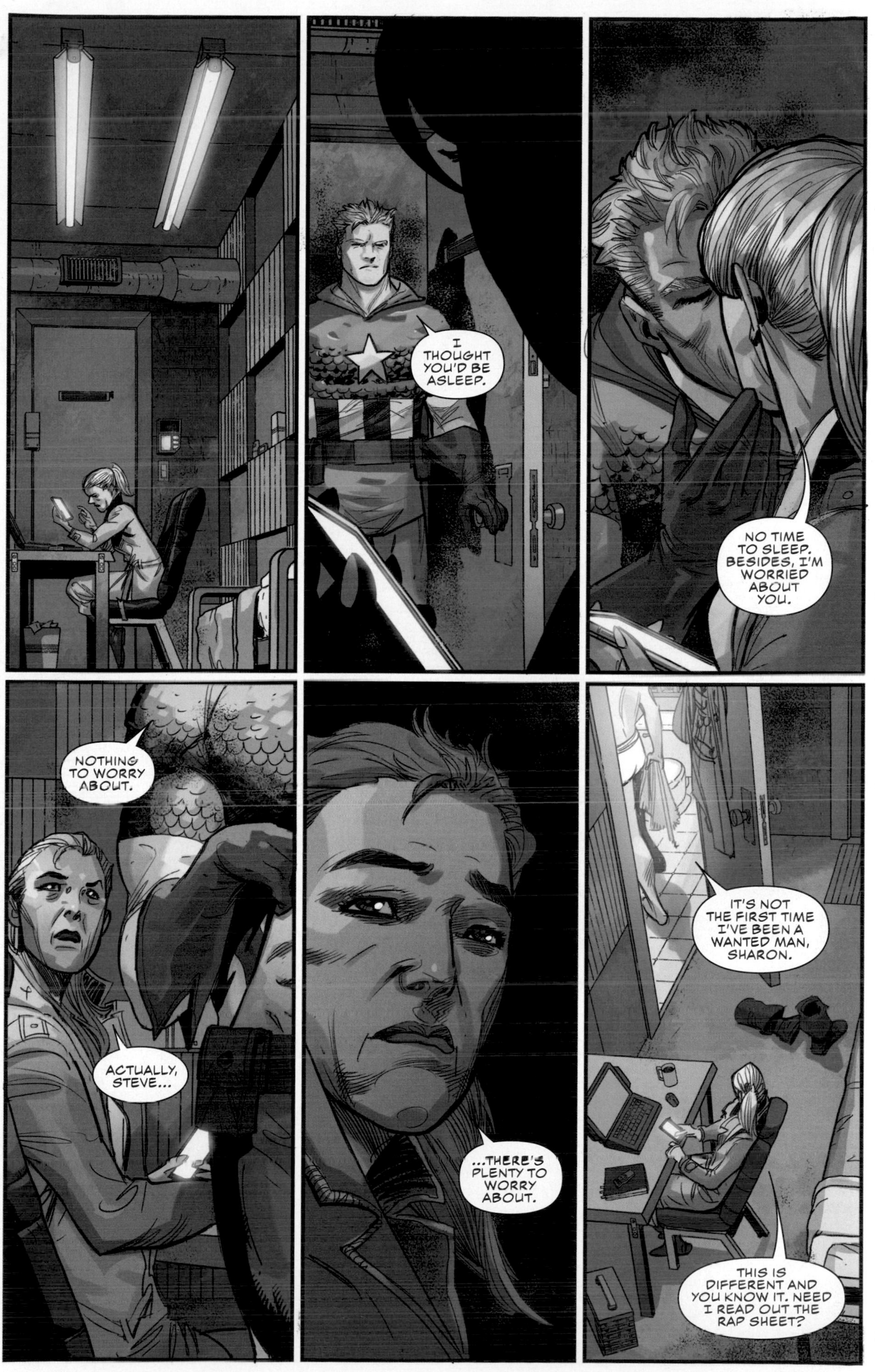
I THOUGHT YOU'D BE ASLEEP.
NO TIME TO SLEEP. BESIDES, I'M WORRIED ABOUT YOU.
NOTHING TO WORRY ABOUT.
ACTUALLY, STEVE...
...THERE'S PLENTY TO WORRY ABOUT.
IT'S NOT THE FIRST TIME I'VE BEEN A WANTED MAN, SHARON.
THIS IS DIFFERENT AND YOU KNOW IT. NEED I READ OUT THE RAP SHEET?

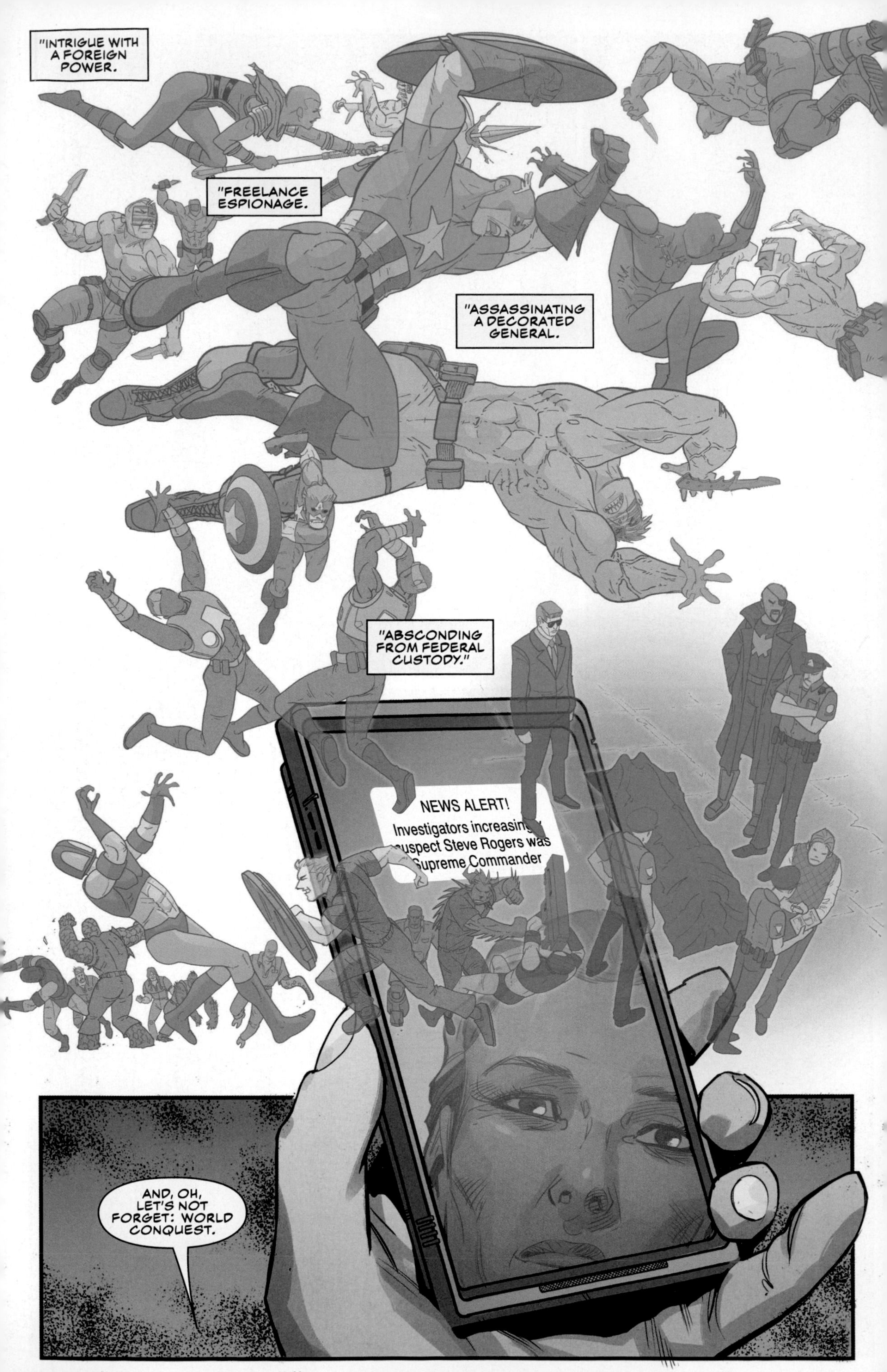
"INTRIGUE WITH A FOREIGN POWER.
"FREELANCE ESPIONAGE.
"ASSASSINATING A DECORATED GENERAL.
"ABSCONDING FROM FEDERAL CUSTODY."
NEWS ALERT!
Investigators increasingly suspect Steve Rogers was Supreme Commander
AND, OH, LET'S NOT FORGET: WORLD CONQUEST.

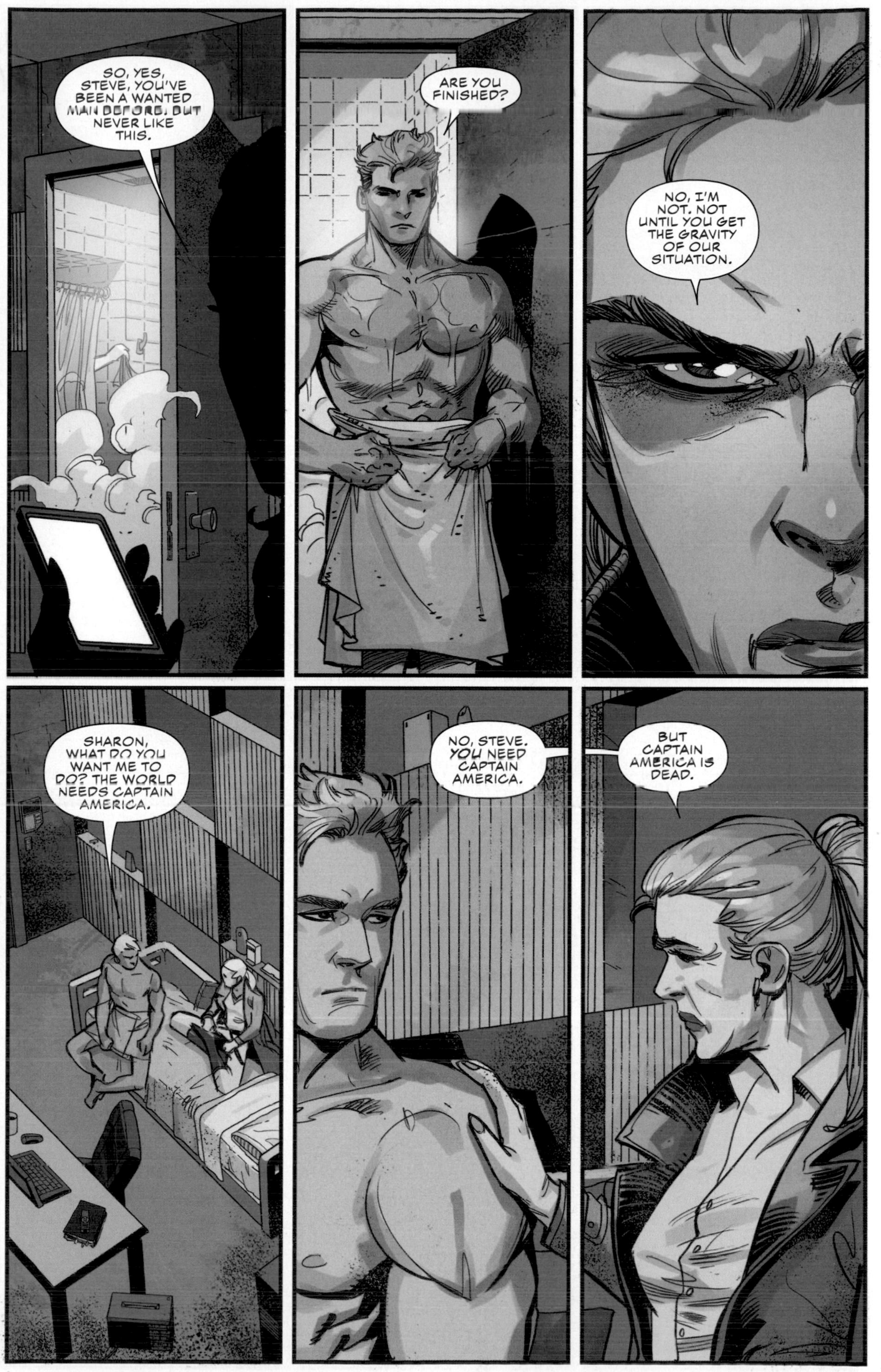
SO, YES, STEVE, YOU'VE BEEN A WANTED MAN BEFORE. BUT NEVER LIKE THIS.
ARE YOU FINISHED?
NO, I'M NOT. NOT UNTIL YOU GET THE GRAVITY OF OUR SITUATION.
SHARON, WHAT DO YOU WANT ME TO DO? THE WORLD NEEDS CAPTAIN AMERICA.
NO, STEVE. YOU NEED CAPTAIN AMERICA.
BUT CAPTAIN AMERICA IS DEAD.

THESE PEOPLE HAVE FRAMED YOU FIVE DIFFERENT WAYS.

AND WE BARELY KNOW WHO "THESE PEOPLE" ARE.

LOOK, YOU'VE BEEN GONE A WHILE. YOU'VE ONLY SEEN WHAT THEY WANTED YOU TO SEE.

YOU DON'T KNOW WHAT'S HAPPENED OUT HERE.

I... I DO.

HYDRA BROKE SOMETHING IN THIS COUNTRY.

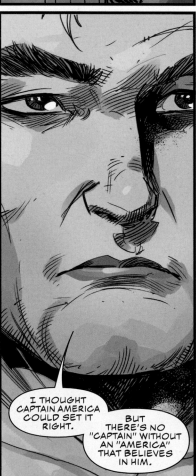

I THOUGHT CAPTAIN AMERICA COULD SET IT RIGHT.

BUT THERE'S NO "CAPTAIN" WITHOUT AN "AMERICA" THAT BELIEVES IN HIM.

THEN PERHAPS WHAT WE NEED RIGHT NOW ISN'T CAPTAIN AMERICA.

MAYBE WHAT WE NEED IS STEVE ROGERS.

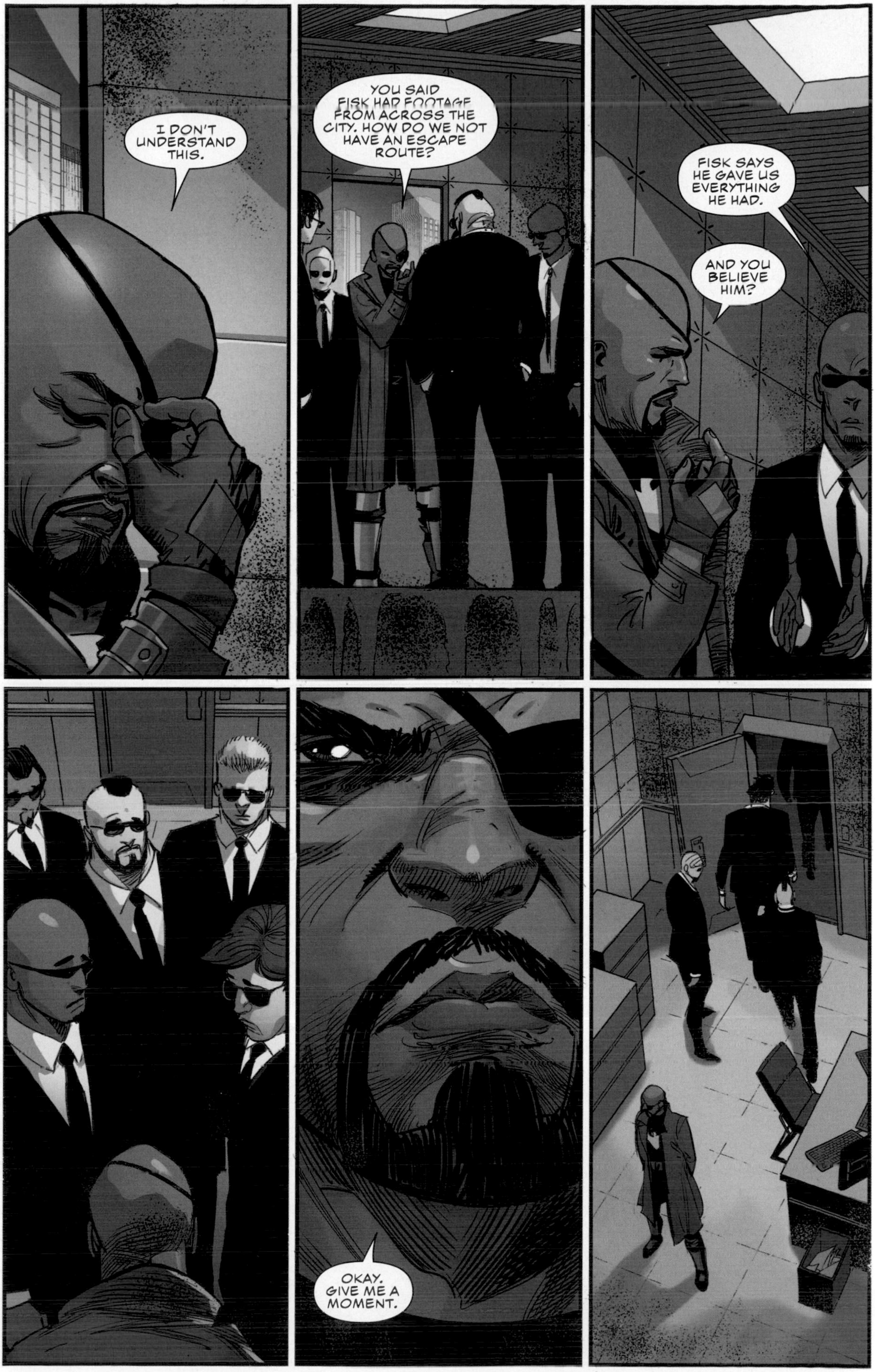
I DON'T UNDERSTAND THIS.
YOU SAID FISK HAD FOOTAGE FROM ACROSS THE CITY. HOW DO WE NOT HAVE AN ESCAPE ROUTE?
FISK SAYS HE GAVE US EVERYTHING HE HAD.
AND YOU BELIEVE HIM?
OKAY. GIVE ME A MOMENT.

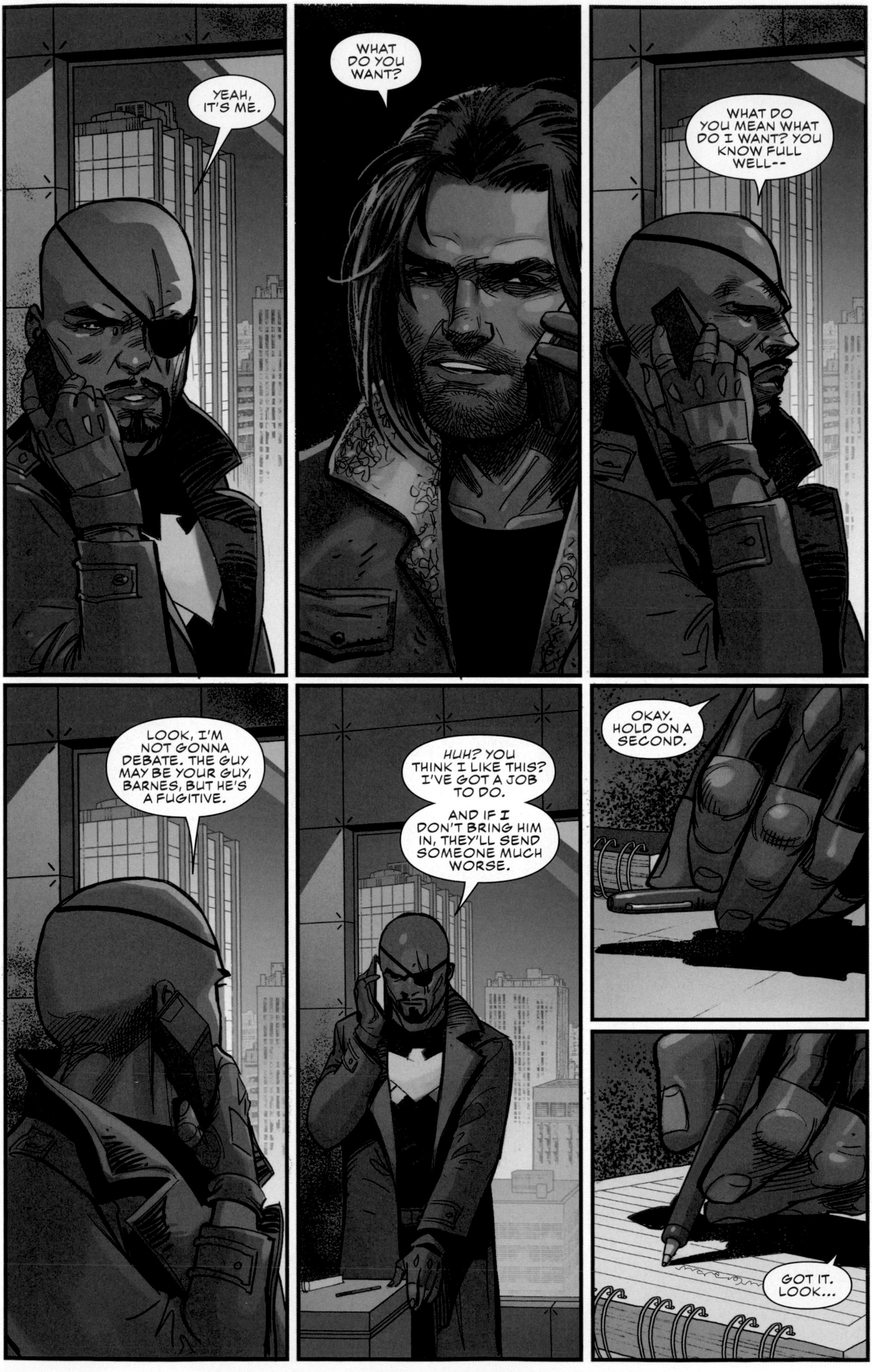
YEAH, IT'S ME.
WHAT DO YOU WANT?
WHAT DO YOU MEAN WHAT DO I WANT? YOU KNOW FULL WELL--
LOOK, I'M NOT GONNA DEBATE. THE GUY MAY BE YOUR GUY, BARNES, BUT HE'S A FUGITIVE.
HUH? YOU THINK I LIKE THIS? I'VE GOT A JOB TO DO.
AND IF I DON'T BRING HIM IN, THEY'LL SEND SOMEONE MUCH WORSE.
OKAY. HOLD ON A SECOND.
GOT IT. LOOK...

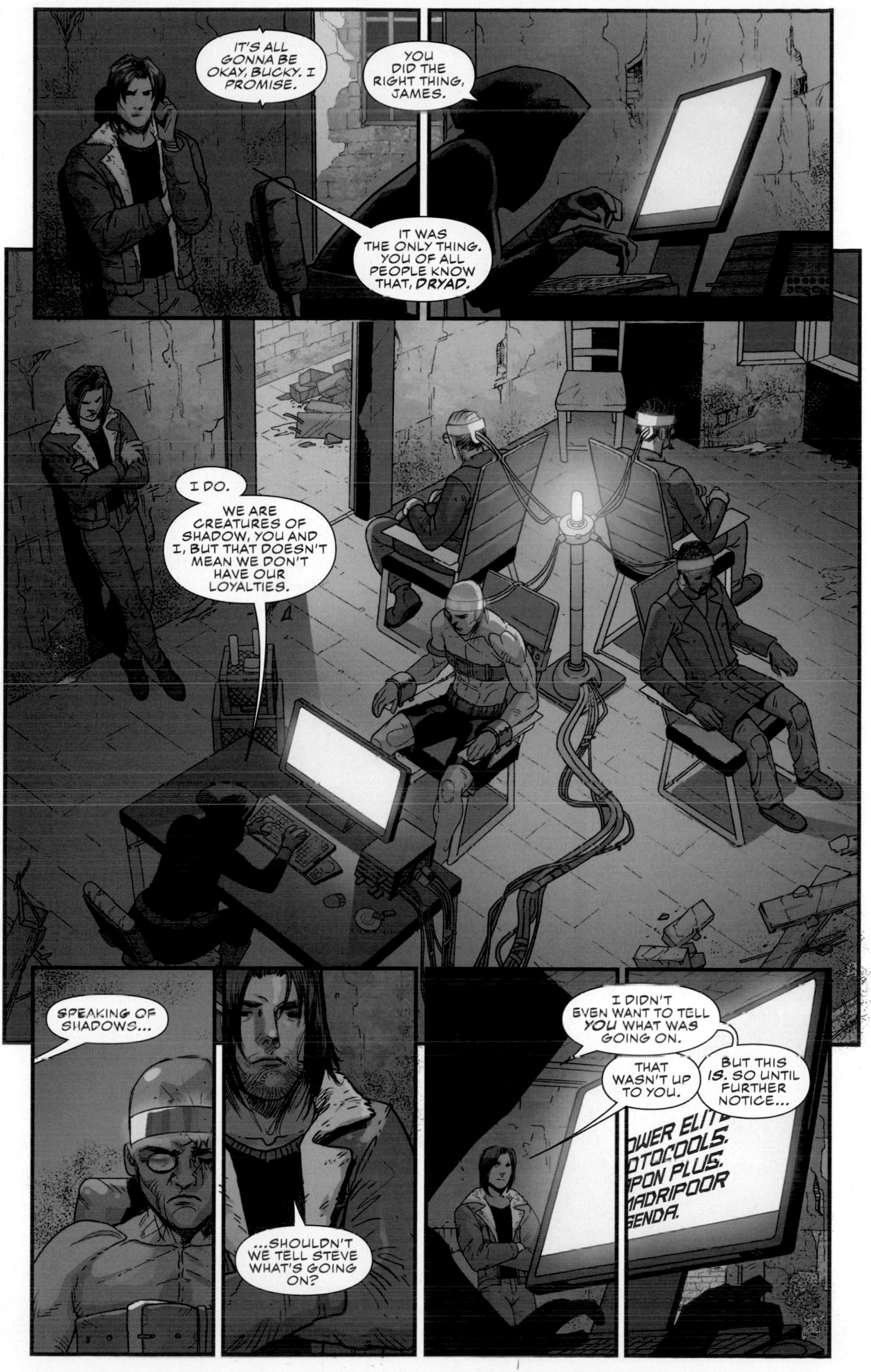
IT'S ALL GONNA BE OKAY, BUCKY. I PROMISE.
YOU DID THE RIGHT THING, JAMES.
IT WAS THE ONLY THING. YOU OF ALL PEOPLE KNOW THAT, DRYAD.
I DO.
WE ARE CREATURES OF SHADOW, YOU AND I, BUT THAT DOESN'T MEAN WE DON'T HAVE OUR LOYALTIES.
SPEAKING OF SHADOWS...
...SHOULDN'T WE TELL STEVE WHAT'S GOING ON?
I DIDN'T EVEN WANT TO TELL YOU WHAT WAS GOING ON.
THAT WASN'T UP TO YOU.
BUT THIS IS. SO UNTIL FURTHER NOTICE...
OWER ELITE
OTOCOOLS.
PON PLUS.
MADRIPOOR
GENDA.

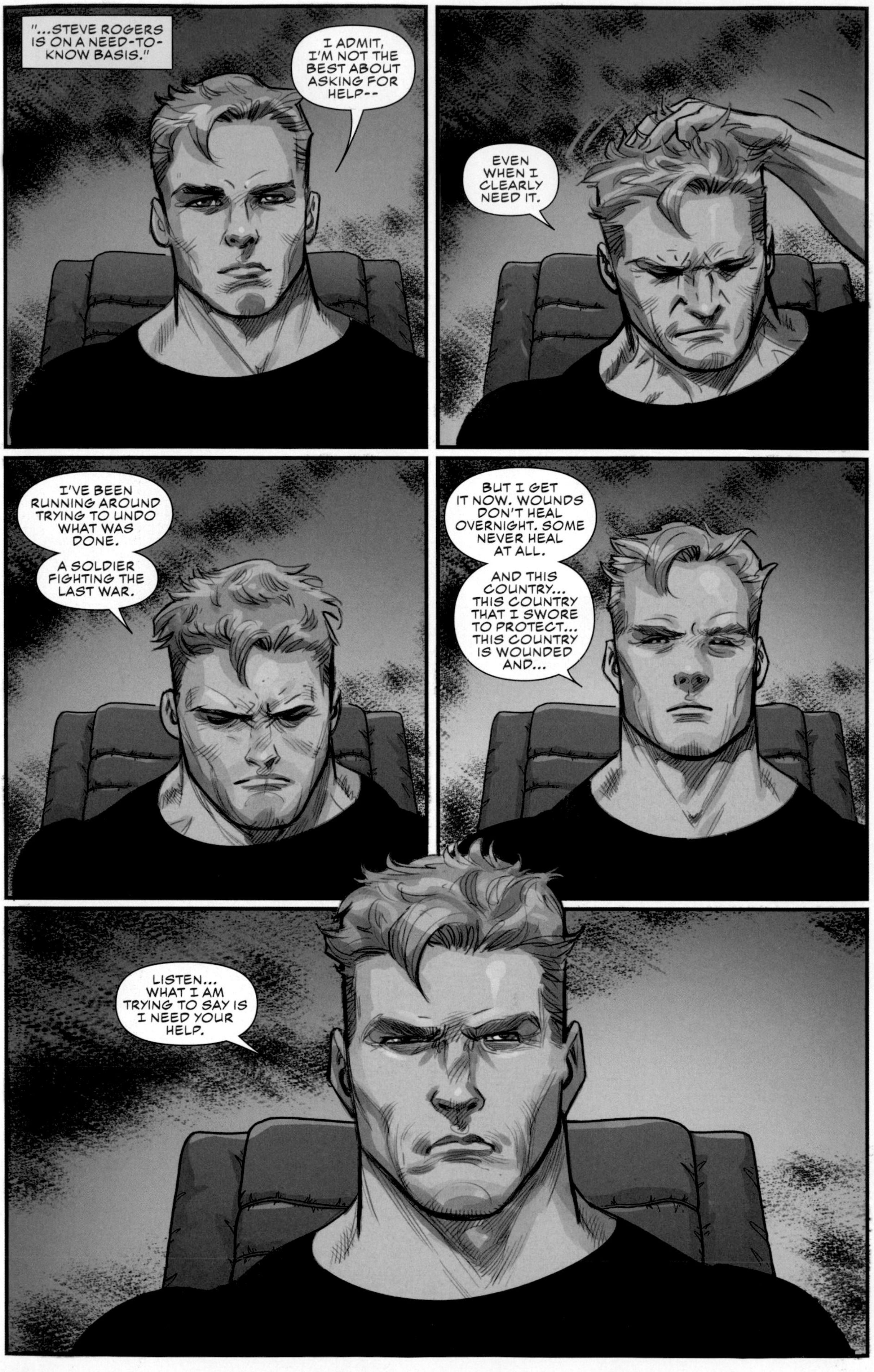
"...STEVE ROGERS IS ON A NEED-TO-KNOW BASIS."
I ADMIT, I'M NOT THE BEST ABOUT ASKING FOR HELP--
EVEN WHEN I CLEARLY NEED IT.
I'VE BEEN RUNNING AROUND TRYING TO UNDO WHAT WAS DONE.
A SOLDIER FIGHTING THE LAST WAR.
BUT I GET IT NOW. WOUNDS DON'T HEAL OVERNIGHT. SOME NEVER HEAL AT ALL.
AND THIS COUNTRY... THIS COUNTRY THAT I SWORE TO PROTECT... THIS COUNTRY IS WOUNDED AND...
LISTEN... WHAT I AM TRYING TO SAY IS I NEED YOUR HELP.

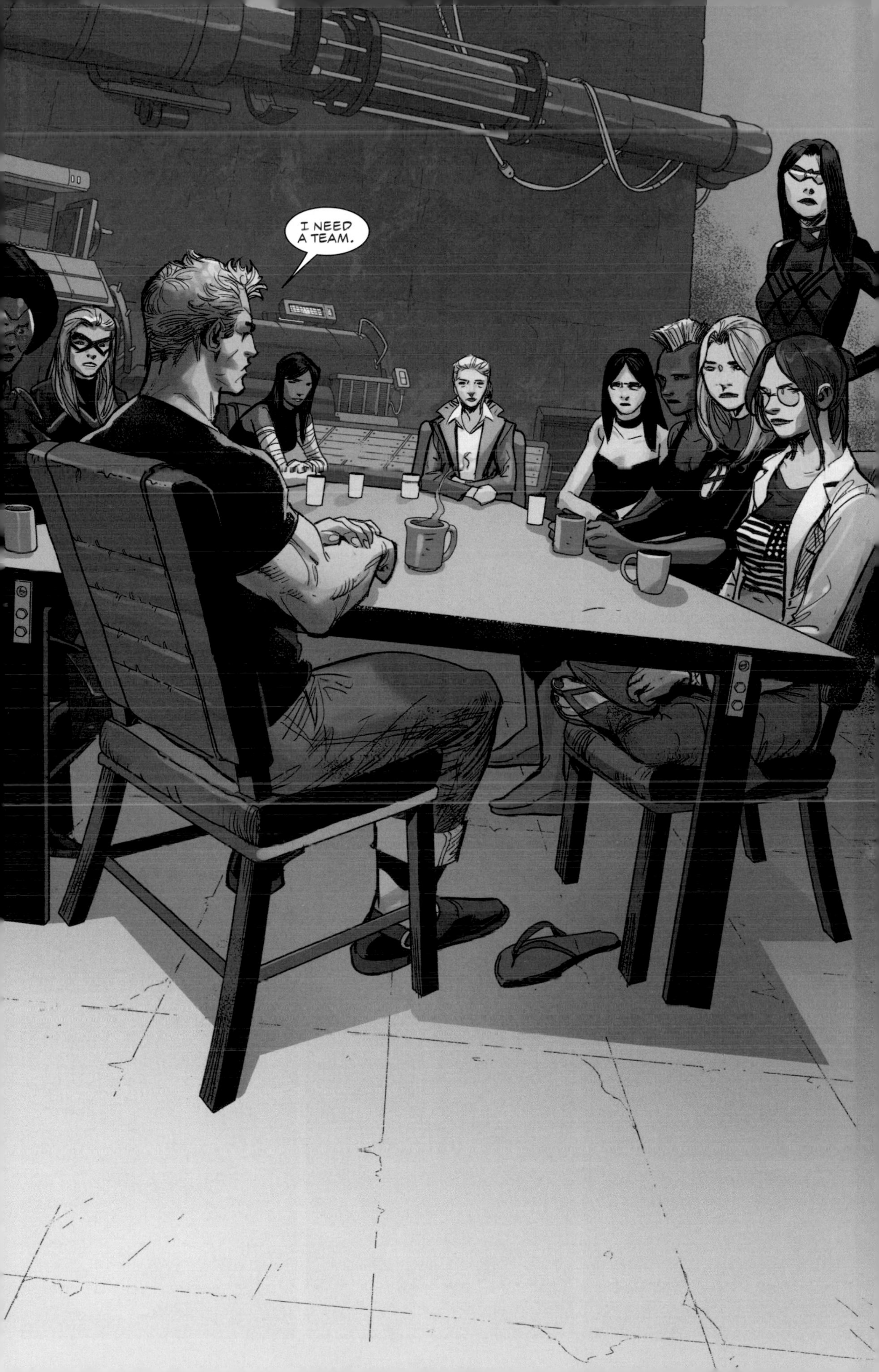
I NEED A TEAM.

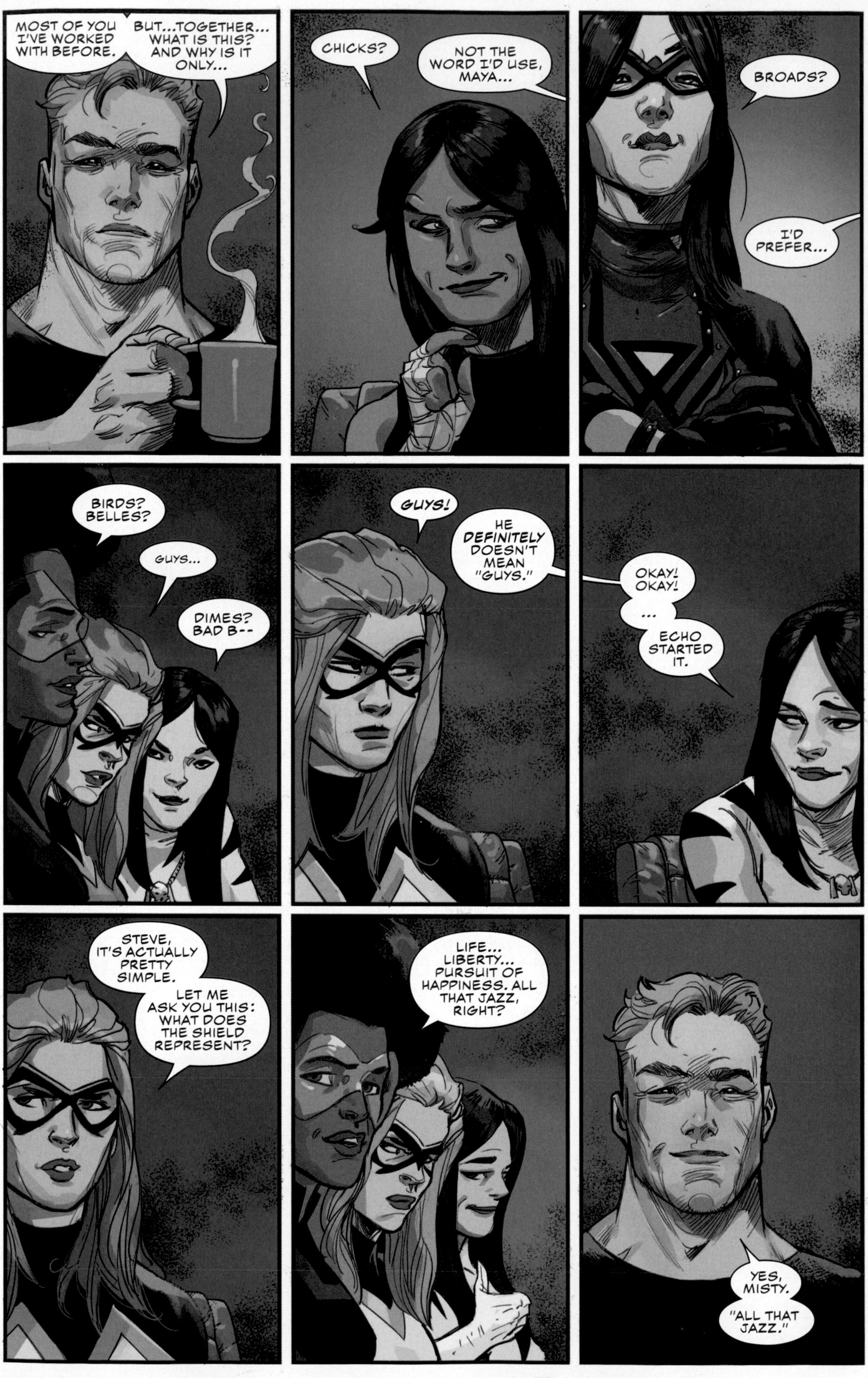
MOST OF YOU I'VE WORKED WITH BEFORE.
BUT...TOGETHER... WHAT IS THIS? AND WHY IS IT ONLY...
CHICKS?
NOT THE WORD I'D USE, MAYA...
BROADS?
I'D PREFER...
BIRDS? BELLES?
GUYS...
DIMES? BAD B--
GUYS!
HE DEFINITELY DOESN'T MEAN "GUYS."
OKAY! OKAY!
...
ECHO STARTED IT.
STEVE, IT'S ACTUALLY PRETTY SIMPLE.
LET ME ASK YOU THIS: WHAT DOES THE SHIELD REPRESENT?
LIFE... LIBERTY... PURSUIT OF HAPPINESS. ALL THAT JAZZ, RIGHT?
YES, MISTY.
"ALL THAT JAZZ."

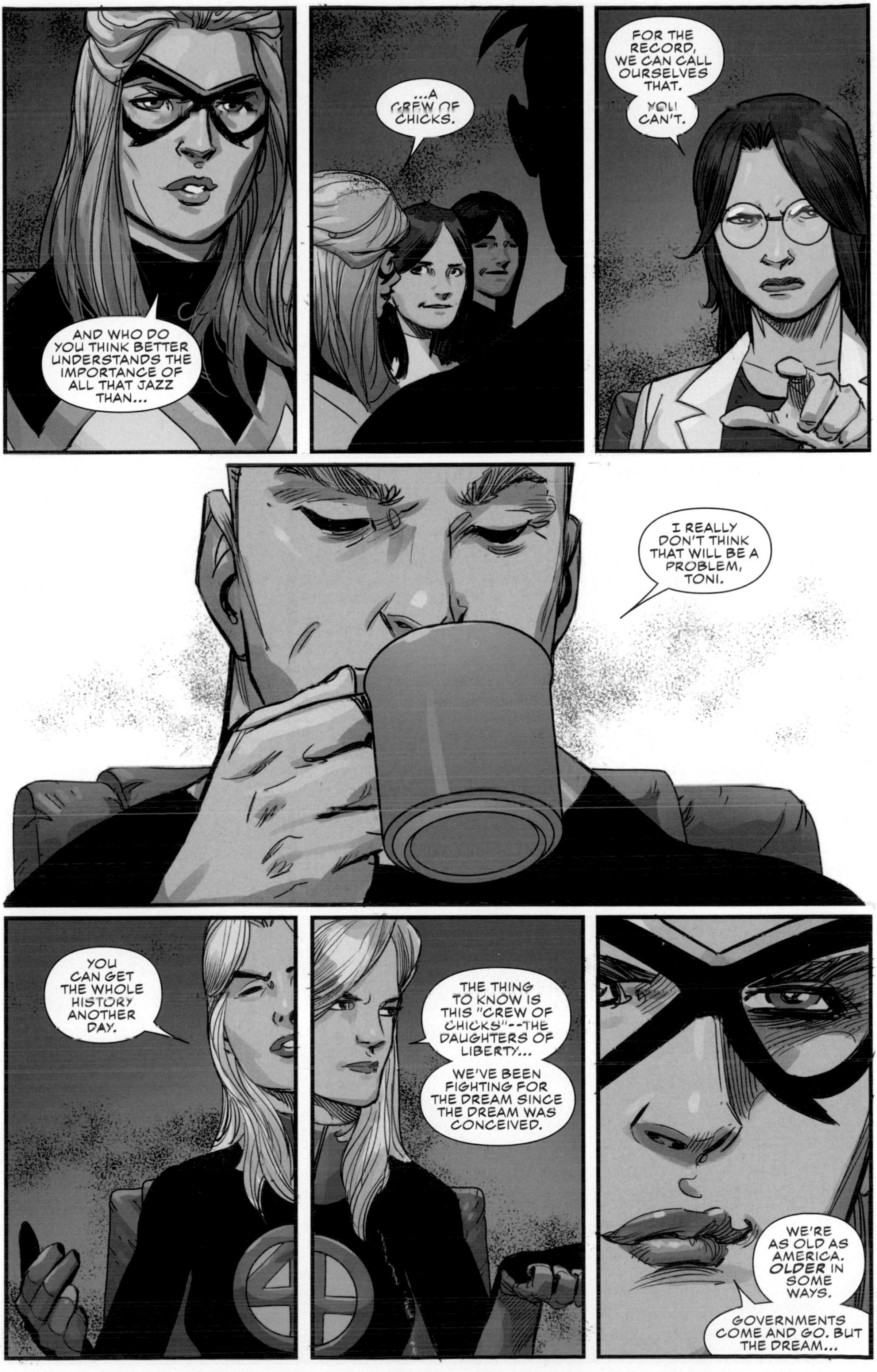
AND WHO DO YOU THINK BETTER UNDERSTANDS THE IMPORTANCE OF ALL THAT JAZZ THAN...
...A CREW OF CHICKS.
FOR THE RECORD, WE CAN CALL OURSELVES THAT.
YOU CAN'T.
I REALLY DON'T THINK THAT WILL BE A PROBLEM, TONI.
YOU CAN GET THE WHOLE HISTORY ANOTHER DAY.
THE THING TO KNOW IS THIS "CREW OF CHICKS"--THE DAUGHTERS OF LIBERTY...
WE'VE BEEN FIGHTING FOR THE DREAM SINCE THE DREAM WAS CONCEIVED.
WE'RE AS OLD AS AMERICA. OLDER IN SOME WAYS.
GOVERNMENTS COME AND GO. BUT THE DREAM...

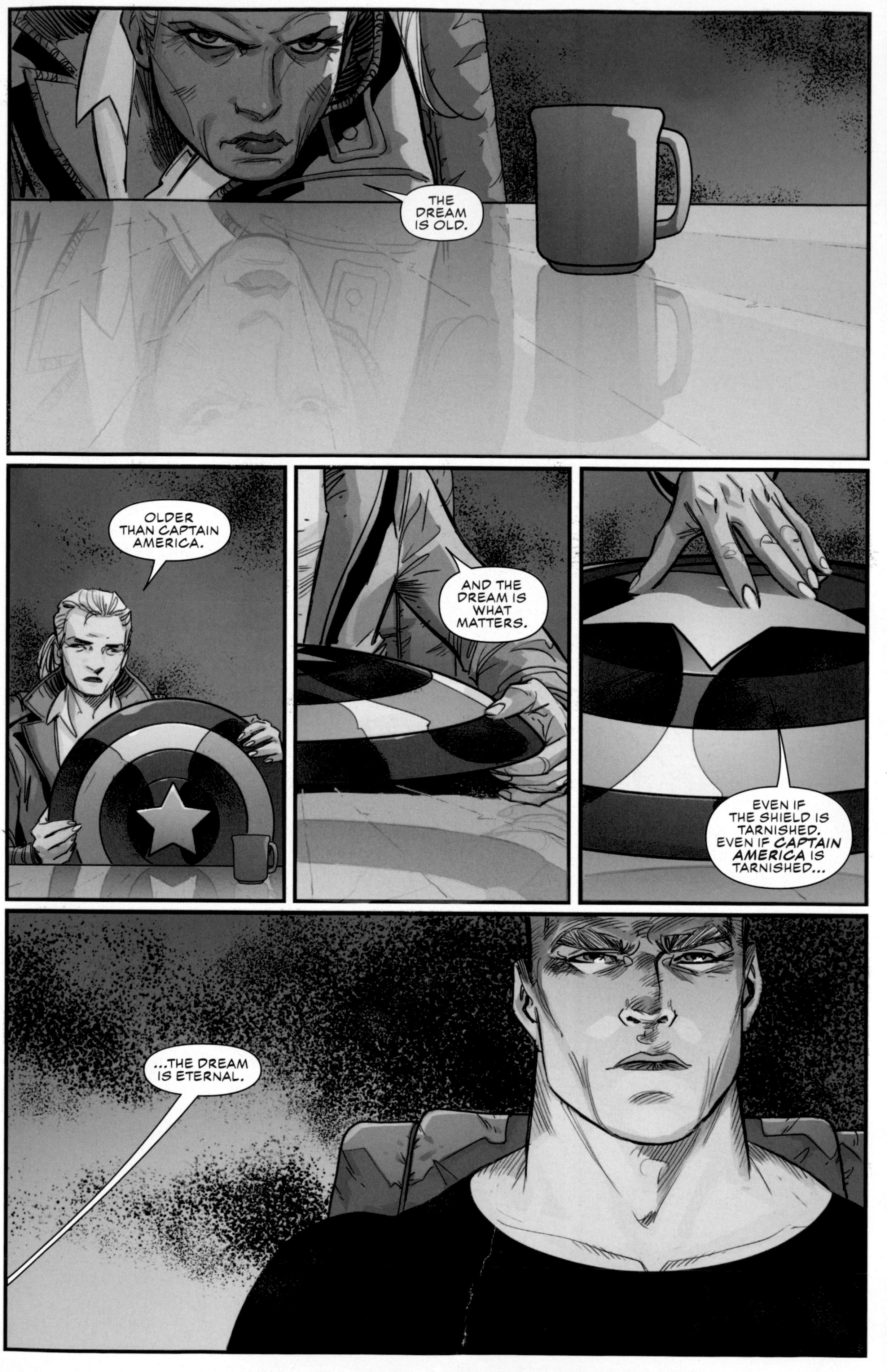
THE DREAM IS OLD.
OLDER THAN CAPTAIN AMERICA.
AND THE DREAM IS WHAT MATTERS.
EVEN IF THE SHIELD IS TARNISHED. EVEN IF CAPTAIN AMERICA IS TARNISHED...
...THE DREAM IS ETERNAL.

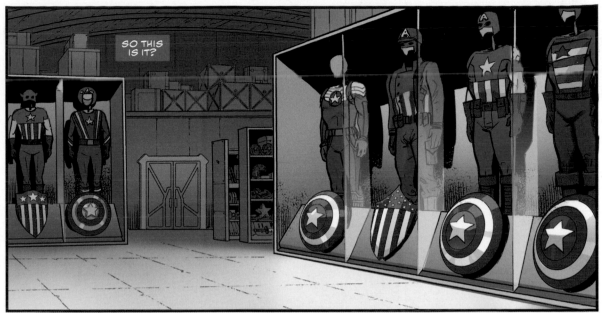

SO THIS IS IT?

ALL THIS TIME I'VE SPENT TRYING TO GET BACK MY NAME.

ALL THIS TIME I'VE SPENT TRYING TO FIX WHAT WAS DONE.

THIS IS IT?

CAPTAIN AMERICA REALLY IS DEAD?

YES.

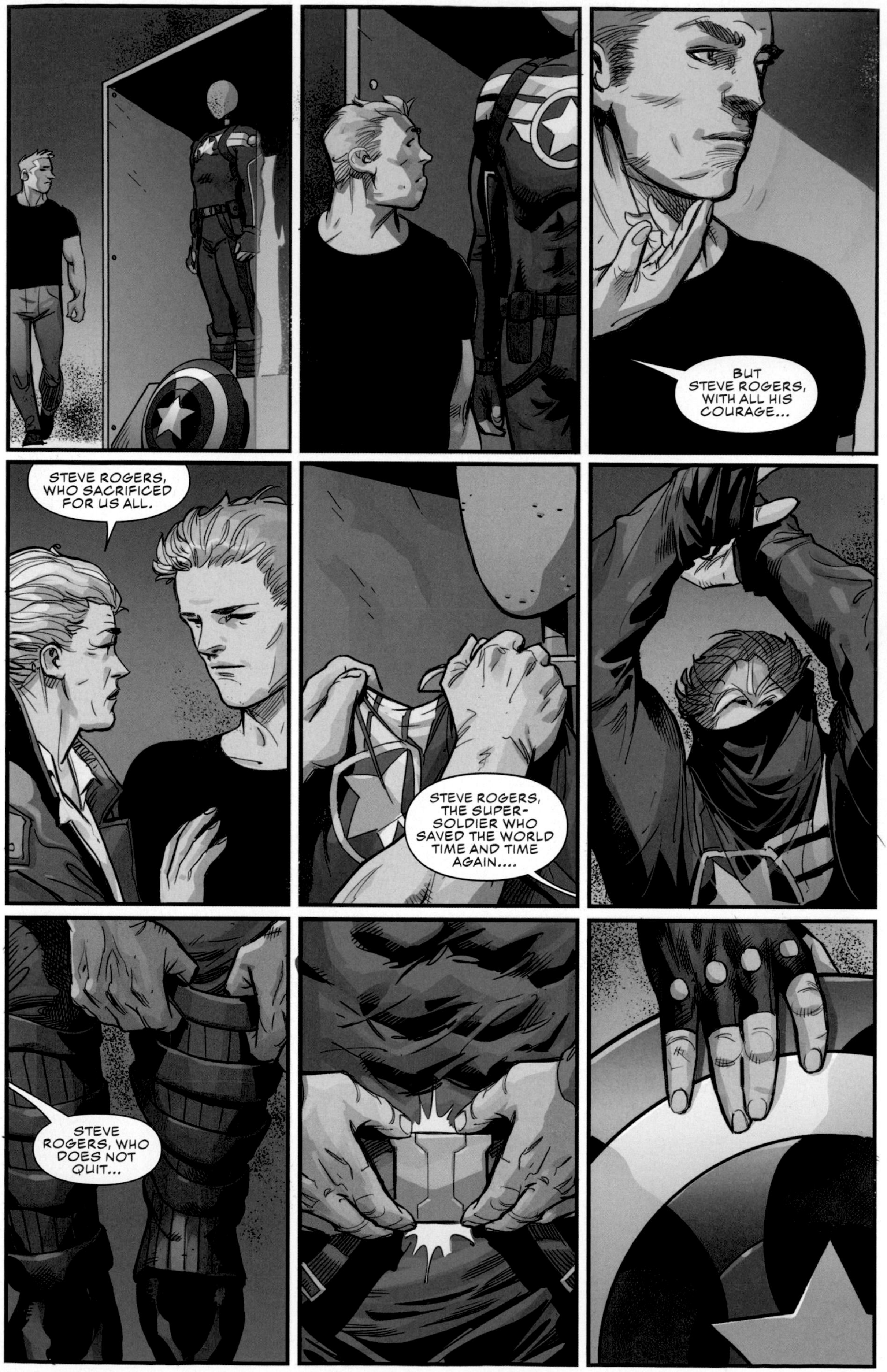
BUT STEVE ROGERS, WITH ALL HIS COURAGE...
STEVE ROGERS, WHO SACRIFICED FOR US ALL.
STEVE ROGERS, THE SUPER-SOLDIER WHO SAVED THE WORLD TIME AND TIME AGAIN....
STEVE ROGERS, WHO DOES NOT QUIT...

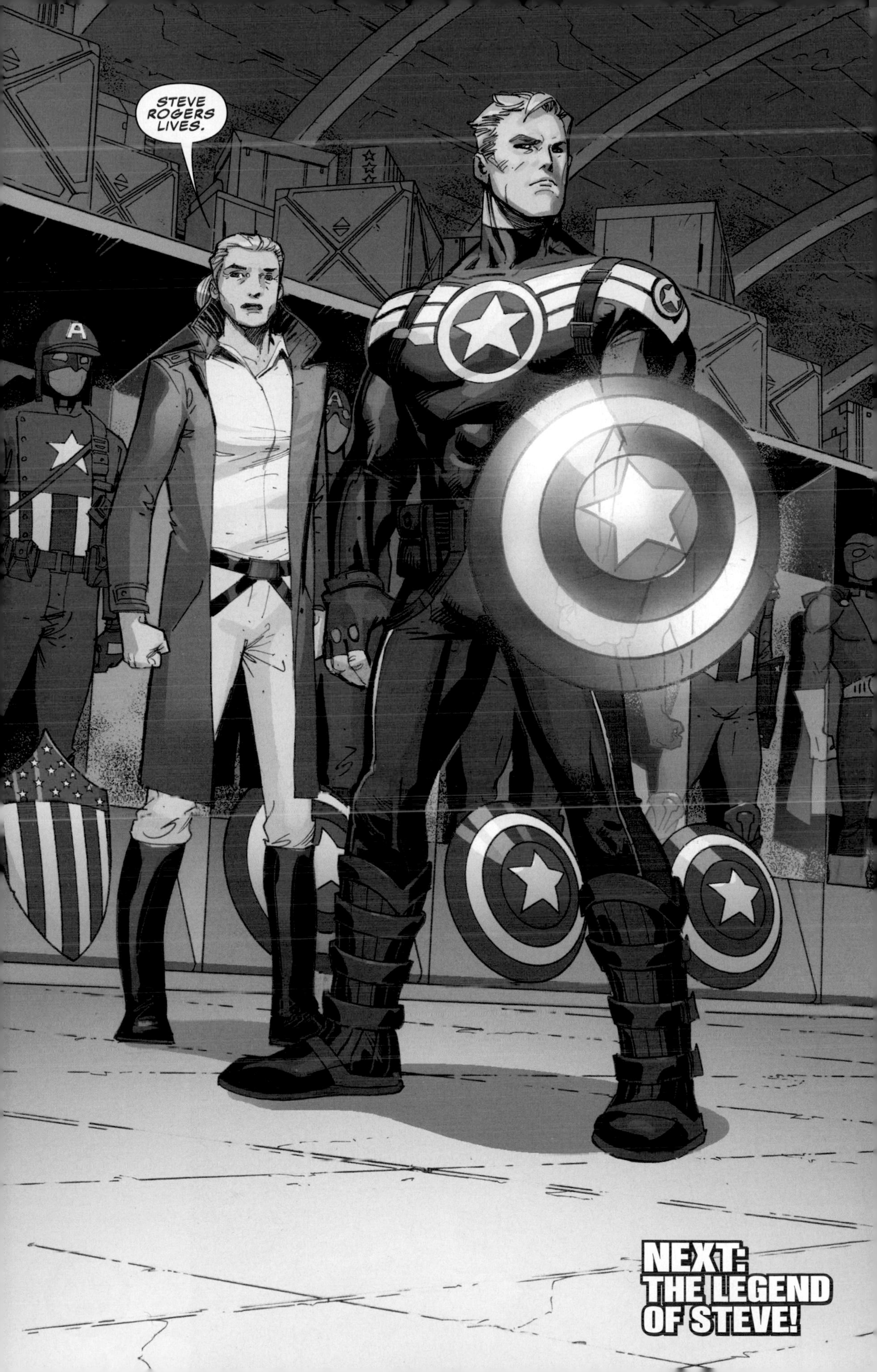
STEVE ROGERS LIVES.
NEXT: THE LEGEND OF STEVE!

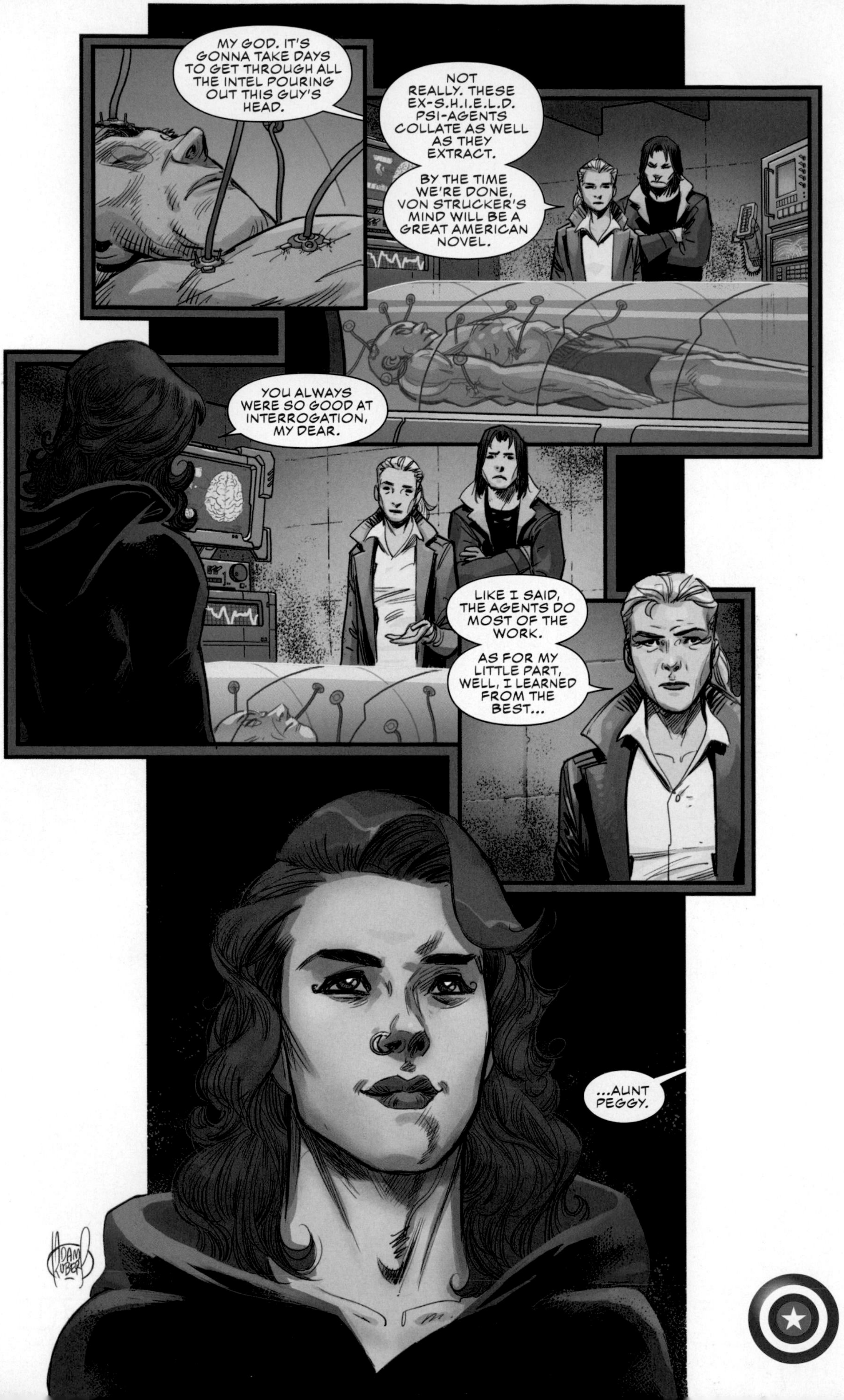
MY GOD. IT'S GONNA TAKE DAYS TO GET THROUGH ALL THE INTEL POURING OUT THIS GUY'S HEAD.
NOT REALLY. THESE EX-S.H.I.E.L.D. PSI-AGENTS COLLATE AS WELL AS THEY EXTRACT.
BY THE TIME WE'RE DONE, VON STRUCKER'S MIND WILL BE A GREAT AMERICAN NOVEL.
YOU ALWAYS WERE SO GOOD AT INTERROGATION, MY DEAR.
LIKE I SAID, THE AGENTS DO MOST OF THE WORK.
AS FOR MY LITTLE PART, WELL, I LEARNED FROM THE BEST...
...AUNT PEGGY.

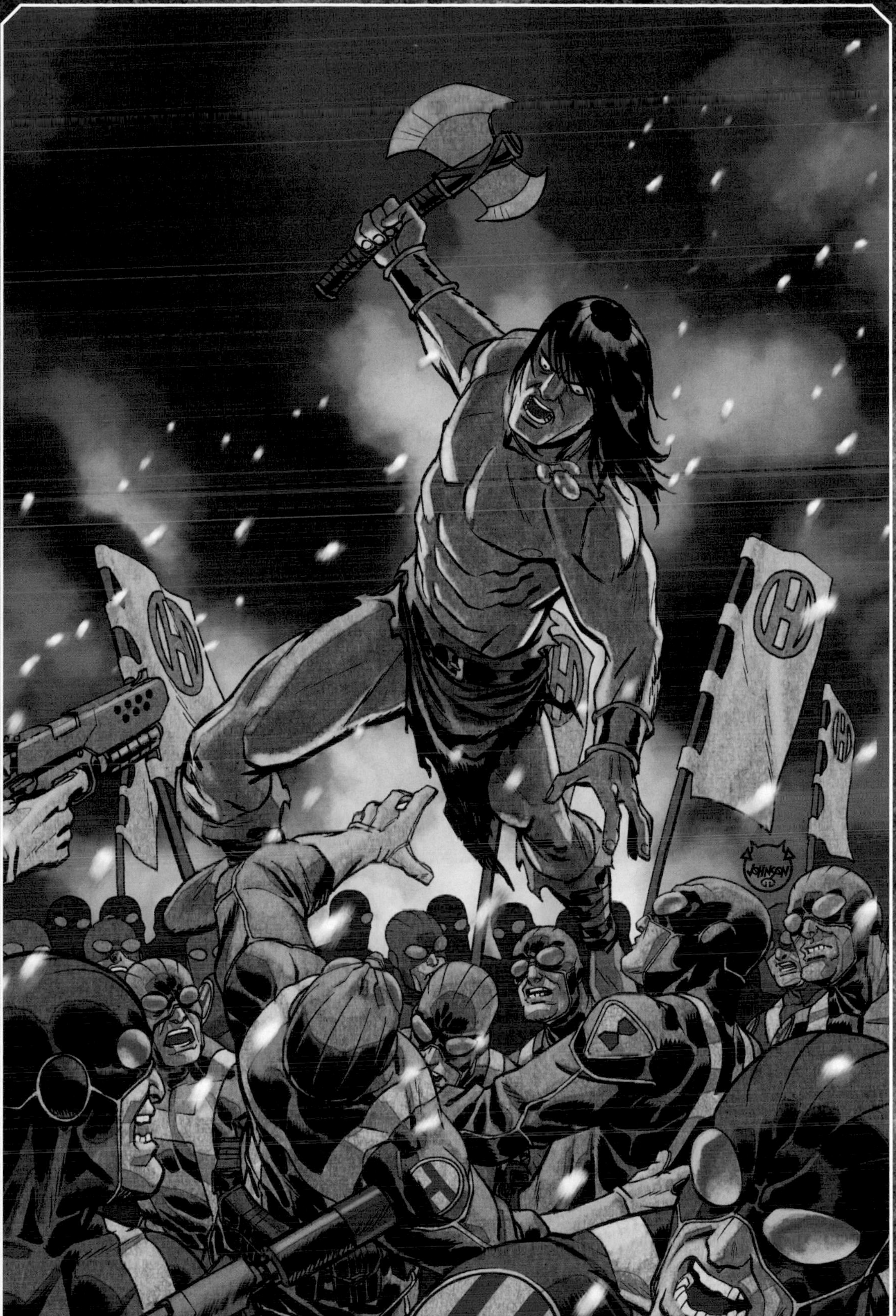
JOHNSON

DAVE JOHNSON

7 CONAN VS. VARIANT

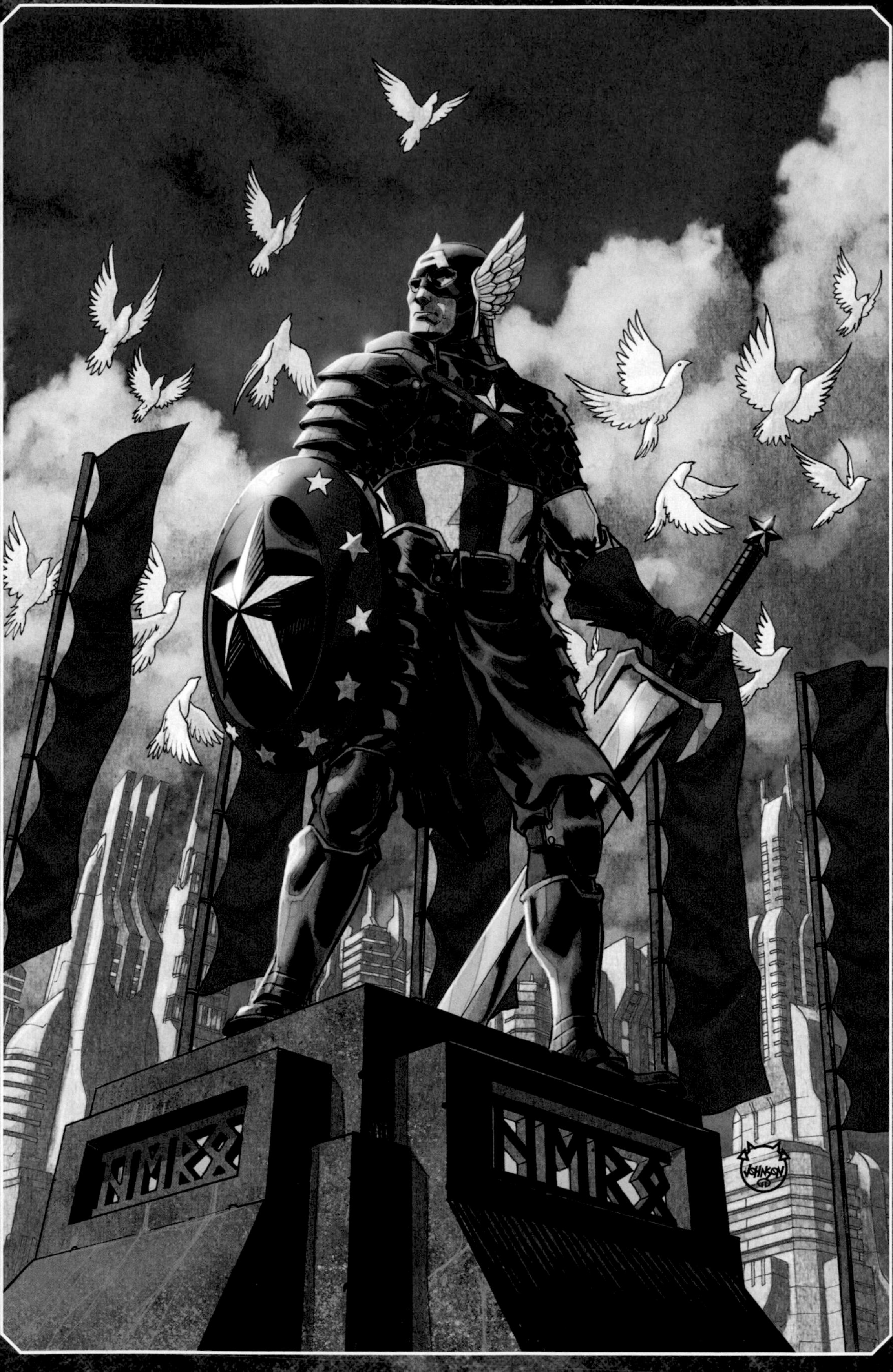

DAVE JOHNSON

10 ASGARDIAN VARIANT

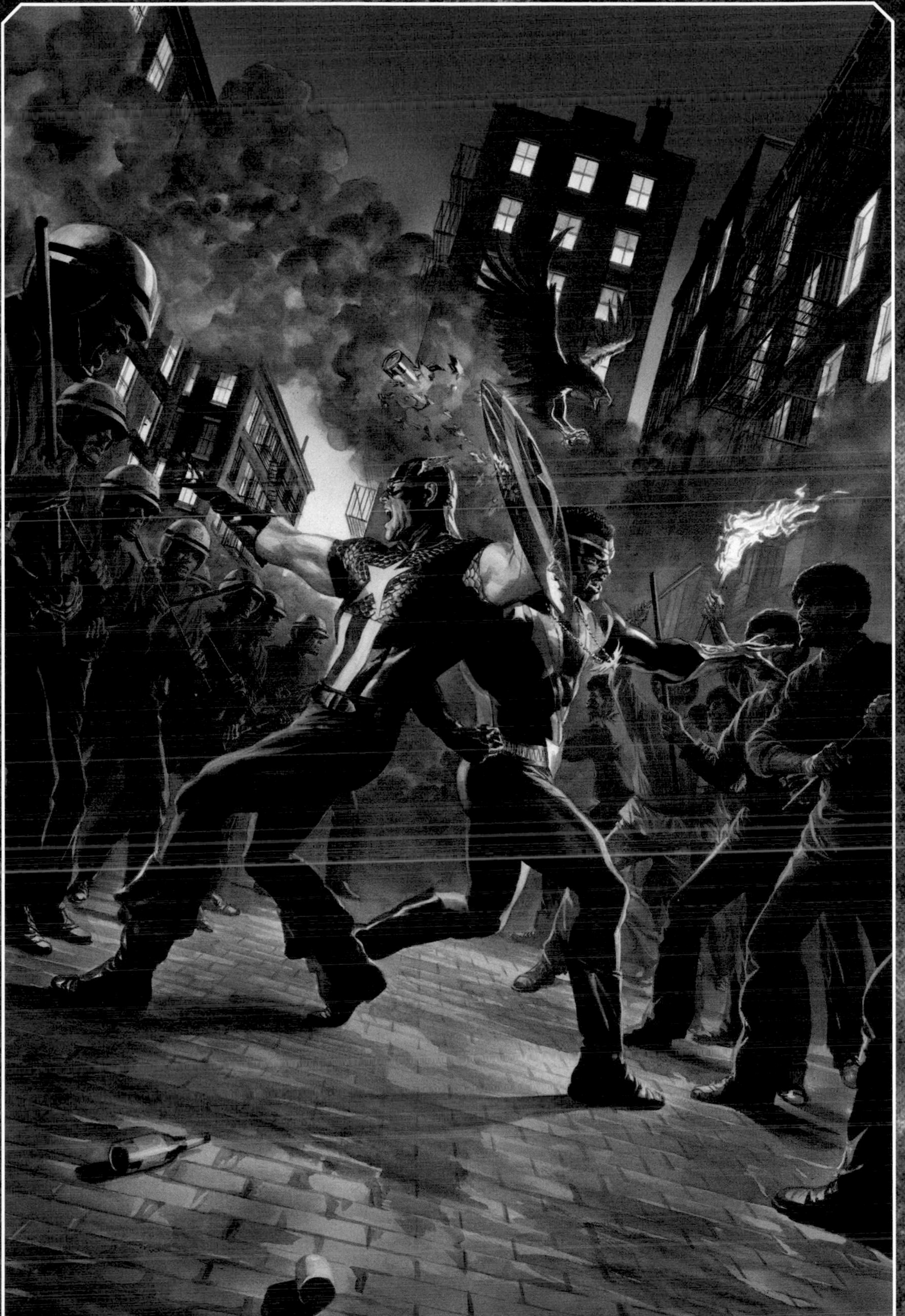

ALEX ROSS

12 MARVELS 25TH ANNIVERSARY VARIANT

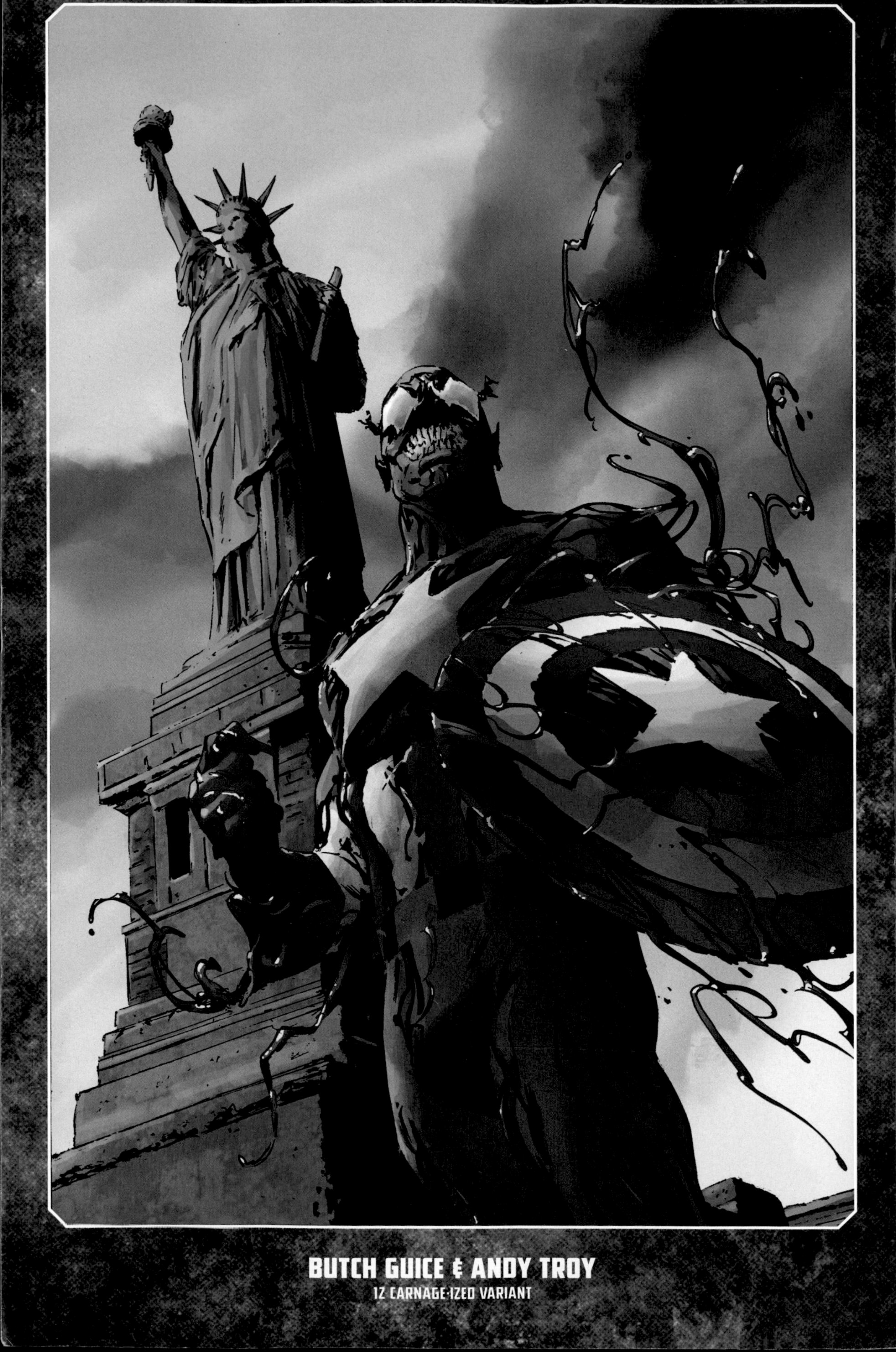

BUTCH GUICE & ANDY TROY
12 CARNAGE-IZED VARIANT